Voices of Angel Island

Voices of Angel Island

Inscriptions and Immigrant Poetry, 1910–1945

Charles Egan

BLOOMSBURY ACADEMIC
NEW YORK • LONDON • OXFORD • NEW DELHI • SYDNEY

BLOOMSBURY ACADEMIC
Bloomsbury Publishing Inc
1385 Broadway, New York, NY 10018, USA
50 Bedford Square, London, WC1B 3DP, UK

BLOOMSBURY, BLOOMSBURY ACADEMIC and the Diana logo are trademarks of
Bloomsbury Publishing Plc

First published in the United States of America 2021
This paperback edition published 2022

Copyright © Charles Egan, 2021

Cover images (clockwise from top): Photo © Michael Nelsen; Jeremiah Feingold's
passport photo, courtesy Michael G. Walsh; Photo of Shizuye Makino, member of the
Cherry Dancing Troupe to the Panama-Pacific International Exposition, 1915; Photo
© Charles Egan; The Yamashita family in 1917, courtesy of Cheryl Yamashita

All rights reserved. No part of this publication may be reproduced or transmitted
in any form or by any means, electronic or mechanical, including photocopying,
recording, or any information storage or retrieval system, without prior permission
in writing from the publishers.

Bloomsbury Publishing Inc does not have any control over, or responsibility for, any
third-party websites referred to or in this book. All internet addresses given in this
book were correct at the time of going to press. The author and publisher regret
any inconvenience caused if addresses have changed or sites have ceased to
exist, but can accept no responsibility for any such changes.

Library of Congress Cataloging-in-Publication Data
Names: Egan, Charles, author.
Title: Voices of Angel Island : inscriptions and immigrant poetry, 1910-1945 / Charles Egan.
Description: New York : Bloomsbury Academic, 2020. | Includes bibliographical
references and index. | This book includes the English translation of selected poems
along with the text in its respective original language. While Chinese remains the
dominant language on the source of the selection, Japanese is also strongly
represented, and Russian, English, Spanish, Italian, French, German, Punjabi (both
Gurmukhi and Urdu scripts), Bengali, and Korean are also found.
Identifiers: LCCN 2020022278 | ISBN 9781501360459 (hardback) |
ISBN 9781501371295 (paperback) | ISBN 9781501360466 (epub) |
ISBN 9781501360473 (pdf) Subjects: LCSH: Poetry—Minority authors—Translations into
English. | Angel Island Immigration Station (Calif.) | Emigration and immigration—Poetry. |
Immigrants' writings. | Inscriptions.
Classification: LCC PN6109.95.M55 E43 2020 | DDC 810.9/895073—dc23
LC record available at https://lccn.loc.gov/2020022278

ISBN:	HB:	978-1-5013-6045-9
	PB:	978-1-5013-7129-5
	ePDF:	978-1-5013-6047-3
	eBook:	978-1-5013-6046-6

Typeset by RefineCatch Limited, Bungay, Suffolk

To find out more about our authors and books visit www.bloomsbury.com
and sign up for our newsletters.

Dedicated to the staff and volunteers of California State Parks

And in memory of Ben Fenkell
Angel Island State Park Historical Interpreter
Educator and friend to all

CONTENTS

List of Figures ix
Acknowledgments xii

Introduction 1

1 Japanese Inscriptions, 1910–1940 19
   Wall Inscriptions 24
   Japaneses Prose and Poetry from *Nichibei Shimbun* 46

2 Korean Inscriptions, 1910–1940 113
   Wall Inscriptions 117
   Korean Poetry from *Sinhan Minbo* 122

3 Chinese Inscriptions, 1910–1940 149
   Wall Inscriptions 155
   An Angel Island Memoir 192

4 Other Inscriptions, 1910–1940 197
   Russian Wall Inscriptions 201
   Russian Poetry from *Russkii Golos* 231
   South Asian Wall Inscriptions 235
   Punjabi Poetry from *Ghadar de Gunj* 237
   Wall Inscriptions in European Languages 239

5 Second World War Wall Inscriptions, 1942–1945 247
   By Japanese Hawaiians 257
   Inscriptions from Yasutaro Soga 266
   By Prisoners-of-War 270
   By Post-war Deportees 281

Appendices 287
    A. Poem Numbers in *Island*, 1st and 2nd Editions 287
    B. Wall Locations of *Island* Poems (*Island* 2nd Edition Order) 289
    C. Wall Locations of *Island* 2nd Edition Poems (Wall Order) 293
    D. Tet Yee Manuscript Poems and Locations 293
    E. Smiley Jann Manuscript Poems and Locations 295
    F. Wall Locations of Pictures 298

Notes (including locations of wall inscriptions) 301
Bibliography 325
Index 331

FIGURES

Introduction

0.1	The barracks in 2020.	2
0.2	Yan Zhenqing, detail of "Yan Qinli Stele."	10
0.3	Detail of *Island* #60. Photo: Michael Nelsen.	11
0.4	Liu Gongquan, detail of "Xuanmi Stupa Stele."	11
0.5	*Island* #2. Photo: Architectural Resources Group (modified for character recognition by Daniel Quan Design).	12
0.6	Detail of Chapter 3, #13 text.	13
0.7	Enrique Piton inscription. See Chapter 4.	13
0.8	Scaly fish. Photo: Michael Nelsen.	14
0.9	The pier and baggage shed in 1971. Photo: Denis Englander.	15
0.10	Barracks map, first floor. Courtesy Daniel Quan.	16
0.11	Barracks map, second floor. Courtesy Daniel Quan.	17

Chapter 1

1.1	Meiji and Xuantong dates. Photo: ARG and Daniel Quan.	24
1.2	Masaru and Kinuyo's wedding day. Courtesy Donna Ebata.	27
1.3	The Hokoda family, about 1926. Courtesy Donna Ebata.	28
1.4	Masaru and Kinuyo in retirement. Photo: Angel Franco / *The New York Times* / Redux.	30
1.5	Ichitaro Yasumi in 1897. Courtesy Catherine Miskow.	32
1.6	"Get me out of here fast!"	39
1.7	The Yamashita family in 1917. Courtesy Cheryl Yamashita.	40
1.8	Bird sketch.	45
1.9	Rooster carving.	45
1.10	Cartoon.	46
1.11	Shimizu Kashin.	68

Chapter 2

2.1	In-Bal Ryu inscription. Photo: ARG and Daniel Quan.	117
2.2	George Hansik Lee's immigration file photo.	120

Chapter 3

3.1	"Clouds and hills all around." Photo: ARG and Daniel Quan.	156
3.2	"Barbering place."	158
3.3	Two birds.	159
3.4	Li Hai poem. Photo: ARG and Daniel Quan.	160
3.5	Sailing ship.	160
3.6	Huang Zuming poem—"Dwelling in the Wooden Building."	166
3.7	"When you go downstairs for meals." Photo: Michael Nelsen.	172
3.8	Detail of "It's hard for Chinese."	175
3.9	"I tended house and home."	181
3.10	Good luck money picture.	183
3.11	Good luck money line drawing.	184
3.12	"There are worms growing." Photo: ARG and Daniel Quan.	188
3.13	Ancestral altar.	189
3.14	Ancestral altar line drawing.	190

Chapter 4

4.1	The Zeitlin (Allen) brothers as children. Jacob is at the center. Courtesy Marilyn Mendoza.	202
4.2	The Zeitlin/Hoppenstein family in Gomel, before 1906. From left to right in the front row: Leib (Louis), father Velvel, Jacob, grandmother Malky Hoppenstein, mother Peshe, and Abram (Joe). Courtesy Evan Allen.	202
4.3	Jacob and Anna Allen in the 1950s. Courtesy Marilyn Mendoza.	203
4.4	Irmia Faingolid's (Jeremiah Feingold) passport photo. Courtesy Michael Walsh.	209
4.5	George (Isaak) and Amelia Fangold in the 1920s. Courtesy Robert Kolbert.	210
4.6	Jerry and Augusta, c. 1965. Courtesy Michael Walsh.	211
4.7	Jerry's and George's parents and sister Ida in Kiev, c. 1940. Courtesy Michael Walsh.	212
4.8	Ida's 1944 telegram to Jerry. Courtesy Michael Walsh.	212
4.9	The Nizenkoffs in Russia, c. 1900. Constantine Z. is sitting front left. Courtesy Erik Nizenkoff.	225
4.10	The Nizenkoffs in America, c. 1936. Constantine Z. at back right, Constantine C. at back left, Anna at front right, and Nina holding Ted at front left. Courtesy Erik Nizenkoff.	226
4.11	Jack and Bella Benoff with son Edward. Courtesy Ethan Benoff.	230
4.12	Tara Singh inscription in Urdu and Gurmukhi.	235

4.13	J.D. Burgess at the Panama Canal, 1930. Courtesy Gerri Burgess.	241
4.14	J.D. Burgess and family, *c.* 1950. Courtesy Gerri Burgess.	242
4.15	Booking photographs of Enrique Piton.	245

Chapter 5

5.1	George Hoshida portrait of Takuji Shindo, left. From the collections of the Japanese American National Museum.	260
5.2	Robert Sueoka inscription. Photo: ARG and Daniel Quan.	261
5.3	"Close the door. There's a draft."	270
5.4	"Long live the Great Japanese Empire!"	272
5.5	Saipan and Tinian inscription.	274
5.6	Japanese POW diary inscription. Photo: ARG and Daniel Quan.	278
5.7	Japanese POW cartoon.	279
5.8	Guard station in the barracks.	280
5.9	Guard tower with machine gun swivel mount, seen from the barracks in 1971. Photo: Denis Englander.	280
5.10	"The time has come for me to fulfill my duty."	285

ACKNOWLEDGMENTS

This book has been years in the making, and would not have been possible without the help, support, and expertise of many people. First of all, grateful thanks to fellow members of the 2003–2004 survey team, Wan Liu, Xing Chu Wang, Newton Liu, and Dan Quan. A special shout out to Xing Chu, who joined me again at Angel Island in 2020 to confirm Chinese readings and discuss problem texts. My friend and colleague Makiko Asano spent countless hours with me deciphering Japanese inscriptions and analyzing poems. Thank you! The Korean chapter would not have been possible without the outstanding contributions of my old friend and classmate Hyong-gyu Rhew and my former student Jikyung Hwang. For Russian, thanks to Svetlana Kristal and her daughter Roza Trilesskaya. For Punjabi, kudos to Jane Singh, and to Chris Chekuri and Nandini Abedin for Bengali. For Chinese, I have my second family to thank—faculty in the Chinese Program at San Francisco State: Clare Cheng, Joyce Liou, Christina Yee, Wen-Chao Li, Fred Green, Yang Xiao-Desai, Josephine Tsao, Hsin-Yun Liu, April Phung, and Mia Segura. Xiexie!

Historian Judy Yung has generously given me advice and support for many years. Many people from AIISF as well: Katherine Toy, Daphne Kwok, Grant Din, Eddie Wong, and Felicia Lowe are just a few. I appreciate all the help. Bill Greene and Marisa Louie Lee at the National Archives and Records Administration have provided help at key moments. Particular thanks—and my admiration—for all the California State Parks personnel at Angel Island, especially Casey Dexter-Lee and the late-Ben Fenkell. I'm very grateful to Kitty Millet for advice and support. I also want to thank Bloomsbury Academic editors Katherine De Chant, Haaris Naqvi, and Amy Martin, and all the production staff.

Last but not least, I am indebted to the many descendants of inscription writers who contributed their stories and photos: Teruku Tamara, Donna Ebata and all the Hokodas, David Yasumi and Catherine Miskow, Cheryl Yamashita, Michael Walsh, Robert Kolbert, Ira Allen, Marilyn Mendoza, Evan Allen, Joan Allen, Seymour Woodnick, Sandra Miller, Devin Gross, the late Ted Nizenkoff, Erik Nizenkoff, Edward Benoff, Ethan Benoff, and Gerri Burgess. Family is everything.

Written in Marshall, California
During the pandemic, 2020

Introduction

My first visit to the Angel Island Immigration Station in San Francisco Bay was in 2003. The site was in a decrepit and neglected state then—the hospital was a near wreck, and the detainee barracks was only marginally better. The scent of mildewed wood and dust permeated the drafty, cold barracks, and our footfalls echoed in the large, empty rooms. Standing in the center of one of the dormitories, not much seemed very remarkable. Yet walking close to the walls, the faint impressions of writing could be discerned, covering almost every square foot of space. Hundreds and hundreds of messages. One could feel the history. One hundred years ago, this room was crowded with up to two hundred people at a time, jostling together or milling about, with nothing to do but wait until their cases were called. Each faced an uncertain future.

The Angel Island Immigration Station officially opened its doors on January 21, 1910. Construction of an immigration station at China Cove had been authorized in 1905, in part to handle the large number of European immigrants expected to pass through the new Panama Canal and land on the west coast. At least that was the way the idea was presented to the public. As reported in the *Washington Post* on July 28, 1911,

> ... it is expected that the all-water route to our Pacific ports will give a great impetus to immigration, inasmuch as the present handicap of high railroad rates will be removed, while the coast States are preparing to offer inducements calculated to draw Europeans here in larger numbers than in the past.[1]

The welcome offered to immigrants from Europe is in contrast to a less publicized reason for the new facility—to stem the tide of Asian immigration. Although often called the "Ellis Island of the West," within the Immigration Service the station was known as "The Guardian of the Western Gate."[2] The island location effectively isolated "undesirable" immigrants while their cases were being adjudicated and their health examined. Unless they could meet the stringent—sometimes unreasonable—requirements set by the authorities, they faced deportation.

FIGURE 0.1 *The barracks in 2020.*

The expected surge in European immigration did not materialize, and the Angel Island Immigration Station never became a portal like the station on Ellis Island. Instead, it functioned as a detention facility for all the years of its operation. Those arriving at the port of San Francisco whose status was not in question and whose papers were in order were processed at the wharves where the passenger ships docked. "Problem" cases were sent to Angel Island, where the wait for adjudication could last a few days or many months. Chinese immigrants tended to be detained the longest, and so at any one time made up the majority of detainees. The longest detention on record is that of Kong Din Quong, who was held for 756 days.[3] Detainees were separated by race, ethnicity, and gender in the crowded two-storey wooden barracks. Dormitories were at the east and west ends of the building. As constructed in 1910, the two large east dormitories had 204 and 192 bunks stacked three high. The west dormitories had sixty bunks each. The middle of the building contained day rooms for the detainees as well as various small rooms for use by station guards and staff.[4] Women detainees were also held in the barracks at first, but were shifted to the Administration Building in late 1911.

In 2010, Erika Lee and Judy Yung published a landmark book, *Angel Island: Immigrant Gateway to America*, which describes the experiences of all the immigrant groups who were processed at the station, in context of legal and social history. Through comparisons of these disparate experiences, this book examines—in the authors' words—"the contradictions inherent in America's celebratory mythos of immigration and the reality that immigration policies reinforced race, class, and gender hierarchies in this country."[5] Though the number of people who were processed through Angel Island cannot be ascertained with certainty, as several government agencies had jurisdiction over detainees, and record-keeping was not standardized, Lee and Yung estimate that 300,000 aliens were sent to Angel Island for immigration inspection between 1910 and 1940: 100,000 Chinese, 85,000 Japanese, 8,000 South Asians, 8,000 Russians and Jews, 1,000 Koreans, 1,000 Filipinos, and 400 Mexicans.[6] Other immigrants were from Australia and New Zealand, the Polynesian islands, Southeast Asia, Europe, South and Central America—people of eighty nationalities entering the port of San Francisco all ended up at Angel Island, sent there when the authorities deemed that their entry applications required investigation.[7] And then there were the large numbers of people who were not *entering* the United States, but *leaving* it, for the station was also the main deportation center for Central and Northern California and Western Nevada. Federal prisoners were sometimes held there. Transients en route to third countries were detained. During both world wars, "enemy aliens" were interned there, and in the Second World War Japanese, Italian, and German prisoners-of-war. The total number of people who were detained at the station may have reached half a million.[8]

Immigration to the United States over the last 150 years is a topic fraught with conflict. When one compares current controversies with the record of the first decades of the twentieth century, it becomes clear that the roots of anti-immigrant sentiment have not changed much from then until now: distrust of "the other," racial and religious bias, and fear that immigrants will take away "American" jobs. As of this writing, the polarization in the country around immigration is the starkest it has been in my lifetime. On the one hand is a trend toward increasing acceptance of diversity, on the other a reactionary impulse—exacerbated by the current leadership—to blame minorities and foreigners for societal ills. The immigration jails on the Mexican border today are eerily similar to the Angel Island of one hundred years ago. This book engages the issues, but does so from a micro level; it is a historical and literary anthology designed to provide a conduit for readers today to connect with the perspectives and experiences of individual immigrants still in the process of "becoming American."

The old station barracks contains an extraordinary archive: hundreds of poems and prose records in multiple languages are on the walls, inscribed by immigrant detainees between 1910 and 1940, and by prisoners-of-war and "enemy aliens" during the Second World War. While Chinese remains the dominant language on the walls, Japanese is also strongly represented, and Russian, English, Spanish, Italian, French, German, Punjabi (both Gurmukhi and Urdu scripts), Bengali, and Korean are also found. A selection is included here, augmented by literary materials from Bay Area ethnic newspapers. Each text tells the story of an individual, but taken together they illuminate historical, economic, and cultural forces that shaped the lives of ordinary people in the early twentieth century.

Laws and policies targeted immigrants in different ways during the period of the immigration station's operation. Chinese immigration was governed by the Exclusion Act of 1882 and subsequent revisions and additions to it. The Gentlemen's Agreement of 1907–1908 regulated Japanese arrivals. A variety of laws, primarily related to class and gender, was brought to bear on arrivals from many countries. In turn, the treatment meted out to immigrants from various countries was not uniform. Thus, following the framework of Lee and Yung's *Angel Island*, this book devotes a separate chapter to each group. The chapters are prefaced by capsule summaries of immigration laws and history that pertain to each. A final chapter is devoted to the Second World War experience at Angel Island.

About this Anthology

This book had its genesis more than fifteen years ago, when the Angel Island Immigration Station Foundation, California State Parks, and the Architectural Resources Group commissioned a new survey of the barracks walls. I was invited to join a project team along with Wan Liu, Xing Chu Wang, and Newton Liu. Our work was supervised and facilitated by Interpretive Consultant Daniel Quan. Among other tasks, we were asked to find the locations of previously published Chinese texts; identify, and if possible transcribe and translate, other Chinese texts; and to transcribe and translate inscriptions in Japanese and other languages. In February 2004, the team submitted its report.[9] While very preliminary in many respects, the report presented a wealth of new information and avenues for research.[10] Hundreds of puzzles waiting to be solved. I was hooked.

Since then, as time has allowed I have continued to study the walls. Conditions in the barracks are poor, making decipherment slow and painstaking. To immigrants, the inscriptions were self-expression, but to the authorities they were merely graffiti. Seven distinct painting campaigns have been documented, and the impressions of the inscriptions were filled with putty. That we can see anything today is a result of shrinkage of the putty over time. Yet this process has not been at all uniform: in some places the writing can be seen relatively clearly, but in others the paint surface remains smooth, or mostly so. Over the years, I have benefited from the input of many people in compiling this anthology, and I am grateful. All remaining errors are my own.

Inscriptions

The Chinese writing at the station is already well known, and is compelling because so much of it is poetry. Chinese detainees expressed their feelings of sadness, anger, and hope in scores of poems in classical forms. Indeed, this was already a tradition when the station opened—there are references to Chinese poems written on the walls of the old "wooden building" on the Pacific Mail Steamship Company wharf in San Francisco, where Chinese immigrants were detained prior to 1910.[11] There are strong cultural reasons that moved Chinese immigrants to inscribe poems on the walls. Poetry was the dominant medium of artistic expression in old China. Public poetry held a special social and ritual function, whether inscribed on a building, a tablet placed at an important site, or even carved on the side of a cliff. Generally, such inscriptions advocated harmony and the common good, and without them the place remained somehow incomplete. The written word was needed to both express and maintain the proper relationships among heaven, earth, and man. A modern counterpart can be seen every Chinese New Year, when people paste *duilian*—New Year's couplets—to the sides of their doors to ensure peace and prosperity for their families. Yet poetry had another public purpose as well: this medium was commonly used by the upright scholar to decry injustice and champion the oppressed. Speaking truth to power, even at personal risk, was demanded by the Confucian moral code.

Moreover, whether invocation or complaint, the beauty of Chinese calligraphy makes public texts not only literary communications but also art objects for viewers to enjoy. It is clear that every poet represented at Angel Island felt a strong responsibility to express the communal feelings of all his fellow immigrants, about their detention and about the future. The poems on the walls reflect a community of shared experiences and values, and were a source of solidarity for detainees trapped in a limbo between the old country and the new.

A group of 135 of these Chinese poems, augmented by individual stories of immigrants and a capsule history of the Chinese experience at the immigration station, formed the 1980 collection, *Island: Poetry and History of Chinese Immigrants on Angel Island, 1910–1940*, by Him Mark Lai, Genny Lim, and Judy Yung. A revised edition was published in 2014. The authors were assisted and encouraged in their task by a whole community of people—former detainees who provided oral histories, dedicated volunteers who painstakingly documented and helped to decipher wall texts, and a host of people who tirelessly advocated the preservation and restoration of the Angel Island Immigration Station site. They also fortuitously discovered manuscripts by Tet Yee and Smiley Jann, two former detainees who copied many poems from the walls in the early 1930s; these became invaluable sources. This pioneering book is a classic in the history of the immigration experience, and many of the issues it raises—concerning policies of exclusion, racial and cultural bias, fear of the immigrant "other," and institutionalized inequality—are as topical today as they were when it was published, or when the poems were written.

Classical Chinese poetry is a lyric tradition, thus most poems are short (generally less than a dozen lines) evocations of human feeling. The great majority of the poems at the station employ the standard *shi* (詩) forms. These forms are unfailingly regular—the line length is either pentasyllabic or heptasyllabic throughout, each line is divided in 2/3 or 4/3 syllable segments, pairs of lines form couplets, and a rhyme falls at the end of every couplet (and sometimes the first line). The *shi* forms derive from a tradition going back 2,000 years; it is notable that none of the Angel Island examples uses the experimental free verse that was in vogue among Chinese urban intellectuals in the early twentieth century. The immigrant authors were mostly boys and young men from rural villages in Guangdong, and they responded to their detention experience in traditional ways.

Several examples from *Island* can illustrate the *shi* forms used at Angel Island—as well as the range of topics and the high quality of expression.[12] The following, #24 in the collection, is a heptasyllabic "ancient verse" (古詩). Ancient verse was the earliest of the *shi* forms to develop, and there are few rules beyond those mentioned above. Length can vary widely.

Random Thoughts Deep at Night

In the quiet of night, I heard, faintly, the whistling of wind.
The forms and shadows saddened me; upon seeing the landscape, I composed a poem.
The floating clouds, the fog, darken the sky.
The moon shines faintly as the insects chirp.
Grief and bitterness entwined are heaven sent.
The sad person sits alone, leaning by a window.
　　　　　　　　　Written by Yee of Toishan

深夜偶感
夜靜微聞風嘯聲
形影傷情見景詠
雲霧濘濘也暗天
蟲聲唧唧月微明
悲苦相連天相遺
愁人獨坐倚窗邊
台山余題
13

The author deftly integrates the images around him with his melancholy. A seamless "union of feeling and scene" was a desired quality in traditional Chinese poetry. The middle couplet is particularly effective. It is nearly parallel, though not quite—parts of speech in the first four positions in the first line match those in the same locations in the second line. Parallel couplets are an elegant way to provide descriptive imagery with emotional resonance.

Island #23 is a pentasyllabic *jueju* (絕句) quatrain. This form is one of the "recent-style verse" (近體詩) forms that expanded "ancient verse" in new ways. The pentasyllabic *jueju* and heptasyllabic *jueju* are limited to four lines, making them the shortest classical poetic forms that were in common use. Brevity forced writers to pare every topic down to a few essential images, and to arrange them subordinate to a single controlling theme. A premium was placed on creating suggestive, thought-provoking language to project meaning and resonance beyond the literal text. Poets reveled in the challenge "to see big within small."

Today is the last day of winter;
Tomorrow morning is the vernal equinox.
One year's prospects have changed to another.
Sadness kills the person in the wooden building.

今日為冬末
明朝是春分
交替兩年景
愁煞木樓人
14

One of the most moving poems in the collection is #112, the second of a pair eulogizing a detainee who had sickened and died at the station.

Shocking news, truly sad reached my ears.
We mourn you. When will they wrap your corpse
    for return?
You cannot close your eyes. On whom are you
    depending to voice your complaints?
If you had foresight, you should have regretted
    coming here.
Now you will be forever sad and forever resentful.
Thinking of the village, one can only futilely face
    the Terrace for Gazing Homeward.
Before you could fulfill your lofty goals, you were
    buried beneath clay and earth.
I know that even death could not destroy your ambition.

噩耗傳聞實可哀
弔君何日裹屍回
無能瞑目憑誰訴
有識應知悔此來
十古含愁千古恨
思鄉空對望鄉台
禾酬壯志埋壞上
知爾雄心死不灰

15

The poet's cry of grief is presented using another of the "recent-style verse" forms, the heptasyllabic regulated verse (律詩). This form and its pentasyllabic counterpart are fixed at eight lines. Particularly challenging is the requirement that strict patterns of the Chinese tones must be followed. To simplify, the tones divide according to sound quality into two groups, level and oblique, and alternation is expected in both the individual line and the couplet. For example, a typical couplet pattern is as follows:

```
- - + + - - +
+ + - - + + -
```

Flexibility is allowed in line positions 1, 3, and 5, but the pattern must be adhered to in positions 2, 4, 6, and 7, as these are stressed syllables. There are other rules for tonal prosody as well. Suffice to say that observing the patterns properly is not easy. The above poem follows the rules perfectly. Regulated verse also stipulates that the middle two couplets be syntactically parallel. The second couplet here is indeed parallel. The third couplet is not, yet it is a powerful statement. The allusion to the Terrace for Gazing Homeward is particularly apt. In Chinese popular mythology, it is the place in the netherworld where the recently deceased can look back at the land of the living for the last time.

Not all the Chinese inscriptions at Angel Island are poems. Another type found in numbers is the extended parallel couplet. These unrhymed prose pieces consist of two sentences presented in syntactic parallelism. The challenge is to maintain the parallelism even when the sentences are quite lengthy. Extended parallel couplets are carved on the walls in an unusual configuration: the sentences are carved vertically, beginning at right and left. They conclude in the middle. *Island* #15 is a fine example:

Abandoning wife and child, I crossed an entire ocean.
   I do not know how much wind
   and frost I've weathered; it was because my family
   was poor that I searched for white jade.
Bidding farewell to relatives and friends, I drifted ten
   thousand *li*. It is difficult to keep
   track of all the rain and snow I've endured; it is all
   due to an empty purse and my reverence for
   copper coins.

拋妻子、重洋歷盡、不知受幾多風霜、
祇為家貧求白璧。
別親朋、萬里飄流、難計捱一切雨雪、
都緣囊澀重青蚨。

16

The calligraphy of the Chinese inscriptions is remarkably good. Traditional education began with the art of the brush, and daily copying of the works of the masters. The revered place of writing in Chinese culture has philosophical roots: it was held that calligraphy, even more than the other arts, is the spontaneous and concrete expression of inner spiritual states. Thus good calligraphy was seen as a mark of personal cultivation, and an indication of moral standing as well. The Angel Island writers were not "scholars" in any traditional sense, but many had obviously received solid educations. The poetic form and content of the inscriptions reveal a sometimes sophisticated understanding of the classical tradition, and the calligraphy reflects many years of training. Yet the poems carved on the walls mark the end of the era of traditional Chinese education. Two or three decades later, and a similar group of ordinary detainees would not have been able to accomplish what they did. Study of the classics had little place in China's modernization efforts, and mostly became the province of university Chinese departments, while the use of pens and pencils in the modern classroom relegated calligraphy to the art studios.

Most of the Angel Island inscriptions reflect the vigorous yet elegant "standard *kaishu*" style used in Qing dynasty woodblock printed books and government documents. This style was designed for efficiency, but also to impress with its bold strength. Long, sweeping lines and sharp angles characterize *kaishu*. The strokes are constructed with multiple discrete movements of the brush, so that each presents a finished structure— angle plays off angle, and straight complements curve. The strokes are added one by one within an imaginary design square such that the proportions always remain in balance, to ensure that the complete character will have integrity and stability. Yet at the same time there is tension and energy, as the various parts play off against each other. An apt metaphor for *kaishu* characters is the drawn bow, which at any moment may unleash the arrow.

There are many calligraphy models to choose from for studying *kaishu*; for convenience let us categorize Angel Island examples using the contrasting styles of the two most influential early *kaishu* masters, Yan Zhenqing (eighth century) and Liu Gongquan (ninth century). Both are outstanding examples of the *kaishu* aesthetic, yet Yan favored thick, almost blocky strokes that gave his characters weight and monumentality (Fig. 0.2). At Angel Island, compare *Island* #60 (Fig. 0.3). Liu, on the other hand, used more slender strokes that are hard and sharp, and which gave his characters lightness and energy (Fig. 0.4). At Angel Island, compare *Island* #2 (Fig. 0.5). The styles of the two calligraphers are seen as complementary: the "muscle of Yan and the bone of Liu" (顏筋柳骨).

Some of the best calligraphic examples at Angel Island reflect a more individual "running standard *xingkai*" style. The "standard *kaishu*" aesthetic remains, but the writer adapts it for rapid brushwork. The strokes tend to run together as the brush moves over the surface, creating a graceful interplay of curves to balance the strong skeletal structure. Each character is a fixed record of the subtle movement of the brush, and as character succeeds character, the piece emerges organically and dynamically. The process is analogous to a dance: a sequence of orderly movements is imbued with

FIGURE 0.2 *Yan Zhenqing, detail of "Yan Qinli Stele."*

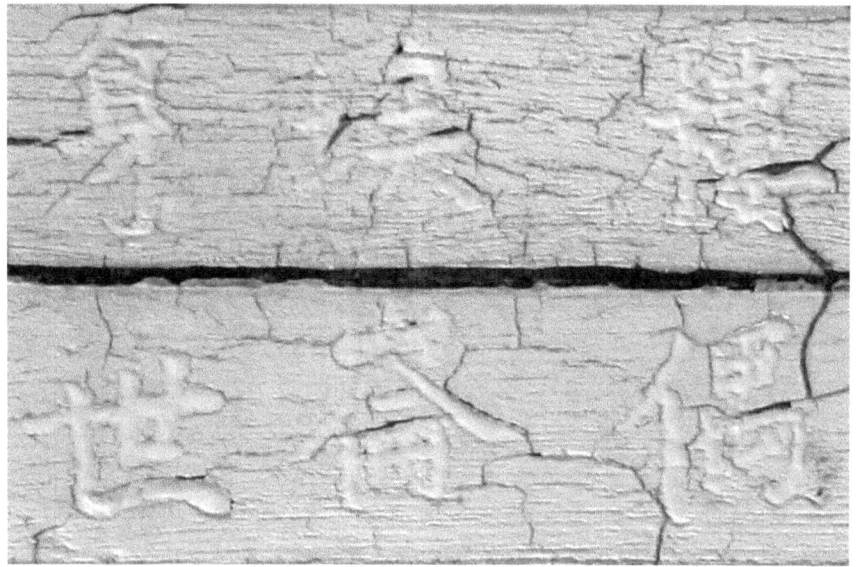

FIGURE 0.3 *Detail of* Island #60. *Photo: Michael Nelsen.*

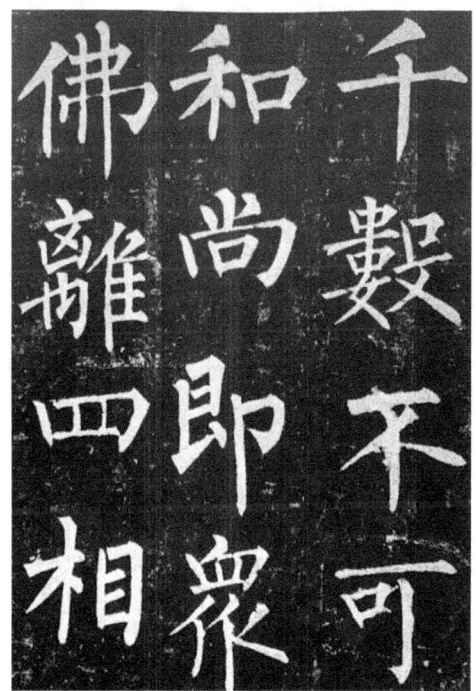

FIGURE 0.4 *Liu Gongquan, detail of* "Xuanmi Stupa Stele."

FIGURE 0.5 Island #2. *Photo: Architectural Resources Group (modified for character recognition by Daniel Quan Design).*

freedom and personal flair (Fig. 0.6). Many of the Japanese carvings show strong calligraphic style as well, and even some of the European inscriptions were created with artistic spirit (Fig. 0.7).

The cultural reasons which led Chinese detainees to write poems on the walls were specific to them. Inscriptions in other languages tend to be straightforward prose, often only names. Yet these, too, are evocative and compelling, for they are tangible records of real people living through a difficult period in their lives. It was enough for some to say, "I was here." There is power in names on a wall. In the nineteenth century, travelers on the Oregon Trail would stop and carve their names on Independence Rock, Wyoming. The site is now a National Historic Monument, and a symbol of the pioneer spirit. Angel Island is the Independence Rock of immigration history.

The United States is a nation of immigrants, so it is only natural—and personal—that we want to know upon whose shoulders we stand. I have researched my own family genealogy, and it has made me feel more connected

FIGURE 0.6 *Detail of Chapter 3, #13 text.*

FIGURE 0.7 *Enrique Piton inscription. See Chapter 4.*

and enriched. The Chinese poems on the walls are powerful and heartfelt, yet no individual author has yet been identified. The names carved by Japanese, Russian, and other detainees are another matter. In many cases, it has been possible to identify the writers, and trace their life stories through public documents. One document can lead to the next, and then the history of an entire family can be discerned. In some cases, I have been fortunate to make contact with living descendants, who have provided their personal

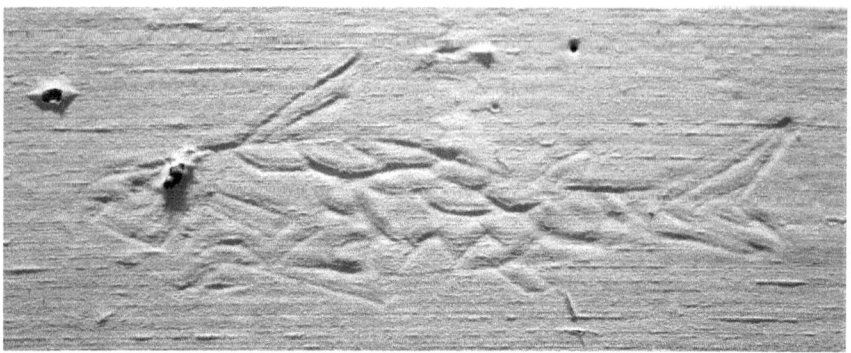

FIGURE 0.8 *Scaly fish. Photo: Michael Nelsen.*

recollections and stories. It has been striking to me how many Angel Island detainees and their families have been swept up in the great events of the last century.

Poetry about the immigration experience was certainly written by groups other than Chinese, even though examples on the walls are few. Ethnic newspapers of the 1910–1940 period contain a great variety of poems and other literary materials by immigrants; some writers mention Angel Island detainment directly, while others complain about government policies, express homesickness, or present perspectives on their new lives in California. A selection of these texts with English translations is also included here.

There are also some forty carved pictures on the walls—birds, ships, human and animal figures, and most surprisingly, two ancestral altars (Fig. 0.8). To see these carved inscriptions and pictures, or the messages penned on top of the paint by Second World War detainees, is to feel a visceral link with those who made them.

Conservation efforts

The Immigration Station was abandoned after the Second World War, and over the years fell into serious disrepair. State Parks had plans to redevelop the site as a campground with recreational facilities, and slated the existing structures for demolition. The wharf was torn down in 1971, as was a Second World War mess hall. A low point was when permission was given for nine old employee cottages to be burned down as a firefighter training exercise—a bitter loss, as they had been designed by acclaimed Hearst Castle architect Julia Morgan. Footage of the fire was used in a Robert Redford film, "The Candidate" (released in 1972). Fortunately, in May of 1970 Park Ranger Alexander Weiss explored the old detainee barracks, and was intrigued by the inscriptions on the walls. As his superiors were unimpressed, he contacted Dr. George Araki at San Francisco State University, who confirmed their historical importance. Araki and photographer Mak Takahashi visited to comprehensively document the wall texts. Members of the local Asian American community became engaged, and led by Paul Chow, formed the Angel Island Immigration Station Historical Advisory Committee to lobby for the preservation of the barracks.

In the summer of 1971, another State Parks employee, Denis Englander, also explored the barracks. He, too, described the inscriptions to his instructor at San Francisco State, who contacted Ethnic Studies faculty. While he was not the first, his efforts are also commendable. A photographer, Denis took multiple shots of the site as it was then, including what may be the last photograph of the wharf and baggage shed before demolition (Fig. 0.9).

The community's efforts were rewarded in 1976, when the California State Legislature appropriated $250,000 to restore and preserve the barracks as a state monument. It was opened to the public in 1983. The non-profit Angel Island Immigration Station Foundation was created at the same time, and in partnership with California State Parks, now oversees preservation and educational efforts. The site was named a National Historic Landmark in 1997, and in 1999 was listed as an official project of the "Save America's Treasures" program. Federal financial support has followed, as well as additional state funding and significant private donations. An ambitious Master Plan for restoration was adopted in 2003, to interpret the entire fifteen-acre site and prepare it as a major educational destination. Phase 1 repaired and restored the barracks, cleaned and stabilized the walls with inscriptions,

FIGURE 0.9 *The pier and baggage shed in 1971. Photo: Denis Englander.*

upgraded utilities, established an interpretive site on the Administration Building "footprint," and restored landscaping; the site reopened to the public in 2009. Phase 2, now almost complete, stabilized and repaired the hospital building to house a multi-purpose learning center, the Angel Island Immigration Museum.[17]

Inscription and Picture Locations

Each of the texts and miscellaneous carvings in this anthology includes a location code in the endnotes, to aid readers in finding them on the barracks walls. A few items were found in the station hospital, and are so noted. These were removed from the walls there during recent renovations, and are now in California State Parks storage. In addition, barracks locations of the *Island* poems are specified in the Appendices, as the published work did not include them.

The coding system is quite basic. Maps of the first and second floors of the barracks will help visitors navigate the building (Figs. 0.10, 0.11). Each room is given a number. The four walls of each room are designated by the cardinal directions, N, S, E, and W. The north wall is that which faces the main courtyard and station hospital. On each wall, a simple numbering sequence differentiates sections, and runs from left to right as the visitor faces it. Usually, but not always, a section is quite distinct, like a portion of a wall between windows. Thus a location code like 205-S-1 will guide one to a text or carving in Room 205 on the second floor (one of the two Chinese men's dormitories), on the south wall, and at far left. These codes will get one close, but a bit of scanning the area may still be needed to find the item.

The wall inscriptions in this book are those that have yielded to decipherment, but it should be remembered that many others have not. Some texts have been partially deciphered, but not enough to be sure of

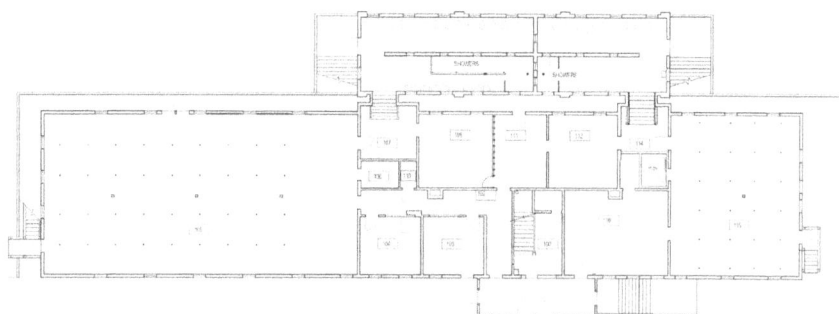

FIGURE 0.10 *Barracks map, first floor. Courtesy Daniel Quan.*

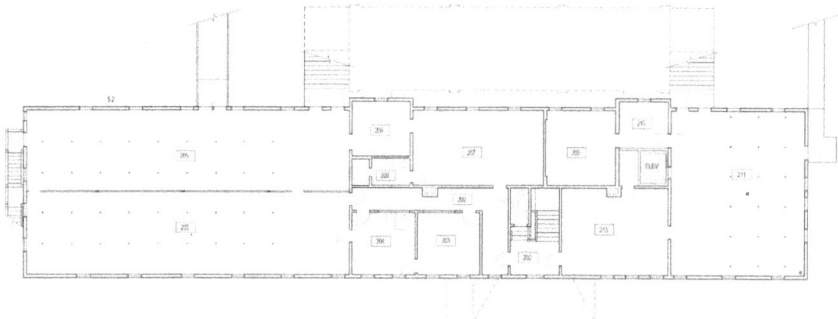

FIGURE 0.11 *Barracks map, second floor. Courtesy Daniel Quan.*

their overall meaning, while some remain completely obscured. Digital photography is helpful, but still has its limits—it cannot help us see beneath the putty and paint. Imaging technologies that *can* penetrate beneath the surface—like X-ray photography and infrared thermography—have not so far worked at Angel Island. Perhaps advances in techniques will change that, and we can look forward to another anthology with new inscriptions. Until then, the walls will keep their remaining secrets.

A Note on Transcription and Translation

When transcribing original texts, characters or letters that have been deciphered with certainty or near-certainty are presented unmarked; those which have been deciphered with less certainty, but based on solid visual and/or contextual evidence, are presented in brackets [ ]; and characters or letters that remain unreadable are marked with a plain square ☐. Replicating the rhyme and meter of poems was not attempted in the translations, which are in prose designed to convey as much of the meaning and tone of the originals as possible. Chinese names and terms are transliterated using the Pinyin system.

1

Japanese Inscriptions, 1910–1940

First dream of the New Year—On the island I meet my picture bride

For Japanese immigrants, the so-called Gentlemen's Agreement of 1907–1908 was the major factor governing immigration practices until 1924. Immigration of Japanese had been relatively free since 1894 under the terms of the US-Japan Treaty of Commerce and Navigation, and the number of Japanese workers in California, Oregon, and Washington had swelled, particularly in agriculture. The Territory of Hawaii attracted even larger numbers—30,000 Japanese contract laborers were there by 1885. Most of the immigrants came from a small number of prefectures in southwestern Japan: Wakayama, Okayama, Hiroshima, Yamaguchi, Nagasaki, Saga, Kumamoto, and (somewhat later than the others) Okinawa.[1] By the early twentieth century, anti-Japanese sentiment had also grown. The Asiatic Exclusion League, a powerful voice for restricting immigration through to the end of the Second World War, was in fact founded in 1905 as the Japanese and Korean Exclusion League. In 1906, the school board in San Francisco voted to ban Japanese and Korean children from public schools that served the general population, and instead required them to attend a newly established "Oriental Public School" along with Chinese children. The Japanese government was offended by this and other acts of discrimination, and so entered negotiations on the immigration issue with President Theodore Roosevelt. Japan agreed not to issue passports to laborers intending to immigrate to the continental US or the territory of Hawaii (professional classes were exempt, as were those laborers returning to a domicile or farm formerly acquired), while Roosevelt agreed to intervene in the San Francisco school plan, and not move forward on a formal exclusion law aimed at the Japanese. A key exception in the agreement was to have far-reaching consequences: parents, spouses, and children of Japanese residents in the US could be allowed passports and entry.[2]

One unanticipated result (from the US perspective) was the coming of the "picture brides," and the ensuing growth of the Japanese community. Young women in Japan were legally married to absent bridegrooms residing in the United States, often with their only previous contact the exchange of photographs and correspondence. The new brides then were given valid passports to travel to the US to meet their husbands. The Japanese government watched over the system. All prospective bridegrooms had to meet a financial standard (in mid-1915 set at $800 in savings). Brides had to be officially registered with their bridegroom's household in Japan at least six months before they could travel abroad, and could not be more than thirteen years younger than their spouses.[3] US authorities were at first perplexed by the practice, and how to reconcile it with domestic marriage law. In April 1911, a San Francisco judge summoned the Japanese Consul General and others to discuss the issues. The *Los Angeles Times* reported,

> Judge Graham stated today he wished to find out if photographic marriages were recognized as legal and customary in Japan, and if there were anything in the treaty between this country and that nation which would bind the authorities here to the admission of girls under age upon marriages performed in this port before arrival. There are now five girls under sixteen years of age who are being held at Angel Island pending a decision in the case of Tane Murase. Proceedings for the appointment of a guardian in order that the five may be given "permission" by the guardian to marry under the American laws are now on file in the Superior Court.[4]

Between 1910 and 1920, when Japan agreed to stop issuing passports to picture brides (the so-called Ladies' Agreement), between 6,000 and 10,000 were processed through Angel Island, in addition to the thousands of Japanese men who applied for entry through various exemptions.[5] Nearly 20,000 picture brides settled in Hawaii in about the same period. At the insistence of the Immigration Service, grooms were required to come in person to Angel Island to meet their brides—the thought of the many happy meetings that occurred there partially counterbalances the weight of heartache of Angel Island detainees. The picture-bride system was not the only way for Japanese men in the US to build families. Many men who had the financial means traveled back to Japan to find brides, and some men who had been previously married in Japan summoned their wives to join them when they decided to become permanent settlers.

The opening of the Angel Island Immigration Station coincided with a transitional period for the Japanese community. As Yuji Ichioka explains, the history of Japanese immigration can be divided into two broad periods: 1885 to 1907, and 1908 to 1924. The first is characterized by the *dekasegi* ideal, which refers to the practice of Japanese laborers leaving their homes temporarily to work elsewhere. Implicit was the idea that the workers would return home to Japan later. Japanese in California at this period were predominantly laborers who engaged in railroad construction or agricultural work, often living in primitive and temporary "camps" (*kyanpu*) in rural areas. Populated at first entirely by men, life there was harsh, and leisure was often devoted to drinking and gambling. Subsequent to the Gentlemen's Agreement, visionary community leaders like Kyutaro Abiko (1865–1936), founder and publisher of the *Nichibei Shimbun* [The Japanese-American News], called for *dochaku eijū* (settlement of the land and permanent residency). A campaign in the newspaper railed against drinking and gambling in the "camps," and encouraged picture-bride marriages and self-sufficiency through agriculture. Abiko and his associates went so far as to purchase land in the Central Valley to foster Japanese utopian agricultural colonies.[6] They bought 3,200 acres of land in Livingston, California, and founded the Yamato Colony in 1907. Two more colonies were established nearby: Cressey in 1918, and Cortez in 1919.[7] Tajiro Kishi was the first Issei to buy land at the Yamato Colony; by 1908, there were thirty colonists. Although life in the colonies was grueling at first, the experiment was ultimately successful: many descendants of the first hardy pioneers still farm the land there.[8]

The amount of land cultivated by Japanese immigrant farmers expanded greatly in the 1910s. Yet a great blow was the 1913 California Alien Land Law, and in particular a stricter 1920 version approved by a ballot initiative, which prohibited "aliens ineligible for citizenship" from purchasing agricultural land, bequeathing or selling it to other immigrants, or leasing it for periods longer than three years. The law was further strengthened in 1923. Though some were able to protect existing holdings through creative legal means like participation in land companies, or even to purchase land in the names of their Nisei children (who were US citizens by birth), the expansion of the Japanese presence in agriculture was effectively curtailed.[9] Between 1920 and 1930, the number of Japanese-operated farms in California fell about 25 percent, and the number of acres farmed fell almost 50 percent.[10] Another major blow was the internment in the Second World War of west coast Japanese Americans. At war's end, many Japanese-American farmers, particularly those who relied on leased land, were unable to resume farming. The total number of Japanese farmers fell by 40 percent between 1940 and 1950, and the number of acres farmed dropped by 25 percent. By 1950, Japanese Americans in California were farming almost the same number of acres as in 1910.[11] The combined effect of the Alien Land Law and the internment precipitated a migration of Japanese Americans to the cities. The California Alien Land Law was finally repealed by popular vote, but not until 1956.

Changes in US law closed the window on almost all Asian immigration. The Immigration Act of 1917 created an "Asiatic barred zone," which covered South and Southeast Asia, the Polynesian islands, Asiatic Russia, and parts of Arabia and Afghanistan. The Act effectively broadened the Chinese Exclusion Act to cover all these localities. Japan was not included (it was an ally in the First World War), but this was to change. The Immigration Act of 1924 included a provision that barred entry to any person who was not eligible for naturalization, which effectively excluded Japanese without having to mention them specifically. Strong protests by the Japanese government were in vain.

The emigration of Japanese in the late-nineteenth and early-twentieth centuries was primarily a working-class phenomenon, caused by the collapse of traditional agricultural economies as commercial farming was introduced by Meiji reformers. Yet Issei leaders in the United States were mostly of the mercantilist class, better educated and closer in outlook with the expansive designs of the home country. A complex dialectic ensued in the formation of the Japanese-American identity. On the one hand, Japanese immigrants were encouraged to remain loyal imperial subjects, and to adopt the ideology of the modern Japanese state. Emigration, for example, became synonymous with colonization, in recognition of Japan's imperialist ambitions. On the other hand, immigrants reacted to their situation as non-white Other by banding together in solidarity to create a distinct Japanese-American community, its identity loosely based on the rugged American pioneer ideal. "Japanese immigrants were often able to navigate through the two state ideologies, not only by turning one against the other but also by conveniently fusing aspects of them."[12]

The thirteen wall inscriptions from the immigration period which lead off the selections in this chapter are mostly found in the small dormitories and sitting rooms that were reserved for Japanese and Europeans (Rooms 115, 116, and 211). Although simple and prosaic (names, places, etc.), some are specific enough to have allowed research to discover the family stories of the writers. Second World War Japanese inscriptions, presented in Chapter 5, are found in most of the rooms in the barracks building.

While Japanese detainees in the 1910–1940 period did not carve poems on the station walls, hundreds and hundreds of poems that describe the immigration experience were published in Japanese newspapers in California. Prose pieces that provide a personal view of the American experience also were frequently included. The remainder of the selections in this chapter are poems and prose published in the Japanese language newspaper *Nichibei Shimbun* [The Japanese-American News]. It was founded in 1899, when publisher Kyutaro Abiko and partners combined two existing dailies. *Nichibei* became the most influential Japanese newspaper in America in the first half of the twentieth century. It ceased publication upon the outbreak of hostilities in 1942, but then was restarted (under different hands) in 1946, and continued to 2009 as the *Nichi Bei Times*. There was to be another rebirth: immediately after the *Nichi Bei Times* shuttered its doors, community leaders and former staff founded the Nichi Bei Foundation, and began to publish the *Nichi Bei Weekly* as a nonprofit newspaper.[13] The foundation also sponsors educational programs, such as a series of Nikkei Angel Island Pilgrimages.[14]

Poems and other literary materials (e.g., serial fiction, essays, anecdotes) were regularly published in *Nichibei*. Many were submitted by readers, and then were selected by the editors for publication. Others were likely written by the editors and staff themselves. Sometimes full names of authors are appended, but much more often pen names appear. Holidays saw particularly large numbers of *haiku*, *tanka*, and other verses. With a few exceptions, the *Nichibei* selections included here are all from the 1910–1924 period. The latter year was when new Japanese immigration was effectively halted. While the Chinese poems in Chapter 3 and in *Island* were composed within the Angel Island Immigration Station barracks, and so reflect the perspective of a group of people in-between countries who had not yet had real experience with American life, the Japanese poems and prose are much more varied. The topics cover the gamut of Japanese immigrant life in the period: Angel Island and picture brides, homesickness for Japan, perspectives on San Francisco and California life and scenery, farm work in the Central Valley, and complaints about discriminatory laws and treatment. A particular focus is on life in "camp." "Camp" refers to any of the temporary work camps in the Central Valley where Japanese migrant laborers found themselves. Yet "camp" in *Nichibei* also refers to the Yamato Colony and similar settlements: many poems document the arrival of wives, the coming of children, and the pride that settlers felt when they saw their heavy labors come to fruition. Taken as a whole, the texts reveal the joys and travails of the Issei as they created something new and permanent. When the Japanese-American experience is discussed in the media these days, invariably the focus is on the tragedy of internment during the Second World War. Yet the Issei experience that these texts represent predates that. Their lives were hard, they were homesick for Japan, and they encountered bias and discrimination, but at the same time they remained focused on building new lives in the US. The emotions they express in the poems and prose selections were mixed, but chief among them was hope.

WALL INSCRIPTIONS

1.

44th Year of Meiji　　明治四拾四年
3rd Year of Xuantong　宣統三年
¹⁵

FIGURE 1.1 *Meiji and Xuantong dates. Photo: ARG and Daniel Quan.*

Side by side on a wall of the station hospital were found these two dates, one Japanese and the other Chinese. Both refer to 1911 (Fig. 1.1). Meiji and Xuantong are imperial reign names, and years are counted from the time an emperor accedes to the throne. Mutsuhito of Japan (1852–1912) became emperor in 1867, using the reign name Meiji (Enlightened Rule). The policies and reforms of his government built the foundation of the modern Japanese state. In contrast, the Chinese Qing dynasty government oversaw a series of failed reforms, and in addition was weakened by internal rebellions and incursions by foreign powers. By the time three-year-old Puyi (1906–1967) was made emperor Xuantong (Manifest Unity), Qing power was spent. An uprising that began at Wuchang in October 1911 quickly spread to the rest of the country, and the Qing was overthrown and succeeded by the Republic of China. Puyi was China's last emperor.

2.

Miyamoto
Nukui Community, Kawauchi Village, Asa District, Hiroshima Prefecture
45th Year

廣島縣安佐郡川內村町溫井ミヤモト
四十五年 [16]

The date in this inscription in Room 211 of the men's barracks refers to the forty-fifth year of the Meiji era, or 1912. This was the last year of Meiji, and since the emperor died on July 30, the inscription must have been carved during the previous seven months. The only male immigrant surnamed Miyamoto detained in that period was teenager Masaru Miyamoto, who arrived with his mother Mitsuyo Miyamoto (born c. 1874) on the *Mongolia* on June 17.[17] Masaru and Mitsuyo were traveling to join husband and father Chiyokichi Miyamoto (born c. 1866), a farmer in Fresno County. Yet both were detained at Angel Island for several weeks, for treatment of uncinariasis—hookworm. They were finally admitted on July 5.[18]

A convoluted search through government documents allowed me to make contact with Masaru's descendants in Los Angeles, and so what follows is partly based on their family memories. The family also fortuitously recorded a moving oral history with Masaru and his wife Kinuyo in 1986, and provided a copy.[19] The Miyamotos were indeed from Nukui, Kawauchi Village, Asa District, Hiroshima Prefecture.[20] The area is now part of the Asaminami Ward of Hiroshima City. Chiyokichi was not born a Miyamoto—he was the second son of Jusaburo Kuramoto and his wife; he was adopted by Tamihei Miyamoto and family, probably because they had no son who could inherit. (An additional benefit for Chiyokichi was that firstborn sons were exempt from army service.) This was not the last name change for the family! When Chiyokichi and Mitsuyo decided to immigrate to Hawaii in 1895 (they had married the same year),[21] they found that applicants from their village were subject to a waiting period before wives could join their husbands. So Chiyokichi borrowed the name of an acquaintance from a nearby village that did not require a waiting period. The 1900 US Census finds Asaboro and Mitsuyo Hokoda (whose ages match those of Chiyokichi and Mitsuyo Miyamoto seen in other records) living in North Kohala on the Big Island of Hawaii, along with their three-year-old son Masaru Hokoda. The Kohala region, comprising North and South Kohala, is the northernmost part of the Big Island. It was a major producer of sugar, and a cane plantation is apparently where Asaboro (Chiyokichi) worked—the Census describes him as a "field laborer," while Mitsuyo took in sewing. Three other children were born to the couple in Hawaii subsequently. Chiyokichi moved the family to California in 1908 and reclaimed the surname Miyamoto.[22] Though Chiyokichi was alone in California at the time of the 1910 Census, working as a hired hand at a Fresno farm,[23] by 1920 he and Mitsuyo—as C. and M. Miomoto—were farming in the Vinland Precinct of Fresno Township 11, and three children were with them, sons Masaru and Minoru (born *c.* 1906), and daughter Misao (born 1914 in California).[24] Another son, Yoshio (born *c.* 1909), was in boarding school in Hawaii, and daughter Chika (born *c.* 1903) was married and living separately in Fresno. The Hokoda name is nowhere to be seen. Passenger manifests of the 1910s and 1920s suggest that members of the Miyamoto family, either singly or severally, made multiple visits to Japan, with their contact address back in Kawauchi Village.[25]

The fact that the 1900 Census in Hawaii lists Masaru as three years old was puzzling to his descendants, as they are certain he was born on May 7, 1899—the date listed in the Social Security system and used in most official records. Yet Social Security cards were not issued until 1937, when Masaru was an adult. The 1900 Census specifically records that Masaru was born in May 1897 (birth month and birth year were among the questions asked). That year the Census was conducted beginning in June—he would have just turned three. Further, when Mitsuyo and Masaru arrived in San Francisco in June 1912, the passenger manifest lists his age as fifteen. Subsequent records show two years shaved off his age. The arrival record also affirms Masaru's birthplace as "Kohara, Hawaii"—certainly Kohala.

FIGURE 1.2 *Masaru and Kinuyo's wedding day. Courtesy Donna Ebata.*

By October of 1920, Masaru Miyamoto was married (Fig. 1.2). His new bride Kinuyo Miyamoto (née Shimonishi) had also been born in Hawaii, and was from a farming family in Fresno. The Shimonishi family returned for a time to Japan, and Kinuyo and her elder sister spent their childhoods there. Kinuyo later recalled her sister as a beauty who died tragically in a typhoid outbreak at age eighteen. In 1918, Kinuyo returned to California with her father Taichi Shimonishi, a farmer in Clovis, Fresno County. Like her future husband, she also had the unenviable experience of Angel Island detention, as she and Taichi were held there for two days.[26] Kinuyo and Masaru's marriage was arranged. She told the story of their first meeting to the family in 1986. One day she was riding her bicycle in Fresno, when an old friend of her father (acting as matchmaker) drove by and offered her a ride. Masaru and his father Chiyokichi were also in the car. Kinuyo had no idea she was being "checked out!"

Masaru decided to make a trip back to Hawaii to locate his birth records, because the Alien Land Laws were then in effect in California, and he wanted to be able to prove US citizenship in order to buy land.[27] In Hawaii, however, he found his birth certificate was in the name of Masaru Hokoda. Rather than fight city hall and attempt to have his name formally changed, he adopted the Hokoda surname and kept it the rest of his life. He added an American given name, and became known as Masaru George Hokoda.[28]

The couple remained in rural Fresno, and their four children were all born there: sons Masato (1921–2012), Hideo (1922–2004), and Katsumi (1927–2013), and daughter Teruko (1925–) (Fig. 1.3). Masaru and family were held at Angel Island once again in 1928, this time for two days.[29] In the late-1920s, the family relocated to Los Angeles, where Masaru found work as a gardener.[30] He was not alone. The California Alien Land Laws drove thousands of Japanese Americans from the farms to the cities. With anti-Japanese sentiment high, not many occupations were open to them, so they used their agricultural skills to carve out a niche for themselves. Throughout California, Japanese Americans dominated the gardening and nursery businesses for decades.

On February 19, 1942, President Franklin D. Roosevelt signed Executive Order 9066, which led to the internment of more than 110,000 Japanese

FIGURE 1.3 *The Hokoda family, about 1926. Courtesy Donna Ebata.*

Americans from the Pacific coast states. The Hokoda family was uprooted and sent to the Gila River War Relocation Center, on the Gila River Indian Reservation about forty miles southeast of Phoenix, Arizona. At its peak, Gila River held 13,348 detainees, when it was only designed for 10,000. Despite the harsh desert environment, the detainees created a flourishing community complete with cultural, civic, and religious institutions, which they ran almost entirely by themselves.[31] Teruko graduated from high school in the camp in 1943, and later attended art school. Unlike most of their fellow camp residents, the Hokodas did not remain for the entire duration of the war. Labor shortages in various sectors and parts of the country led to the opportunity for some detainees to gain work release. In late 1943, Masato was allowed to take a job in Dayton, Ohio, and soon thereafter Hideo found a job in Michigan. In 1944, the rest of the family still at Gila River joined Masato in Dayton, where they were sponsored by the Stroop family and given work on the farms managed by the Stroop Agricultural Company.[32] Fred Stroop even offered financial support for Katsumi's education. All three of the Hokoda sons then joined the US Armed Forces, and served during and after the last months of the war. Katsumi served Stateside. Hideo was posted to Europe, where he served as a guard during the war crimes trial of the major Nazi political and military leaders at Nuremberg. Hideo had daily contact with the accused, and a dozen of them autographed his notebook in exchange for cigarettes, including Reich Marshal Hermann Göring, Deputy Führer Rudolf Hess, Field Marshall and Chief of the Armed Forces High Command Wilhelm Keitel, and General and Chief-of-Operations of the Armed Forces High Command Alfred Yodl. Masato was recruited to use his Japanese skills in the US Military Intelligence Service.

At war's end, Masaru and Kinuyo returned to Los Angeles, bought a home, and restarted the gardening business. Their children also all returned to the city and started families of their own. Masaru and Kinuyo enjoyed a long life together, with a large family surrounding them that eventually included eleven grandchildren and eight great-grandchildren. In August 1989, when Masaru and Kinuyo were residents of the Keiro Japanese Retirement Home in downtown Los Angeles, they and other residents were featured in a *New York Times* story about the delay in payment of reparations to former Second World War Japanese-American internees, despite approval in August 1988 by Congressional action (Fig. 1.4). The promise of $20,000 to every internee had been accompanied by a formal apology from President Ronald Reagan. Yet one year later, not a single payment had been forthcoming (and in fact payments did not begin to be made until 1991, and were not completed until 1998). In the article Kinuyo is quoted as saying, "We trust America, but we doubt. We expect the American Government to give to us, but too long over the years now. We doubt. We doubt. We are not sure now." The article concludes as follows:

Mr. Hokoda is growing deaf with age, and leaves most of the talking to his wife. But in their small and tidy room, it was he who seized and proudly displayed the photographs of their three sons, all in uniform, from the days when they fought with the United States Army while their parents waited behind barbed wire in the Gila, Ariz., relocation camp.

"They're getting old, too," he said, clearly pleased. "Two of them are retired." After the war, one son went on to own a lawnmower shop, one to work in a chick hatchery and one to become a commercial artist.

"Forty years ago we had a struggle, yes, but we managed it because my husband is a hard-working man," Mrs. Hokoda said. "We had a bitter experience but we are still loyal to the United States, that is sure."[33]

FIGURE 1.4 *Masaru and Kinuyo in retirement. Photo: Angel Franco / The New York Times / Redux.*

Masaru died on December 23, 1995, and Kinuyo on April 9, 1999.

The location of the Miyamoto/Hokoda family home in Japan itself tells a tragic story. Nukui had previously been a separate village, until merged with another, Nakachoshi, to form Kawauchi Village in 1889. Kawauchi was in the countryside about ten kilometers north of Hiroshima City, and was well known for its production of green vegetables. At the end of July 1945, the Kawauchi Village Volunteer Citizen Corps was summoned for national service. Members from the former Nakachoshi were sent further north, away from the city, to do airport construction work in present Akitakata; the Nukui members, on the other hand, were dispatched to the city center of Hiroshima to help in demolition activities. At approximately 8:15am on August 6, the atomic bomb was dropped, and at least 174 people from Nukui—mostly men and some women—were killed instantly. They had been working at almost exact ground zero. Thereafter, Kawauchi became popularly known as the "Widows' Village." A monument memorializing the dead of Nukui stands today in Hiroshima's Peace Park.[34]

There are other sad twists to this story. In Fresno in 1920, Masaru's younger sister Misao was just six years old. When she grew to adulthood she married, and before the war she and her husband moved to Japan. The couple ran a business in Hiroshima City, but as the cities became dangerous in wartime, they closed it and moved to the relative safety of the countryside. Yet on the morning of August 6, they went into the city with their ten-year-old daughter. All three were killed by the atomic blast. Two sons, a four-year-old and a five-year-old, were safe with Misao's parents-in-law. Family lore has it that both boys died young of radiation sickness. And Kinuyo's father Taichi Shimonishi had retired to Hiroshima after three decades in Hawaii and California. On the day of the explosion, he had borrowed a handcart to take luggage to the Hiroshima railway station. His body was never found, only the handcart.

Kinuyo's younger brother Toshio Shimonishi, born 1914 in California, was held during the war at the Heart Mountain internment camp in Wyoming, and later at Tule Lake in California. At war's end, he renounced his US citizenship and requested repatriation to Japan, one of 5,589 Japanese Americans to do so. He took with him his wife Mildred and three children. Yet when they reached Hiroshima, they found little welcome, and their relatives near starving.[35]

Masaru and Kinuyo's eldest son Masato was posted to Japan with the Military Intelligence Service, and served as a translator during the American Occupation. About eight months after the atomic bomb was dropped, he visited the city and viewed the massive destruction to his ancestral home province firsthand. On this and subsequent trips, he shared his army rations with surviving family. Though he did not speak of it in later years, it must have been a sadly ironic experience: Masato in his American uniform walking among the ruins where his relatives died.

3.

Passenger on the *Tenyō Maru*
Ichitarō Yasumi

大洋丸舩客
休一太郎[36]

This inscription dates to 1915. Ichitaro Yasumi, who listed his occupation as "hotel keeper," arrived on the *Tenyo Maru* on February 22, and was held at Angel Island for treatment of uncinariasis—hookworm.[37] He was detained for two weeks, until his medical release was authorized on March 8 (Fig. 1.5).

Tracing the movements of Ichitaro and his family, and the ups and downs of their employment histories, it is striking how many personal sacrifices

FIGURE 1.5 *Ichitaro Yasumi in 1897. Courtesy Catherine Miskow.*

they made to build a life in America. Arduous labor and long family separations were the foundation that allowed ensuing generations to thrive. Yet, as described below, the separations and vicissitudes of the family still influence the lives of Ichitaro's descendants.

Originally from Hera Village (平良村) in Hiroshima Prefecture (now part of the city of Hatsukaichi), Ichitaro was a longtime resident of the United States. He and wife Hide Okamura Yasumi first arrived in the 1890s (records differ on exactly when—Ichitaro's Angel Island detention record says 1895), and settled in Los Angeles. A travel record in 1907 lists Ichitaro's occupation as laborer in a boarding house.[38] In the 1910 Census, he and Hide are together in domestic service; Ichitaro was the cook, and Hide was the housekeeper in the home of James W. and Lillian McKinley. James was former City Attorney for Los Angeles and a Superior Court judge. Among the questions asked that year was the number of years couples had been married. Though Ichitaro was only thirty-two, and Hide thirty-four, their answer was seventeen, which suggests they married at ages fifteen and seventeen respectively! The 1910 Census enumeration was held in April. On September 22 of that year, the couple's son Hideo was born. Another son, Saburo, was born May 23, 1913. About this time Ichitaro became the proprietor of a boarding house in what is now the Koreatown section of the city.[39] In 1914, the family returned to Japan. Hide and the two boys remained there, and only saw Ichitaro on his infrequent journeys home. While Ichitaro's Angel Island detention file says he planned to return to his boarding house, the business apparently did not long survive his year-long absence in Japan. Records in 1917[40] and 1920[41] have him back in domestic service as a cook. The boarding house was no money maker anyway—he netted only $80 to $90 per month, and had no savings in the bank.

Although Hide, Hideo, and Saburo were back in Hera Village, Ichitaro was not alone in America. Another son, Yorito, had been born in 1894 in Japan before Ichitaro and Hide emigrated. They left him behind in the care of Ichitaro's father Genhichi Yasumi and family. He grew up there, and married a woman from the same village, Chika Yoshimura (born 1899). At age twenty, Yorito left alone for California, arriving in San Francisco on February 2, 1914.[42] He also had to spend time at Angel Island, but only for a day; he was admitted February 3. Meanwhile, back in Hera Village, Chika was pregnant. She gave birth to their daughter Fumi on August 20. Chika stayed in Japan to care for Fumi for four years, but then left her in the care of the family and embarked for America to rejoin her husband.[43]

In Los Angeles, Yorito and Chika followed in Ichitaro's occupation. In 1917, Yorito was a "houseman" at the original Hotel Hollywood, which hosted a steady stream of silent film stars.[44] Rudolph Valentino lived in Room 264. After Chika's arrival, the couple took jobs as cook and housemaid for a private family.[45] In the next decade, the family finally began to prosper. By 1930, they settled in the heart of Hollywood, and Yorito was running his own restaurant.[46] The couple had three more children, Sachiko (born 1921), Midori (born 1923), and Takashi (Tom) (born 1930). Also living with them was Yorito's brother Hideo, who arrived in 1928 after growing up in Japan.

In 1940, the family was doing well. Yorito was the owner/operator of a chop suey parlor, where Chika was the cook and sixty-three-year-old Ichitaro helped out as handyman. Midori married Henry Hiroshi Kano late that year. Hideo had married Michiko Naganuma in 1938, and the couple had a daughter, Joanne Chizumi, in 1939. In 1940, they lived with Michiko's parents, and Hideo worked in their grocery store.[47] Hideo took his wife's surname, and was adopted into the family.

With the advent of the war, things fell apart. Hideo and the Naganuma family traveled back to Japan in mid-1940, and were still there when Pearl Harbor was attacked. Return to California became impossible. Hideo, Michiko, and other California-born Naganumas had to renounce their US citizenship; only Joanne Chizumi was excepted, as she was still an infant. Hideo and Michiko never again stepped foot on American shores.

Back in Los Angeles, Yorito and family were given only a week to wrap up their affairs and report to the "assembly center" at Santa Anita Racetrack for relocation. There was no way he could sell the business in that short a time, so he had no recourse but to close it. It was while at Santa Anita—notorious for housing many internees in horse stalls—that Yorito had to file his Second World War draft registration. It is depressing to see Yorito describe himself as "Former Proprietor, Cherry House Chopsuey." The family, Ichitaro included, was sent to the internment camp at Heart Mountain, Wyoming. Midori was not with them, as she and her husband were sent to Manzanar instead. Another separation.

In late 1944, Yorito and the family at Heart Mountain gained work release to Cleveland, Ohio. At war's end, there was no reason to return to California, so they remained for several years. Ichitaro died in Ohio in 1948.[48]

Meanwhile, Yorito and Chika's eldest child Fumi had grown up in Japan. She did immigrate to the United States, but only after her marriage to Yoshiki Onoyama, a Buddhist priest. The couple arrived in 1934,[49] and had three children. The family lived and served in several locations in Northern California where there were Buddhist congregations. They were in Reedley at the start of the Second World War. When the order came to assemble for evacuation, Reverend Onoyama carried the Buddha image from the Reedley Buddhist Church with him, so that religious services for the community could continue at its bleak new accommodations, the Poston War Relocation Center in southwestern Arizona. From 1960 until his retirement in 1965, Reverend Onoyama was pastor of the Buddhist Church of Lodi. He and Fumi remained there the rest of their lives. Onoyama descendants still call Lodi home.

Family separations that begin as temporary can become long-lasting breaks. Research on Ichitaro's Angel Island inscription led me to make contact with two descendants from different family branches. Hideo and

Michiko's daughter Joanne Chizumi Naganuma grew up in Japan, graduating high school there in 1959, and then attending college in the US. Skilled in three languages, she was hired as a flight attendant by Pan Am in its glory days. Through her work she met her husband, airline pilot Ken Miskow. Their daughter Catherine Miskow is now a university teacher of French and Japanese. I sent her a message about Ichitaro's inscription and related family history. She replied that she had no idea that a member of her family had ever been detained on Angel Island, and continued, "The revelation that Ichitaro Yasumi had family in the United States was quite a shock to both my mother and me. Everyone in Japan thought that she was the only person who lived in the United States." I also spoke with David Yasumi, youngest child of Tom Takashi Yasumi. Though he grew up in close contact with aunts Sachiko and Midori and their families, he had no idea who Hideo was, let alone that Hideo and Michiko had a daughter and granddaughter in California. He also said that he, his siblings, and his cousins had heard they had another aunt, but did not know she was Fumi Yasumi Onoyama, or that there were Onoyama descendants living in Northern California. Ichitaro carved his name on a wall, and it has led to the opportunity for his descendants to reconnect. If he had known this would be the result, perhaps Ichitaro would have felt his Angel Island detention was a fair price to pay.⁵⁰

4.

September 30, 11th Year of Taishō
Hakui District, Ishikawa Prefecture
Kinzō Tsujitaka

大正十一年九月卅日
石川縣羽咋郡
辻高金造⁵¹

Yoshihito of Japan (1879–1926) was crowned Emperor Taishō on July 30, 1912. Thus the 11th year of Taishō is 1922. Kinzō Tsujitaka was nineteen in that year. He was a sailor who had joined the crew of the freighter *Washington Maru* at Kobe in September 1921. His first landing in America was at Astoria, Oregon the following month. He was still employed on the ship when on a subsequent voyage it arrived at the Port of New York from Liverpool on June 30, 1922. However, when the ship departed on July 28, he was not on it—the master of the vessel reported Kinzō as a deserter! Except for the inscription on the wall, no records have yet come to light which describe Kinzō's detention at Angel Island. Presumably he was picked up by the authorities after a month or two on the lam, and sent to the Immigration Station prior to deportation.

5.

Person from Mie Prefecture
Isaburō Hamaguchi
Shima District, Katada Village

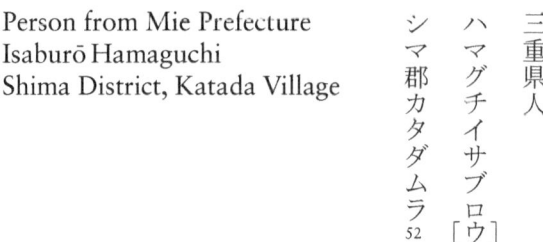

三重県人
ハマグチイサブロ[ウ]
シマ郡カタダムラ⁵²

Twenty-eight-year-old Isaburō Hamaguchi arrived in San Francisco aboard the *Asama Maru* on January 2, 1930. The ship's list confirms he was born in Mie Prefecture, and describes him as a fisherman on his way to Ensenada, Mexico. He appears to have been joining family—between 1926 and 1930, at least ten Hamaguchis from Katada Village, all fishermen, arrived in California.[53] Two of them, Matsubei Hamaguchi and Yashichi Hamaguchi, also indicated they were on their way to Ensenada.[54] Several of these Katada Village Hamaguchis also appear on the 1930 US Census as residents of the San Pedro District of Los Angeles. Before the Second World War, a very large number of the fishing boats on the California coast were operated by Japanese fishermen. In Southern California, the Japanese fishing community on Terminal Island in San Pedro alone numbered 3,000 people. The primary catch in the area was abalone and albacore tuna. When the local fisheries declined in Southern California, attention shifted to the waters off Baja California in Mexico.

Terminal Island has strategic importance as a center for US naval facilities and industry, and so at the outset of the Second World War many of the male Japanese residents were immediately rounded up by the FBI, even before the implementation of Executive Order 9066 to intern Pacific coast Japanese. When the internment order came down, the remaining residents were given 48 hours to evacuate. The Terminal Island Japanese residents were not allowed to return after the war, and their houses were razed.[55]

6.

[Masa]mi Miyata

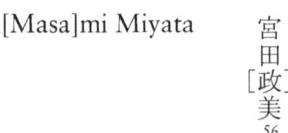

宮田[政]美⁵⁶

The third character is very battered, so the reading here is tentative. There is indeed a Masami Miyata in immigration records. Born in Tamori Village, Hiroshima Prefecture in about 1875, by 1910 he was living with his brother in Berkeley, California, and working as a house cleaner.[57] He had first immigrated in 1904. He was held at Angel Island at least once: he and his wife Toshie arrived on the *Mongolia* on May 6, 1914, and were detained for a day for medical examination. Six years later he was still in Berkeley, living with Toshie and their three children, and working as a gardener.[58] A 1925 arrival record has his occupation as "laundryman." When war broke out, Masami R. Miyata, a widowed sixty-seven-year-old, was interned at the Topaz War Relocation Center in central Utah.

Alternatively, this inscription could be a Japanese woman's name—the final character is a suffix, meaning "beauty," used mostly (but not always) in given names for women. The inscription is found in Room 211, one of two small rooms that were used as women's dormitories only during the first year or two of the station's operation. Subsequently, women were all housed in the Administration Building. Whether or not any women left behind inscriptions there is indeterminable, because the Administration Building burned down in 1940. This inscription is the only one yet found at the station that may have been written by a woman.

7.

M. Oku
Sakamura[59]

In English letters. Motoichi Oku (born January 7, 1878)[60] immigrated to the US in 1906.[61] He moved to the Los Angeles area, and in 1910 was working as a domestic servant in Rowland (now Rowland Heights), east of the city.[62] Motoichi was at Angel Island twice, each time for one night for medical observation. The first time was after arriving on April 3, 1914 aboard the *Chiyo Maru*. He and his young wife Ume (born c. 1896) were both detained. We can surmise that he had gone back to Japan to find a bride. The second time was after arriving on the *Korea Maru* on June 11, 1922. This time he traveled alone. On both occasions, Motoichi gave as his nearest relative in Japan his father, Naojiro Oku, in Sakamura [Saka Village], Hiroshima Prefecture. Sakamura is now Sakachō [Saka Town] in Hiroshima's Aki District.

Motoichi and Ume settled in South Pasadena, where in 1920 he worked as a gardener and she as a washerwoman.[63] Sometime in the 1920s, Ume either died or the couple separated, for by the 1930 Census Motoichi had remarried. Shizuno Iriye (born March 30, 1893)[64] had first arrived in America at San Francisco on March 29, 1914 on the *Siberia*. With her was her then husband Tokuzo Iriye (born c. 1879).[65] They were held at Angel Island for two days for medical examinations. Tokuzo had first immigrated to the US Territory of Hawaii in 1903.[66] The couple had six children together. Tokuzo suddenly died on November 22, 1929, leaving Shizuno a widow.[67] The 1930 Census was conducted during the month of April, and it shows Motoichi and Shizuno living on North Lake Avenue in Pasadena with five young children—Shizuko

(Katherine) (born 1918), Kazunori (Henry) (born 1920), Yuriko (Lily) (born 1922), Tsuginori (born 1923), and Haruye (Marienne) (born 1926). The sixth Iriye child, Uraye (Grace), was born on May 27, 1930, after the Census had been completed and six months after her father had died.

Motoichi and Shizuno had two more children together, sons Hisao (Jack) Oku (born 1932), and Sadao (George) Oku (born 1934). By 1935, the whole family had moved to Compton, south of downtown Los Angeles, where Motoichi became owner/operator of a truck farm. Compton today is not at all known as a center for agriculture, but in fact until the mid-twentieth century it was a mixed rural/urban community, and even today agricultural pursuits continue in the Richland Farms neighborhood. At the time of the 1940 Census, all ten Iriyes and Okus were in Compton. Many of their neighbors were also Japanese Americans.

The Second World War Japanese internment uprooted the whole family. Motoichi, Shizuno, and seven children were all were transported to the Rohwer War Relocation Center in rural southeastern Arkansas. Shizuko had married Teruo (Arthur) Murayama, and they were sent to Rohwer as well. With them was their infant daughter Keiko (Eunice); a son, Norihiko (Daniel) was born at Rohwer in 1944. Except for Yuriko, who was released in 1943 to attend Madison College in Tennessee, all the Okus, Iriyes, and Murayamas were detained at Rohwer until May, 1944, when they were transferred to the Tule Lake War Relocation Center in northeastern California, near the Oregon border. Tule Lake was the largest of the war's internment camps, and had the highest level of military security. It was where detainees from around the system were sent if they refused to swear unqualified loyalty to the United States, or refused to fill out the questionnaire in which the loyalty questions were asked. At war's end, Motoichi renounced his American residency and elected to return to Japan; he took Shizuno and the two Oku boys with him. Shizuno, Hisao, and Sadao later returned to live in California, but Motoichi never did. All of the Iriyes and Murayamas elected to remain in the United States after the war.

8.

Is racial bias justifiable? 人種的偏見正當ナリヤ？
68

9.

Person from Kagawa Prefecture
Yamashita
Get me out of here fast!

香川縣人
山下
早ク出タイ
69

A very likely candidate for the writer of this inscription is Tsurukichi Yamashita from Kusakabe, on the Inland Sea island of Shodoshima, Kagawa Prefecture (Fig. 1.6). Tsurukichi (1892–1975), wife Nao (1895–1953), and daughter Kimiye (born *c.* 1914) arrived together in San Francisco aboard the *China* on July 13, 1915. They were on their way to join father Matsukichi Yamashita (born *c.* 1867, and who immigrated 1905), a foreman and tenant farmer on the Irvine Ranch in Orange County, California. Matsukichi was not Tsurukichi's birth father, but Nao's. Tsurukichi's birth surname was Ikegami. He was adopted into the Yamashita family upon his marriage to

FIGURE 1.6 *"Get me out of here fast!"*

Nao, and took her surname.[70] This was a common practice in Japan for households with daughters but no sons to inherit. Upon arrival, the three were sent to Angel Island. There Tsurukichi met a fellow detainee named Masanosuke Yasui, who published a diary of his immigration experience in the *Nichibei Shimbun* newspaper (the diary is translated in this anthology – see below). Yasui suggests that Tsurukichi and his family were detained because immigration authorities did not recognize the adoption. They were judged "liable to become a public charge at time of entry" (LPC), and ordered deported. Tsurukichi appealed, and the family was admitted—but not until August 24.

At the time of the 1920 Census, they were living with Matsukichi in Santa Ana, engaged in farming work (Nao's mother Iwa Yamashita had joined them in 1917) (Fig. 1.7). Yet when the California Alien Land Law of 1913 was revised and made more restrictive that year, it became increasingly difficult to remain in farming. Matsukichi and Iwa threw in the towel and retired to Shodoshima in 1921. They took with them Tsurukichi and Nao's daughter Kimiye and son Shigeru (born 1918). The children thrived there until Iwa died in 1923, and Matsukichi in 1928. Subsequently, they endured a difficult and bitter childhood in Japan, as they had no close relatives to take care of them. Kimiye grew up to become an elementary school teacher. She remained in Japan, and married in 1935; the couple raised five daughters

FIGURE 1.7 *The Yamashita family in 1917. Courtesy Cheryl Yamashita.*

there. A lifelong regret was that she never saw her mother again. Shigeru stayed in Japan until he finished high school, and then in 1937 returned to the US to rejoin the rest of the family.

Tsurukichi and Nao toiled on as tenant farmers on the Irvine Ranch until 1925, and had three other children in California, but they then picked up and moved to Overton, Nevada, where they had—sight unseen—purchased farmland. Times were hard at first, but they prospered, producing cantaloupes, tomatoes, cucumbers, and other crops, and raising turkeys for sale in Las Vegas. Tsurukichi and Nao had even more children—making twelve in all! One daughter tragically died in infancy, but the rest all grew to adulthood and started families of their own.

Son Junwo "Jimmy" Yamashita later recalled that the small local community was tolerant and supportive of their new neighbors, and were "always ready to lend a helping hand." "Even though there was a language barrier, it didn't prevent us from becoming an integral part of the community." Jimmy was even elected Student Body President of Moapa Valley High School in 1941. During the war, the family was spared relocation. Jimmy recalled, "Our friends and neighbors were very tolerant and assured us that they would be there to quell any safety concerns."[71] The Yamashitas were even able to assist other Japanese families they had known in California to gain release from War Relocation Authority camps to work in Overton.

Though Shigeru "Shig" Yamashita had already finished high school in Japan, the principal of the Moapa Valley High School welcomed him to attend classes, to improve his English skills and to get to know the community. He graduated, and continued studies in Los Angeles at the Polytechnic High School, until he was drafted in early 1941. (The Selective Service Act was passed in September 1940, more than a year *before* Pearl Harbor.) He was selected for intensive training as a military translator, along with fifty-seven other Nisei. Their training program was accelerated after the Hawaiian attack.

In May 1942, Shigeru shipped out for New Caledonia, where he joined the Americal Division. He served as a military translator for the unit throughout the Pacific war, participating in operations in New Caledonia, Guadalcanal, Bouganville, and the Philippines. He was awarded both the Bronze Star and the Legion of Merit.[72] Jimmy joined the army in 1943, and became a platoon leader in the 442nd Regimental Combat Team, made up almost entirely of Japanese-American soldiers. For its exploits in multiple major battles of the European war, including the rescue of the "Lost Battalion," the 442nd became the most decorated unit in American history.[73] Another brother, Kiyoshi, also served in the armed forces late in the war.[74]

After the war, four Yamashita siblings (Masako, Kiyoshi, Roy, and Mitzi) remained in Nevada. Kiyoshi and Roy continued farming. Their children and children's children now mostly live in Nevada, Utah, and parts of Washington and Idaho. One sibling, Nobuko, married in San Jose. The other five in the United States (Shigeru, Jimmy, George, Meri, and Lily) all relocated to Southern California to pursue employment and education. Nao died in 1953, Tsurukichi in 1975. The Yamashita clan, including four surviving siblings—Jimmy (93), Meri (91), Lily (88), and George (80)—now numbers over 200 people, and is in its sixth generation in the United States. Ties among them remain close, and big family reunions are held every two or three years.

10.

Sakoi
Nagata Village
Takata District
Hiroshima Prefecture
Entered Detention on September 3, 3rd Year of Shōwa (1928)

Taiyō Maru

大洋丸
昭和三年九月三日入監ス
ヒロシマケン
タカタグン
ナガタムラ
サコイ 75

Maichi Sakoi, a thirty-three-year-old carpenter from Hiroshima Prefecture, arrived aboard the *Taiyo Maru* on September 3, 1928. He was held at Angel Island for a month for treatment of hookworm, and was landed on October 3. Maichi was a temporary visitor for business purposes, not an immigrant, and he was admitted for six months after posting a bond. His wife Hisa remained behind in Hiroshima. Yet besides business, Maichi was visiting relatives as well. His destination was Lodi in San Joaquin County, where his brother Joichi Sakoi (born 1891) was a farmer. Joichi and his wife Haruka (born 1902) had three sons born in California, Toshio (Ted), George, and Shunso (Jim). During the war, Joichi and family were first interned at Rohwer, and then at Tule Lake.

Maichi was granted an extension to his stay, and on October 24, 1930 returned to Japan aboard the *President Jackson*.[76]

Takata District (高田郡) (including Nagata Village [長田村]) was merged into Akitakata City (安芸高田市) in 2004.

11.

People of Yamato

大和民族 77

Yamato is an ancient name for Japan. Beginning in the late nineteenth century, "people of Yamato" became a term used by the dominant ethnic group of Japan to refer to itself, and to distinguish it from minority groups in Japan and other peoples of the expanding Japanese empire. It had connotations of separateness and superiority, and figured frequently in propaganda of the period.

12.

Fourteen years old	五月三十日ヨリ78	六月三日廣島縣人	五月卅日	久保田登ンデ 1936	十四歳

Noboru Kubota
1936
From May 30 to June 3
Person from Hiroshima Prefecture
Since May 30

The fourteen-year-old writer arrived in San Francisco aboard the *Asama Maru* from Kobe on January 29, 1936. He was the son of Katsumi Kubota (born 1885) and Kame Kubota (born 1892), who had operated a boarding house in the old Japantown area of downtown Sacramento at least since 1917.[79] Japantown was a small but thriving community in the first half of the twentieth century. Covering roughly twelve square blocks, it was centered at Fourth and M Streets, a few blocks east of the Tower Bridge and the Sacramento River. The Kubotas' boarding house was in the heart of the district, at 315 M Street between Third and Fourth. Japantown is gone now—it never recovered from the internment of the Japanese population during the Second World War, and much of the area was transformed by redevelopment in the 1950s and 1960s. Capitol Mall—the grand boulevard that leads from Tower Bridge to the Capitol building—now covers much of old Japantown.

Upon his arrival in 1936, Noboru carried a US passport, and the manifest lists his birth in California, yet he was caught up in legal wrangling about his status, and so was detained at Angel Island. The Kubotas and their children (Noboru had two elder sisters) had made multiple trips to the family seat in Tomo Village, Asa (now Aki) District, Hiroshima Prefecture, and immigration inspectors thoroughly reviewed the records. It was discovered that Noboru was only a three-month-old infant when he and his mother took passage from Japan to California on the *Siberia Maru*, arriving in San Francisco on September 26, 1921. Noboru's entry on the manifest for that voyage clearly states he was of Japanese nationality, not US, and that his place of birth was Tomo Village.

Two attorneys in succession argued on Noboru's behalf, but his petition for entry was denied on March 25, 1936. He appealed on March 30, and the case was referred for further adjudication, but was ultimately denied on May 20. Noboru was ordered deported on the *Asama Maru*, which sailed June 3.

13.

Overthrow American imperialism!
~~Overthrow~~ Long live communism!
[Overthrow] Japanese imperialism!

打倒米國帝國主義
打倒共産主義萬歳
□□日本帝國主義
80

This inscription has been defaced and altered, which seems to indicate the political passions it aroused. Although all in characters, it is likely by a Japanese writer, as the word for "America" in the first line follows Japanese usage. It is also possible that three or more writers contributed a line each, as the calligraphy differs somewhat. What is noteworthy is that to date this is the *only* mention of communism found anywhere on the barracks walls. The Japanese Communist Party was founded in 1922, and came under almost immediate repression by the increasingly militaristic authorities. It survived, however, and remains a force today in left-wing Japanese politics. The Chinese Communist Party was founded in 1921. The remains of the characters for "overthrow" (打倒) are hazily visible preceding "communism," but an attempt has been made to rub them out. The characters for "long live" (萬歳—ten thousand years) have then been added to the end of the line. The two characters preceding "Japanese imperialism," which presumably were "overthrow" (打倒), are completely missing, and it appears a knife was used to gouge them out.

JAPANESE INSCRIPTIONS, 1910–1940 45

FIGURE 1.8 *Bird sketch.*

FIGURE 1.9 *Rooster carving.*

FIGURE 1.10 *Cartoon.*

JAPANESE PROSE AND POETRY FROM *NICHIBEI SHIMBUN*

Translations by Makiko Asano and Charles Egan

The selections below are grouped in several broad categories to reflect the variety of the Japanese immigrant experience: (1) Angel Island, Immigration, and Picture Brides; (2) New Life and Old Memories; (3) Camp and Colony; and (4) History, the Law, and Discrimination." Poem translations are accompanied by the original Japanese texts.[81]

Angel Island, Immigration, and Picture Brides

14. From an Angel Island Window: A compatriot's diary about his detention by the Immigration Service [1915; excerpted]

Masanosuke Yasui, a twenty-seven-year-old cake and candy maker, spent a little more than one month on Angel Island in July/August 1915, before withdrawing his appeal of a deportation order and voluntarily returning to Japan. While at the station he wrote a diary about his experiences, which *Nichibei* published serially between August 22 and September 1, 1915. Details of people mentioned will follow the text.

Published here is the diary of Masanosuke Yasui, who crossed to America and entered port on the 21 of last month aboard the Manchuria, and is being detained on Angel Island. Immigration officials ordered him deported because they feared he was likely to become a public charge. He is currently appealing the decision. From the diary one can perhaps understand what life is like for typical Japanese detainees at the Immigration Station, and sympathize with them.

July 21

Clear and windy skies. The customs officials started inspecting the luggage at about 8:00. Arrived at Angel Island at 1:00pm. The trees and shrubs on the mountain behind the Immigration Station are luxuriant, and the clipped grass in the courtyard is verdant green. Moss rose, hydrangea, hollyhock, and other flowers vie with each other in bloom, and somehow remind me of my home country. We were escorted to a large room on the second floor. Both sides of the corridors were covered in thick iron mesh. Not only the windows, but also the walkways to the toilets and baths were all covered this way.

Somebody said, "It's as if we've been put in prison." Similar sentiments could be heard from others all around me. Weary of more than twenty monotonous days of life at sea, my joy at seeing the beautiful blooming flowers and scenery turns to sadness at my captivity in this prison-like place. After 2:00pm I was told it was time for the midday meal.

Went to the dining hall. Rice and a cooked dish were mounded up in separate metal tubs. The porcelain bowls looked like Buddhist begging bowls, and were covered with red and black tea stains. I put rice and some of the cooked dish in two separate bowls, and picked up a bit with my chopsticks and tasted. The rice was Saigon rice, and it had a foul smell. The cooked dish was glistening fat on top of some unknown green vegetable and pork meat. The vegetables were half cooked and tasted of salt. "Ugh!" we all said, in disgust. At that point I put down my chopsticks and returned to the room. It seems that most of the others left without eating, too.

There are five or six kids staying in the room. Most of them had been summoned here by their fathers. Yet because their answers in interrogations did not match those of their fathers, they were detained. I understand they are currently appealing.

At 4:00pm the evening meal was announced, and I again went to the dining hall. It looked to be the same food as at lunch. I was disgusted.

Then someone said that a western meal was available for fifteen cents. I ordered it, but found it was a "western meal" in name only—a slice of meat, a potato, some beans, and as much bread and coffee as you want. It tasted terrible.

In the evening I was given a blanket and a mattress to spread on the bunk. Lying in bed I gazed at the lights on the far shore, while I worried about tomorrow's interrogation.

July 22

Thick fog. Breakfast at 5:30. As the food was the same again, I ordered the western meal. At 8:00 we all went to the hospital, where each person was given a basin with a numbered tally in it. We wrote the numbers of our tallies on our ship tickets and gave them to the guard. Then we had to leave fecal samples in the basins. We were told to wait in a small courtyard surrounded by iron mesh, until everyone was finished. Then we had eye examinations, and when those were finished we were led to a room where we were told to take off our shirts. We waited until a doctor came to check our lungs. Then we were lined up, and one after another the doctor examined our private parts behind a screen.

After the physical examination, we returned to the second floor room, and shortly thereafter was the midday meal. Those who had passed the fecal examination were allowed to land. At 2:30 my name was called, and then I waited about an hour but no interview took place. I then returned to the second floor. After finishing dinner at 3:30, for some reason I began to feel anxious and unsettled. In the evening the room was filled with lively conversation. Last night I was exhausted, and went to sleep about 9:00pm, but tonight my mind was filled with all sorts of worries about my future, and though the electricity in the room was turned off, I could not sleep.

July 23

Clear. After lying awake all last night, as dawn broke I finally fell asleep. Yet almost immediately I was awakened by the guard for breakfast, which as before was a western meal. A little after 9:00 I was called downstairs, and after waiting for an hour and a half with no instructions, was told to return to the second floor. Lunch was a western meal again. About 1:00 I was called out again, and for about an hour the inspector asked me about my reasons for crossing to America, whether this was the first time I had ever worn western clothes, whether my home was closer to Yokohama or San Francisco, and other stupid questions like that. Finally, because I had little money with me, and no relatives here who could provide assistance in case I committed a crime or became sick, I was ordered deported.

The interpreter told me that I had a choice of returning to Japan without any ship fare charges, or appealing the decision, which would take about a week. I replied that I would appeal, and returned to the second floor room. Lying in my bunk, I bit my lips as all kinds of thoughts one after the other ran through and overwhelmed my mind.

I was not happy about coming here, for I would not be home for the final send-off for my beloved grandmother, to whom I owe even more than I owe my mother, and whose remaining span of life is short. Yet somehow I persuaded her, and she gave her consent for me to cross to America. If I am deported now, I will have no face to meet her again.

Come to think of it, I blame myself for the awful way I answered the questions put to me. Oh, how could I have said such things? I even resented the inspector for ordering the deportation just because of my slips of the tongue. When the dinner was called, I was in no mood for eating. I went back to the room, but my head was heavy and anxiety kept me tossing and turning all night.

July 24

Thick fog. After breakfast I asked those who had been detained longer than me about various things, but all are in the midst of appeals, and they said they didn't know what was going on. They are children of probably fifteen to sixteen years of age, who were called here by their fathers. There are altogether five of them, and among them two are adopted sons. One of these was a fifteen- or sixteen-year-old boy named Kawakita, who was called here by Chairman Ushijima of the Japanese Association. Yet Chairman Ushijima did not come to meet him, denying that he had ever summoned such a person, nor did he come even once to visit. There must be something to the story, but at any rate since the boy had come this far, I thought Chairman Ushijima could have at least come once to visit, or taken him home. Yet Kawakita said that he was to be deported on the next sailing of the *Manchuria*.

There is another boy called Hatanaka from Osaka, whose father went back to Japan last year and then took passage back here again in a certain month this year. Yet the father said that he crossed to America five or six years ago and had not been back to Japan, while the boy said he went back last year. Their stories did not match, and so the immigration officer ordered the boy deported, on the grounds that a parent who tells lies cannot raise a child.

There is also a detainee named Yamashita who was summoned here by his adoptive father. He is appealing an order of deportation he received, made on the grounds that an insufficient number of years had elapsed since the adoption was registered.

The remaining two boys said they would be deported for similar reasons. It seems to me that the immigration official's primary job is to ensure that as few people as possible land in this country!

At 1:00pm I was told someone had come to see me. It was the Secretary of the Japanese Association, who said, "I heard you were refused permission to land. How sad!" He consoled me, and asked why I was refused. So I told him all the details. He said, "In order to appeal, I must compare what you said and what the immigration officer said. Then I can make the appeal based on reasons. Do you want to entrust it to me, or do you want another lawyer?" I decided to entrust it to him, and paid him the five-dollar handling fee. He said he would come see me on Monday or Tuesday, and left . . .

I think that to make children lead this kind of life for long is extremely bad. Imprisoned within iron bars they cannot help but be bored, and with nothing else to do, they smoke cigarettes which they don't even feel like smoking, or buy things to eat. One said he was scolded by his parents because during the seventy-odd days he was here he had exhausted the $50 he brought with him. I don't blame him, for it's only natural. Others have been here more than thirty days, and during such a long period became involved in improper activities. In these days when people are so concerned about public morals, it is a shame that young boys with promise and potential are imprisoned for so long in such a place, so that they pick up bad habits. I hope that those in authority will give serious thought to this matter.

There are some people who had their watches stolen when they weren't paying attention. And it's not unusual for shaving mirrors and other things to go missing. When we tell the guards they don't even bother to look, so we can't leave things lying around here even for a little while . . .

I cancel my appeal.

After consultation with a certain friend who came to visit, I decided to go back home. I asked Mr. Haworth of the Japanese Association to cancel my appeal. I had to pay $7.50 for telegrams and so on.

Every day as many as five groups of foreigners—both men and women—come to observe. It's unpleasant for me to see the manner of those young women chattering and laughing loudly. Although such behavior may be typical in the West, in the eyes of Orientals it looks to be terribly lacking in manners. Someone said we had better dress our best, because if they see Orientals dressed like we are now, they will go back and use it as evidence for Japanese exclusion. It was not our intention to stay in such a place for long, so we hadn't prepared anything. Yet they come to observe us, and what's more, use what they see as evidence for Japanese exclusion. So I think that Americans are heartless and shallow.

The rage of the Chinese.

At dinner on August 7, the Chinese men began to riot because of the food. They broke their rice bowls and threw rice everywhere, and it was wild and disorderly. In the end they went up to the second floor without eating. After the women had finished their meal, the men were calmed down and were called back again to eat. I think they made use of American ways really well. If Japanese people had known how to apply such methods in diplomacy, then I think that Japanese-American problems would have been solved long ago. In the evening many of the Chinese brought out musical instruments and they were all jumping around. I guess they were probably celebrating their victory.[82]

* * *

Masanosuke Yasui, the author of the diary, was twenty-seven when he arrived in San Francisco on July 20, 1915 aboard the *Manchuria*. He was a native of Wakayama Prefecture, in the southern-central region of the main Japanese island of Honshū, where he had been apprenticed to a cake and candy maker for nine years. His stated goal of coming to America was not immigration, but a short-term stay to "learn American candy-making"—he had an introduction to the proprietor of the Surugaya shop at 1670 Post Street in San Francisco. (The Surugaya Company, based in Wakayama, was one of the oldest and best-known sweets makers in Japan, with a history of over five hundred years; it went bankrupt in 2014.) Masanosuke left his wife and daughter behind in Japan. His immigration file is extant, and includes the transcript of his interview.[83] The "stupid questions" he ridicules were in fact asked, but it appears from the full transcript that the officers had their reasons for asking them. They wanted to ascertain whether Masanosuke had come to *study* or to *work* at the Surugaya shop, as he had arrived with just $50 in his pocket. He hemmed and hawed in his answers, which made the officers suspect that he was planning permanent residence and a career in San Francisco. They asked him about his wages back in Japan, and appeared unsatisfied when he said he did not receive any as an apprentice—presumably the question was asked to see if Masanosuke had a stable job to which he would return. (In fact, the officers did not show an understanding of the Japanese craft tradition, in which long apprenticeships were common.) The question about his Western suit was similar—the officers seemed to want to know if he had it made as preparation for his new life in America. The questions about Yokohama and its relative proximity to his hometown concern whether or not Masanosuke's trip to America was necessary at all:

Q Did you enquire in Yokohama, Japan, as to whether there were any American cake or candy makers?
A No, because Yokohama is too far from my hometown.
Q Is it not a fact that Yokohama is nearer to your hometown than San Francisco?
A Yes.
Q Why did you not investigate as to whether or not you could learn the American cake and candy manufacturing business in your home country rather than in this country?
A Because I understood that American candies made in Japan are of very inferior quality.

At the end of the interview, the officers were so suspicious of Masanosuke's answers that they went so far as to ask him—given that the date of his marriage was in June 1914, and the birth of his child was in November 1914—whether his wife's father had demanded the marriage to make the child legitimate! Masanosuke replied "no," that it was only that the registration of the marriage had been delayed. The officers then abruptly terminated the interview, and ordered Masanosuke deported as LPC—likely to become a public charge. As he describes in the diary, Masanosuke withdrew his appeal on August 5. He was deported on the *Mongolia* on August 25.

Shigeto Kawakita, a sixteen-year-old boy from Fukuoka Prefecture, arrived in San Francisco on June 29, 1915 aboard the *Siberia*. His immigration file contains a single document, a medical certificate dated July 7, which states he was afflicted with ichthyosis—a skin disease.[84] An order of deportation for him (sent to the steamship company) is also extant; the reason for the order given is that he was LPC—likely to become a public charge. He was deported on the *China* on July 24. Still, the claim in the diary that young Kawakita had come to join Chairman Ushijima may have a kernel of merit. Both were from Fukuoka—the passenger manifest for the *Siberia* lists Shigeto's home village as Yamaharu, which is now incorporated in the city of Ukiha; Chairman Ushijima was born in the adjacent city of Kurume. And though only 16, Shigeto lists his occupation as "Overseer of farm labor" and his destination as Stockton, which might make sense if he had a connection with Chairman Ushijima, and a job lined up on the older man's vast holdings in the Stockton area. For Chairman Ushijima was the most successful and wealthiest Japanese immigrant in California. Born Kinji Ushijima in 1864, he arrived in Northern California in 1889, and after a stint as a domestic servant, worked as a migrant farm laborer for several years, and then as a labor contractor. He took an American name, George Shima, and by the late 1890s was engaged in draining and diking land in the swampy San Joaquin Delta. He found the new farmland was perfect for growing potatoes. A savvy businessman as well as a talented farmer, he had nearly 29,000 acres under cultivation by 1913, and by 1920 controlled

85 percent of the California potato crop. Lauded as the "Potato King," George Shima was named the first chairman of the Japanese Association in 1909, and for the rest of his life was at the forefront of efforts challenging Japanese exclusion and California's succession of Alien Land Laws. He died in 1926.[85]

Choichiro Hatanaka was only thirteen (born October 21, 1901) when he was detained at Angel Island after arriving in San Francisco aboard the *Nippon Maru* on May 25, 1915.[86] The Hatanaka family was from Nichitottori Village in Osaka Prefecture. As the diary states, Choichiro's long detention (more than two months) was not due to anything he had said or done, but because the immigration authorities distrusted his father. Chosaburo Hatanaka (born 1871) was a partner in a leased apricot orchard in Guinda, Yolo County, California. Chosaburo had first immigrated to America in 1903, arriving April 8 at Seattle on the *Aki Maru*. He returned to Japan for a long period, from 1908 to 1914. Yet when he applied for his son to join him, he did indeed falsely state he had been in the US continuously since 1903. Through interviews with both Choichiro and Chosaburo, the Board of Inquiry discovered the discrepancy. The officers then began to doubt other aspects of Chosaburo's story, including the father-son relationship itself. Chosaburo then claimed he had lost his second passport (later recovered), so his false story was due to the fact he was using his old one, which did not mention the 1908–1914 trip to Japan. Yet the damage was done, and the Board ordered Choichiro's deportation. The boy returned to Japan on August 7, 1915, on the *Tenyo Maru*. All was not lost for Choichiro Hatanaka, however. He took ship for America again in 1917, arriving at Seattle on July 22 aboard the *Mexico Maru*. This time he was admitted. At the time of the 1920 Census, he and his father resided in Suisun City, Solano County, and worked as farm laborers.

Yamashita—Tsurukichi Yamashita. See Wall Inscription #9.

Mr. Haworth is the Reverend B.C. Haworth, a former missionary and official Japanese translator for the Immigration Service, who became Secretary of the Japanese Association in early 1915. The *Los Angeles Times* once described him as "one of the two white men in the West who are able to read and write the Japanese script or 'running hand.'"[87]

15. A Day at Angel Island: Traveling companions take care of each other [1914]

The brief diary of Kotoko Tominaga published in the San Francisco *Shin Sekai* [New World] newspaper provides a unique contemporary perspective on Japanese women's experiences at Angel Island, and a sympathetic portrayal of young picture brides awaiting their first glimpse of their new husbands.

At 3:00 on the afternoon of May 8, my breast filled with high hopes, I embarked from the wharf at Yokohama. After seventeen days at sea, where we entrusted our lives to the 6,000 ton ship *Persia Maru*, before dawn on the 25th we entered the port of San Francisco. Before long the passengers were all detained at the Angel Island Immigration Station. I had not expected life behind iron bars. This must be how Monk Shunkan of olden times felt—knowing only the sorrow of the sound of waves. I vainly envied the seagulls who come and go through the air to San Francisco.

At eleven o'clock came the call for the midday meal. In Japanese with a curious accent, the matron said, "Quickly, quickly!" to hurry us up. When we went to the dining hall, there were tubs filled with mountains of bread, jelly, and pudding, and tea that was tea in name only. To those of us who were facing such a meal for the first time, there was no more bitter experience imaginable. Yet it looked to me like the twenty or more women who had arrived in port on the 23rd on the *Hong Kong Maru* did not find the meal so awful, and were actually enjoying it. I recalled the old saying, "When you are starving, there is nothing that doesn't taste good." I felt very sad to see them like this.

After the meal, the forty women in the dormitory talked together about their travels. Whether they had set out from Hanasaki, or from Kobe, or from Yokohama, they had undergone multiple trials and examinations together, and some seemed to be well acquainted. Indeed, it is true that "traveling companions take care of each other."

Arrangements had been made for all the *Hong Kong Maru* passengers—except for the picture brides—to be landed that afternoon. Although it was only a few short days that they had become friends through sharing the dangers of the voyage across the wide sea, the eyes of those departing and those sending them off were all unexpectedly dripping with tears.

After the evening meal, the matron led us on a walk in the courtyard. All sorts of beautiful flowers were in chaotic bloom. Underneath the trees on the hill, people waited expectantly for their turn on the swings. The natural athletes among us immediately rushed straight over. Looking down on the ocean beneath their eyes, for a while they were happy to become innocent children again. Basking in this lingering feeling, they were led unwillingly back on the return path. Before long, we caught the graceful scent of roses about to bloom. It was like the quiet pride of women soon to marry.

Feeling anxious about the landing, at 8:00pm I went to bed. Suddenly, especially boisterous peals of laughter erupted from the bathroom. The image of unladylike little princesses appeared unbidden in my mind's eye. From somewhere wafted the faint sounds of Western music. Is that what is popular these days? After a while, the road of dreams led to the old country . . . parents who are missed, the smiling faces of beloved children left behind . . . the image of a child asking for milk disappears . . . perhaps there are mothers, the sleeves of their nightdresses wet with tears? . . .

I awoke to the small sounds of dawn. Already most of the women were up and dressed beautifully. I'm an experienced traveler, yet still I rose later than the others; I'm disappointed in myself for not acting my age. Through the window I saw the island bathed in the fresh light of the morning sun.

I rushed downstairs to the dining hall. There was only miserable Chinese food that had a particularly nasty taste to it.

About 10:00am we saw a crowd of people on the wharf. Anxiety was on the faces of the women looking down on the scene, as each inwardly asked herself, "Which one is my husband?" I was moved to pity by their fear. As a layer of fencing was between them, there was no way the women could speak with those coming to meet them, so they just chitchatted about various things to divert their minds. I found this very touching.

In simple Japanese, a grey-haired American passed along the news that I had permission to land. Ahead of my friends, I began preparations for departure. Well, what is precious now at the hour of our parting is to remember the old saying, "Even chance meetings can create lasting bonds." For close to twenty days, we depended on each other to bear the bitter, harsh ocean crossing. Soon all will settle in different places, some west and some east. Will we ever meet again? My friends, I wish you every happiness. Amidst the sounds of goodbye, we take our final leave of Angel Island. Suitcases in hand, we journey through this floating world. When wind blows, let it blow; when rain falls, let it fall. This is our long-cherished dream: striding across the American land.[88]

* * *

The author, Koto Tominaga, had come to America as a twenty-two-year-old bride in 1907, accompanied by her husband Gusuke Tominaga, a forty-one-year-old farmer. The age disparity was typical of the time, for like many of his immigrant contemporaries, Gusuke had first come to California as a younger man, and worked until he earned enough to marry. After seven years in Sacramento, he had returned to Japan in 1905. Both he and Koto were from Jonan village in Yamaguchi Prefecture, which is part of the present-day town of Tabuse. Gusuke and Koto's marriage was a failure. At the time of the 1910 Census, Koto was working as a live-in domestic servant in Los Angeles. She describes herself as married with one child, yet neither Gusuke nor the child was with her. Koto wrote this diary after returning to California from Japan on May 25, 1914. The passenger manifest does not mention her husband at all; rather, it says she is going to work as an "assistant at the Japanese Ladies' Society" at 1350 Burlington Avenue in Los Angeles. This was the Jane Couch Memorial Home, operated by the Women's Home Missionary Society of the Methodist Episcopal Church. It served as a shelter for Japanese and Korean women who had fled abusive or unhappy marriages, or who otherwise had ended up with no means of support, and their children. This information led me back to the 1910 Census to look for Koto's child. And there she is—one-year-old Sumi Tominaga was being cared for at another of the Women's Home Missionary Society shelters, on W. 12th Place in Los Angeles. We can guess that Koto had also been a resident for a time, and now was returning to help carry on the good work. The diary text suggests Koto left Sumi with her parents when she returned in 1914. In 1920, Gusuke arrived once more in California with a new bride, twenty-five-year-old Matsuyo. He was then fifty-three.

Shunkan (c. 1143–1179) was a Japanese monk who was exiled after participating in a coup attempt. He spent part of his exile alone on an island in the former Satsuma Province.

16. From All the Women Detained on Angel Island: "It's too cruel to be sent back after all that we have been through!" [1920]

The following plea arrived at our offices:

We humbly speak from Angel Island:

Congratulations on the flourishing prosperity of your newspaper. Ever since we arrived from across the ocean in October of last year, we have troubled you many times for your assistance, for which we sincerely apologize. We were called by our husbands to this place, and we thought that together with them we would be building a new world from then on. We crossed 4,000 miles of towering waves, and we thought that—barring illness—we would be allowed to land right away. Yet to our surprise, we were sent to this Angel Island, and were told such things as the husbands who had summoned us did not have passports, or they were illegal immigrants to this country, and so we have experienced hardship we did not expect. In fact, our situation is the same as that of imprisoned Japanese criminals. First, the food at this Angel Island is really rank, and we can't stand it. At the beginning we thought that this is the way that people in America eat every day, but as we heard more we realized that this is not so at all, and that this Angel Island is particularly awful. Indeed it's like what they feed pigs. There's nobody to whom we can appeal and express our pain, and there's no way we can blame our husbands, so we try to console ourselves by thinking we just had the bad luck of coming here at the wrong time. However, we heard that if a man had been here more than five years, even if he had come illegally, he would have the same rights as a legal immigrant. If that's really the case, then we feel truly aggrieved by the actions of the immigration officials. In this world there are many people who feel warm sympathy for us, yet we don't know curses enough to deal with the cruelty of our present situation. Not only that, we have been in tears night after night wondering where we go from here. Then the order came for our deportation, and we felt sadness on top of sadness, and cried until no more tears came. This may just be our whining, but if they were going to deport us, why didn't they do it sooner? Isn't it just too cruel to deport us *after* caging us up on this island for two to three months? A certain newspaper opines that wives who are summoned by men without passports are violating the Gentlemen's Agreement. What the heck is the Gentlemen's Agreement? We haven't been able to understand it at all. The people at the Japanese Association have helped us tremendously. We've heard that any matter can be taken to court, and so all of us are writing this letter now, although the style of our words is poor, to ask those at the Japanese Association to do the following. Please do not spare any efforts, and make effective use of the power of the People of Yamato in order to craft a strong defense accompanied by righteous arguments. We also ask those at the *Nichibei Shimbun* [Japanese-American News] to understand our sincere feelings, and to support us. We bow to you nine times.

All the women at Angel Island
February 7

* * *

Between the years 1908 and 1920, an estimated 10,000 picture brides were summoned by their husbands to America.[89] Yet, particularly in the latter years of that period, the practice had become a flashpoint in race relations in California. In an attempt to reduce anti-Japanese sentiments, in 1919 Consul Tamekichi Ota recommended to his government that the practice be stopped. The Japanese government concurred, and on December 17 declared that passports would no longer be issued to Japanese picture brides, effective March 1, 1920. Increased scrutiny of the practice worked to the disadvantage of seventeen picture brides and four children of Japanese men in California who had arrived in October and November. They were detained at Angel Island because immigration authorities charged that the men who had summoned them were in the country illegally, contrary to the Gentlemen's Agreement. The men had come without passports by way of Mexico to work on farms in the Imperial Valley. Yet there was a loophole in immigration regulations: persons who had been in the country for five years were not subject to deportation, even if they had entered illegally. Thus the Japanese men waited five years before involving the Japanese Consulate to send for dependents. A writ of habeas corpus was filed in the US District Court on behalf of the women and children on February 4, 1920. They were eventually released to start their new lives in California.[90]

17. Suicide Note of a Picture Bride [1917]

Whether waking or sleeping, this is something for which I cannot apologize enough. While on the ship I was seasick, and I started to feel itchy. I waited, thinking that I would recover, but it didn't go away easily. I was so worried I developed a fever. Although I said I didn't mind, other people couldn't stand to see me this way, and took me to the hospital on the night of the 1st. At 4:00 on the 2nd I was examined by a doctor, who said I had scabies or something like that, and that I should go back to Japan on the *Shinyō Maru*. I have no idea how I got such a disease. I don't care what happens to me, but cannot apologize enough to you, the shipping company, and my husband. Please forgive me.

Tamiye

こんな申し訳ない事は寝ても起きてもありません、船の中で船酔ひしてカイガリが出てなをるかと思ふて待つゐたのになかなかになをりませんでそれで心配して[91]

On the morning of May 8, 1917, twenty-four-year-old picture bride Tamiye Furukawa (古川タミエ) was found dead in the women detainee's dormitory at the Angel Island Immigration Station. She had hanged herself at her bunk with the narrow under-sash (*hoso-obi*) of her kimono. Tamiye (American records have Tomiye) was a native of Minamihiro Village in Wakayama Prefecture, and had arrived in San Francisco aboard the *Shinyō Maru* on April 28.[92] She had come to join her new husband Kisuke Furukawa (古川喜助), also a Wakayama native, whom she had never met. The marriage ceremony for Kisuke and Tamiye had been performed in Japan in February 1917, and she had been added to his household register. Kisuke had immigrated to the United States in 1906, and worked in farming in Hanford, the county seat of King's County, California.[93]

Tamiye's death was particularly tragic, as it appears it was the result of cultural miscommunication, and could easily have been prevented. The Japanese Association carried out a full investigation, and the results were the basis for a series of articles in *Nichibei*. As she writes in her suicide note, Tamiye had been sick on the ship, and then developed a high fever. She was hospitalized at the Angel Island Immigration Station on May 1. When she saw the doctor on May 2, she mistakenly believed he ordered her deported on the *Shinyō*

Maru, scheduled to depart on May 9. Previously, while still on the journey outbound from Japan, Tamiye had read in a newspaper that women who arrived in America with any type of venereal disease were subject to immediate deportation. In her fevered mind Tamiye somehow jumped to the conclusion that she had received such a diagnosis, though this was not the case. In fact, the bureaucratic machinery was already moving to have her released to her new husband. The authorities summoned Kisuke to the station, and set the immigration interview for May 5. Yet on the 4th Tamiye's fever spiked to over 100 degrees, and she was sent back to the hospital. The immigration interview was postponed. Events hit another snag on May 7, when Tamiye and Kisuke met for the first time at the station. The interview could not be completed because the regular translator was unavailable. The immigration inspector told them the interview would be rescheduled for the 8th, when Mrs. Terasawa (Fuku Terasawa, matron and interpreter, and wife of Reverend Barnabas Terasawa) could attend. Kisuke and Tamiye spoke no English, and did not understand this message. As Tamiye left the room to return to the dormitory, the last words she said to Kisuke were, "I want to die." Tamiye's roommate Tomishima Shige discovered the body and the suicide note the next morning.[94] Shamed to have contracted a disease she did not understand, Tamiye had ultimately decided she could neither go forward nor go back.

The marriage to Tamiye was not Kisuke's first. Kisuke was forty-two in 1917, and had already undergone a picture marriage two years previously with another woman from Minamihiro Village, which ended in divorce within one month. After two failed picture marriages, Kisuke gave up on the practice, but not on marriage. He traveled back to Minamihiro Village, and returned to the US on June 12, 1918 with his twenty-three-year-old bride, Ei Furukawa. The 1930 Census shows the couple and their five children still in Hanford, where they managed a truck farm. By the time of the Second World War internment of Japanese Americans, Ei was a widow.[95]

18.

Regulations
are especially cruel
on cold mornings at Angel Island.

by Tahara

田原[96]

掟むごきを殊に朝寒う天使島

19.

Without even Toso wine,
New Year's first dawn rises
Over Angel Island.

        by Hikawa

氷川 屠蘇もなく天使島の初日の出
97

Toso wine is a type of *sake* that is imbued with medicinal herbs. It is traditionally consumed at the New Year, as a way of ensuring health and prosperity in the coming year.

20.

The bride on the island
And the groom at the inn
Grow a year older.

        by Akei

阿惠生 妻は島婿は旅館で年を取
98

21. A Night at Angel Island

In a stone prison on Angel
    Island
A Japanese girl is crying.
Leaving muddy streaks on
    her pale face,
As she clings to a chill
    window.

From the chill window
    what can be seen?
Pale, eerie moonlight that
    keeps her from sleep.
From the chill window
    what can be heard?
Dreamlike in the distance,
    white gulls faintly cry
The lingering sound of
    tears.

A Japanese girl is crying.
Clinging to a chill window,
Muddy streaks on her face
In a stone prison on Angel
    Island.

          by Chinami Itoshima

22.

Kind angel—
That's the name of the island.
A Western lady comes ashore
With a duck-tail waddle.

          by Futaba

The juxtaposition of these two lines suggests a connection. We can speculate that the poem refers to United Methodist Deaconess Katherine Maurer (1881–1962), known as the "Angel of Angel Island" for her tireless efforts on behalf of the detainees' welfare. She was a constant visitor from her appointment by the Women's Home Missionary Society in 1912 until the station closed in 1940.

23.

She sends a wireless telegram
To her picture husband,
And waits at the ship,
Hoping he will come.

She is worried
She'll be rejected by her husband,
Whose face and heart
She has never seen.

Although he said
This season is not the best,
She has counted on her fingers,
And this is the joyful month.

For the sake
Of her husband's success,
She's taken jobs she's not used to,
Washing dishes and scrubbing floors.

She yearns for
Her beloved husband in the picture,
Yet upon arrival, she sees only
The heartless immigration official.

by Pantsu

24.

First dream of the New Year—
On the island I meet
My picture bride.

    by Kanzan from
      "A–" City

亞市　閑山生 102

初夢は寫真の妻に島で逢ひ

25.

Ceremony at the Immigration Station,
In the New Year's dawn light.
The violet glow of mountains.

    by Asei

亞生 103

紫匂ふ移民校舎の式初日輝く

26.

The suspicion
Of a disease of the eye—
On the island, a long night.

    by Meizan

鳴山 104

眼病の嫌疑に嶋のよや長し

Diagnosis of common eye diseases such as trachoma was grounds for deportation.

27.

Even the shit
Is thoroughly looked after
By the Immigration Service

      by Kagebenkei

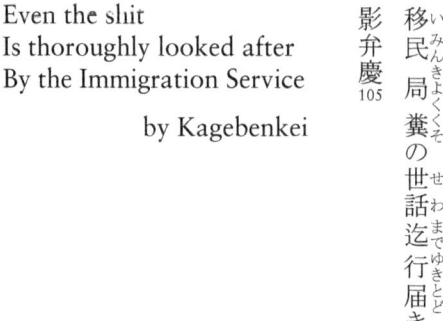

Probably a wry reference to the fecal samples required during the medical examinations.

28.

When they told me
I don't have to worry,
And tomorrow I can land in America,
My heart was filled with joy.

At the ship,
I catch a glimpse of his face,
Yet my husband's heart
Is not yet revealed.

Before the happy meeting
At the wharf,
The bitterness
Of a heartless examination.

My sufferings on a lonely island
Are all forgotten now,
In the happiness
Of my new life.

Discretely I pull out the picture
And take a look—
On the deck of the ship,
Where is my husband?

Three years apart:
When you summoned me,
Joyful tears
began to fall.

My thoughts
Cross four thousand miles,
Delivered there
At the tip of my joyful brush.

by Fundora

明日は上陸する心配すなと、聞て嬉しい胸の内。
主の心は未だ見えぬ。
會ふて嬉しい波止場の見合、つれない檢査に一苦勞。
沖の孤島の苦勞も今は、忘れて嬉しい新世帶。
主は何處と船の上。
三年別れて呼寄せられりや、嬉し淚が先に立つ。
妾の思ひが四千哩外に、届いて嬉しい筆の先き。

ふんどら生
106

船でちらりとお顏は見たが、
人目忍んで寫真を出して、

29.

By an Immigration Station window,
I wait for the sky to clear,
To see Vega, the Weaving Maid.

by Kuniko

移民舎の窓に女星の晴れ待てり

洲子[107]

In East Asian folklore, the Weaving Maid (the star Vega) and her husband the Herdboy (the star Altair) are separated by the Milky Way (the "River of Stars"). They meet only once a year, on the seventh night of the seventh lunar month, when magpies form a bridge across the span between them.

30.

Arriving at Angel Island,
I realize
It's the Isle of Demons.

On Angel Island,
Demon angels with protruding horns
Are wailing.

On Angel Island,
Specters of demon angels
All disappear.

On Angel Island,
In the dippers and the mortars
Demon angels dwell still.

by Kagebenkei

天使島來て見て鬼ケ嶋と知れ。
天使嶋天女も角を出して泣き。
天使島天女の姿皆無なり。
天使島杓子や臼の天女棲み。

影辯慶[108]

The "Isle of Demons" features in the popular Japanese folktale, *Momo Tarō* (Peach Boy). Momo Tarō was born from a large peach, and was raised by the old couple who found him. Aided by a dog, a monkey, and a pheasant, Momo Tarō defeats all the monsters on the Isle of Demons, and captures their riches.

"Demon angels with protruding horns" most familiarly recalls the grinning, horned mask of Hannya, a jealous female demon in Noh drama.

In Japanese folklore, *oni* (the general term for ghosts, demons, and monsters) frequently haunt ordinary objects, and attack the unwary. Hyōtankozō, the *oni* found in calabash ladles, is often depicted along with Nyūbachibō, the *oni* who inhabits mortars.[109]

31.

At the New Year,
My wife makes the first temple visit—
At the Immigration Station.

           by Kuniko

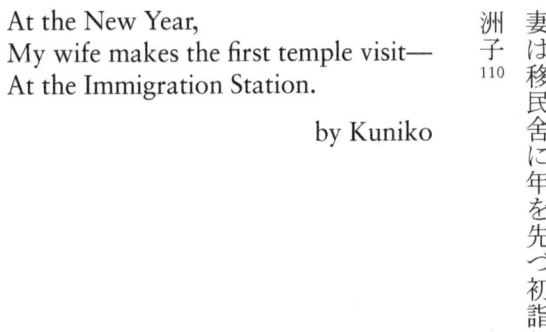

[110]

Hatsumōde (First Visit) is a Japanese New Year's tradition. On the first, second, or third day, people visit Shinto or Buddhist shrines to pray for peace and prosperity in the coming year.

32. The Month of March

Ah! March last year
Was the month when I,
Raised in the mountains,
First took ship across the ocean,
The hated month when I gazed
   at the hills
Through the iron bars of Angel
   Island.

       by Kashin Shimizu

[111]

Kashin Shimizu is the pen name for Terukichi [Thomas] Shimizu (born 1894), who arrived in San Francisco on March 16, 1915, after crossing on the *Mongolia*. He had traveled from his home in Mine Village, Usui District, Gunma Prefecture (in central Honshū) to join his father Shinsaku [Frank] Shimizu, at the time a bicycle dealer who resided at 2413 Shattuck Avenue, Berkeley, California.[112] He hoped to become a dentist. Terukichi was detained at Angel Island not because of a problem with his immigration application, but because he was diagnosed with the hookworm parasite—uncinariasis—which was grounds for deportation. After a hearing, he was indeed ordered deported, but with the caveat that, "... if hospital treatment is applied for and granted and a cure effected you may be admitted under the immigration law." His father provided a $50 bond to pay for medical treatment, and after hospital care at Angel Island for six days, Terukichi was given a medical release on March 26, 1915.[113] As Kashin, which means "Summer Morning," Terukichi frequently published poetry in *Nichibei* in the ensuing months and years. In the early 1920s, he also published two books of his poetry. The striking woodblock portrait of the author in this volume, by Matsubara Chōyū, is from his first book, published locally in 1921 (Fig. 1.11). His 1923 book was written in English, and includes illustrations by the well-known Bay Area Japanese artist Chiura Obata.[114]

象印の晨夏

FIGURE 1.11 *Shimizu Kashin.*

33.

Why do I see such despair?
Late summer
At Angel Island.

          by Fuki

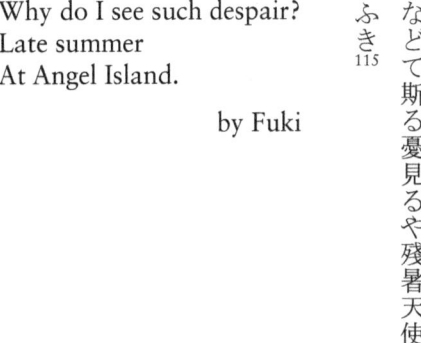

34.

When the new bride
Was allowed to land in America,
She made sushi.

          by Kashio

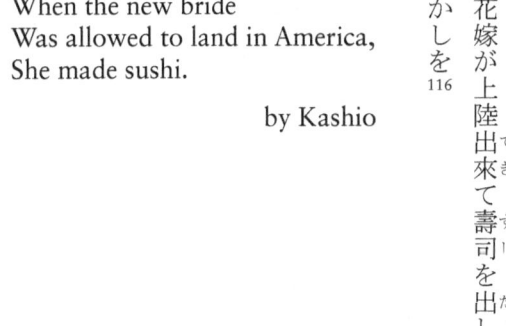

Angel Island Poems by Karl Yoneda

Labor activist Karl Goso Yoneda (1906–1999) was a young man of twenty when he spent two months in captivity at the Immigration Station. Born in 1906 in California, he accompanied his immigrant parents when they decided to return to Japan in 1913. After spending his formative years there, he took ship back to America in 1926, to avoid being drafted into the Japanese Imperial Army. Although he carried his US birth certificate with him, still he was locked up at Angel Island, until his cousin and sister in Los Angeles vouched for his identity. To while away the hours he composed poetry, and after he was released he published selections in *Nichibei* in early 1927, under the pseudonym Kiyohi Hama. He joined the American Communist Party, and was a leader in the International Longshoremen's and Warehousemen's Union (ILWU), and an organizer for the Congress of

Industrial Organizations (CIO). During the Second World War, he was interned at Manzanar, so has the dubious distinction of having been imprisoned twice by his own government. He volunteered for the US Army in November 1942, and joined the Military Intelligence Service. He served as a Japanese language specialist in the China-Burma-India theater. In 1983, he published his autobiography, *Ganbatte: Sixty-Year Struggle of a Kibei Worker*.[117]

Not all Yoneda's poems (#35–49) are *about* Angel Island, but all were written at the Immigration Station.

35.

At dusk on one of the sad days,
As my eyes devoured a newspaper,
I felt there
The breath of my girl in Japan.

悲しい或る日の
たそがれに食った新聞紙に
故國の女の臭覺を
私は感じた

36.

On New Year's Day,
Nine Japanese wrapped in blankets
In an immigration jail
Send off the calm sea waves of the New Year from Angel Island.

正月の元旦
ここの九つの東邦人が
移民監で毛布と共に
海上静波の新年を
天使島から見送っていた

37.

Hara-kiri,
Wandering emptiness monks,
And Daisuke Namba,
Are the reality of Japan.
All three are pictured in the newspaper
On the wall of the immigration jail.

ハラキリと
虚無僧と難波大助
之が日の丸の國の實相です
この三様の寫真を刷り込んだ新聞が
移民監に貼り出されてありました

Hara-kiri, formally called *seppuku*, is the practice of ritual suicide by disemboweling. It was especially associated with the samurai class in old Japan.

Followers of the Fuke sect of Zen Buddhism, often called "emptiness monks" (as here), played the *shakuhachi* flute as a form of meditation during pilgrimages around Japan.

In late 1923, Daisuke Namba (1899–1924), son of a member of the Japanese Diet, attempted to assassinate Prince Regent Hirohito at the Toranomon intersection in Tokyo. When he was sentenced to hang, he defiantly shouted, "Long live the Japanese Communist Party! Long live Russian socialism and the Soviet Republic! Long live the Communist Internationale!" The three images that Karl Yoneda chooses are very different, which is precisely the point: he describes Japan as a land of contradictions.

38.

I rode in on the ocean tides
And was thrown in an
   immigration jail.
In spite of all the investigations,
After two months, I'm to be
   sent back.
I think she will come
To the Yokohama docks
To welcome me back from
   across the sea.

海潮を乗り切つて來て
すぐさま移民監に抛り込まれ
二ヶ月の後には元へ逆もどりです
それでも視察はどつさりと
洋行歸りの私を
彼の女はヨコハマに
迎えてくれるでせう

39.

Over ten months of calamity
On this island.
The coming of the New Year
Makes me feel old.

わざわひのとつき餘りをこの島で
暮して年を取りし正月

There is likely a typographical error in the newspaper text, as the author spent only two months on Angel Island, not ten. Only a slight change in the first phrase, from のとつき餘り to のひとつき餘り, would yield "over one month."

40.

New Year arrived quietly, without event.
At twenty-one, I guess
This can be called happiness.

正月があつけなくすぎし二十一は
さちにも見えねかくあらまほし

41.

Writing a poem again
After a long time,
So much discontent
Disappears from my weary mind.

久々に歌作りしは我胸の
わだかまりいたく疲れ消えしか

42.

Lately, bit by bit, I've forgotten
That people in the village
Hated me so.

このわれをいたく厭ひし村人の
事をとやうやく忘れしこの頃

43.

The promise that you made
Without regard to country, yours or mine,
Is just like
The evening of the day.

君はとて國もしらずてかわせしは
ちぎりにも似しある日の夕べ

44.

Lately,
Even when now and again my tears fall,
They are without feeling, insipid,
Just like a lie.

ときたまに落る涙もこの頃は
味氣なくてしいつわりに似る

45.

There was a girl I met on the ship
And parted from on the ship,
In late night conversations
Never knowing her name.

船に見て船に別れし女あり
夜の語りに名も知らずして

46.

Angel Island—
What a beautiful name.
Yet today, surrounded by wire fences,
The sadness of prisoners.

天使島名よくしてよけれあみがこひ
囚はれ人のものうき今日なり

47.

Between the waves
In the distant sea,
The red sun and your heart
Are sinking.

沖つべに波がかりつゝ沈み行く
陽の赤々とかの君ごころ

48.

The sound of waves
On a winter day falling into darkness
Makes my eyes fill with tears
While I think of you.

冬日落闇の波音にさそわれて
泪ににじみぬ君思ふまま

49.

I can't tell the color—
Is it crimson or purple?
That is reflected in the sea
As the sun falls in.

何の色赤か紫か知らずして
落ち行入り日海に映ゆ見る

New Life and Old Memories

50.

In the New Year's dawn,
San Francisco looks just like Nagasaki
Wrapped in mountains!

     by Sanfurō

桑市は長崎に似て山包初日哉
三府ろう [118]

51.

Sleeping in the big city,
I wake as the first dawn's light
Shines on skyscrapers.

     by Kojin

大都眠り覺めで初日摩天樓に映り
虚人 [119]

52.

Sweat!
Sweat!
Sweat is the jewel
That turns into gold.

汗を流せよ流せよ汗を、
汗は黄金を結ぶ玉。 [120]

53. Autumn Grass

If you come
To America,
Where gold falls from the sky,
Don't despair
When you tread on withered grass.

    by Tōkirō

「秋草」
黄金ふる等アメリカへ行かばやと悲しがらずや醜草踏めば。
藤枝郎

54.

Even advocates of assimilation
Want to eat
The rice cake soup!

    by Fundoshi-ikkan

お雑煮を同化論者も喰ひたがり
褌一貫

Zōni (or *ozōni*) is a Japanese soup containing *mochi* rice cakes that is traditionally eaten at the New Year.

55.

She crosses to America
And finds her husband
Is a dishwasher.

    by Bōroku
    Los Angeles

羅府 望鹿

渡米して見ば亭主は皿洗ひ 123

56.

When I left my home country
I was dreaming;
After ten years in America
I'm still not awake.

    By Nonkibō

呑氣坊

國を出る時や夢みて居たが、在米十年まだ覺めぬ。 124

57. Watching a Friend Send Her Children Back to Japan

Her face is desolate with loneliness
As she sends off her infant child
Who knows nothing
Except love for his parents.

She is grief-stricken
By the love of her child
Who is now walking away
Into the dim light
Of a second-class stateroom.

    by Ijūin Ijiri

「友の子供送還を見て」
父母戀ふる何も知らざる乳哺子を送る妻の顔や淋しき。
うす暗き中等室の一室に今別れ行く子の愛を悲しむ。

井尻伊集院

58.

His wife is here now,
So he answers the telephone
In English.

    by Bōroku
    Los Angeles

羅府　望鹿

妻が居て電話の返答英語でし

59. The Coming of Autumn

Autumn has come lately—
I long for the singer
In the foggy San Francisco night.

    Written in the wilds of Northern California

                by Kyōsen Suzuki

60. Love Songs

All at once,
For a little while,
The bitterness of my labors
Releases me,
When I see you, my love.

In the past,
I couldn't stand that man of mine;
But now,
A lonely traveler,
I long for him.

                by Tanaka

61.

On New Year's Day,
In the corner of a saloon,
Alone.

        by Harei

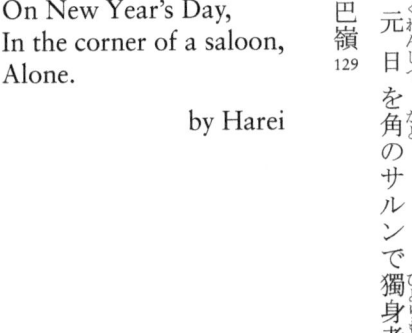

巴嶺 129

62.

Talking about
The San Francisco Earthquake
Through the long night.

        by Bogyū

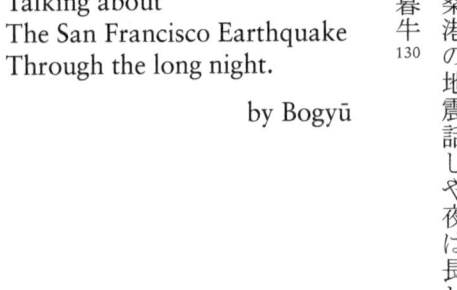

暮牛 130

63.

Below a half moon
We run with the tide,
And sing a song
Of the Monterey sardine boat.

        by Tōmenrō

島面樓 131

The sardine industry centered in Monterey, described most famously in John Steinbeck's *Cannery Row*, peaked in 1945 and dwindled thereafter. Sicilians dominated the fleet, but at any one time up to one-quarter of the fishermen were Japanese.

64.

In this year of national mourning,
New Year's celebrations
Are a bit lacking.

    by Dondonbō

The Meiji Emperor died on July 30, 1912, and was succeeded by his son Yoshihito, who became the Taishō Emperor.

65. To Leave or Not?

As the sun sets,
The children cry out in grief.
The ocean grows dark,
And following the ship's way,
My soul is lost.

The smell of the sea,
And my children's faces,
And the great ship,
And my wife, and me—
Still we cannot leave.

    by Chinami Itoshima
      "A–" City

66.

Born subjects of the emperor,
We live in a foreign land.
At the New Year, we make a toast:
"May your reign last forever!"

   by Keiko Kodama

兒玉桂子134

大君の民と生れて異國に君が代千代を祝ふ初春。

The last line is a paraphrase from a line in the Japanese national anthem.

67.

In my hometown,
My family is searching
For my bride.

  by Hijitetsubō

肱鉄坊135

故郷では内々嫁を探して居

68.

Over a month in America—
Still crying over the broken mirror
Through the long night.

                by Kinshū

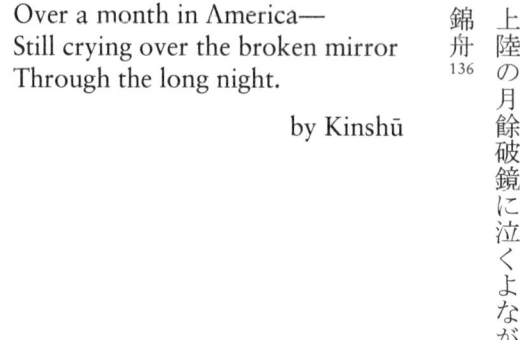

Mirrors in old China and Japan were round, and so became a symbol of unity, particularly marriage and family unity. A "broken mirror" signifies a breakup, or a divorce.

69. My Hometown

Slurping the *hiyamugi*
    wheat flour noodles—
Smooth, slippery
    (Gobble! Smack!)
Slippery, smooth
    (Swallow! Gulp!)
Somehow it's like I've
    returned to Japan.

Western food, Chinese
    food, Japanese food—
Our digestive organs can
    handle anything,
But the one thing that's
    hard to digest
Is the spirit of American
    people.

This utopia of freedom in
    the world
Is a place where the living
    standard is high,
Yet we are not happy.
When I slurp the flour
    noodles,
I start to miss my home.

          by Kōsō

70.

New Year's greetings
Were sent off to Japan
Half a month ago!

        by Kimyōan

71.

A poor student celebrates New Year
With a nickel's worth
Of rice cake soup.

    by Shōei

72.

After a round of New Year's visits,
Downtown, on the road home,
Lost.

    by Kakumaru

73.

The telegram arrived three days ago,
In this South Park hotel
The night is long.

A steam whistle in the harbor in the long
 night,
Teased by the wind at the window,
Waiting for my bride.

    by Tanoji

South Park is in the South of Market area of San Francisco. Nearby were the wharves where most trans-Pacific passengers landed. After the San Francisco Earthquake, the neighborhood was dominated by warehouses, cheap hotels, and businesses catering to longshoremen and immigrants.

74.

At the New Year,
I get drunk on wine
Poured by my new wife.

    by Hikawa

氷川 142

新たなる年を新婦の酌に酔ひ

75.

In America,
Even mortuaries
Send New Year's greetings!

    by Dondonbō

吞々坊 143

アメリカの葬儀社春を祝って來

76.

In my New Year's letter,
The name of my wife
Is written first.

        by Umeshō

77.

Every year they say,
"This year for sure
I'm going home!"

        by Teruo Sakata
             Los Angeles

A thirty-four-year-old single man by this name was aboard the *Chiyo Maru* when it docked in Honolulu on January 9, 1913. The passenger list states that his next destination was San Francisco. At the time he registered for the First World War draft, he was working as a janitor in Los Angeles.

78.

He: My bride
　　Is even prettier than her picture!
　　Drinking Toso wine.
She: My bridegroom
　　Is hiding something . . .
　　Eating rice cake soup.

　　　　　　by Akei

女房は寫真以上と屠蘇機嫌
花婿が猫をかぶつて雑煮喰い

阿惠
146

79.

Even though you have no money,
I will never leave you,
For I've fallen in love
With your sincere heart.

　　　　　by Shihyō
　　　　　Los Angeles

黄金（かね）がないとて縁（えんきり）切はせぬ、
主（ぬし）の實意（じつい）に惚（ほ）れた妾（わし）。

在羅府

思漂生
147

80.

As long as you
Are in this world,
I don't mind
Having nothing.

　　　　by Yoshio

生ける世中に主（よじゅぬし）さへあれば、
何（なに）がないとて氣（き）にならぬ。

よしを
148

81.

This year
Finally comes to an end,
Like the sufferings
Of a chicken
With its head cut off.

       by Hikarisō

Camp and Colony

82.

In camp
Men cook and men dance—
It's spring everywhere.

       by Shisei

83.

Staying up all night in camp,
I'm getting used to
The sound of mosquitoes.

   by Sanshō

蚊の聲になれてキャンプの徹夜かな
三笑 151

84.

My first attempt
At digging potatoes
On a cold morning.

   by Taizan

處女事業の芋の試掘や朝寒み
泰山 152

85.

Cold morning—
The dew, in a night,
Has rusted the farm tools.

   by Takebō

朝寒や農具に露の一夜錆
竹坊 153

86.

A newcomer
Breaks through spider webs
To find his place.

            by Chiroku

新参は蜘蛛巣分けし潜り込み

池鹿

87. Camp

Plum leaves are falling in San Jose
In the last gleams of a pale setting sun.
In the distance, from the top of a bush,
The broken cries of a shrike.
In our corner of the tiny storeroom,
I've grown tired of hearing Chico's stories
Of the strong liquors and the women—
I wonder what the San Francisco night is really like?
Only five o'clock, and already the sun is gone;
Somehow my world seems so small.
I light the kerosene lamp and cook the meal.
I'm on duty tomorrow:
These attacks of rain and frost—
The tomatoes won't stand them for long.
I hated leaving my old hometown,
But I am worried about my future.
As I hear the sound of the train whistle,
I take off my dusty, sweaty shirt.
Tomorrow may see frost,
For tonight I feel a cold wind.

by Heki

88.

City fellows say
Where we live
Is like a pig sty.

Underneath
That camp bed
A pig is squealing.

      by Shōei

豚小屋の様だと町の奴つい云ひ
其のキヤンプベツドの下で豚が鳴き

省英
157

89.

The shadows of wild horses
In the Sierra Nevada foothills
On New Year's Day.

      by Shinji

ネバタ裾の野馬群を初日影哉

針時
158

90.

Line by line, wild geese
Cross an ancient marsh
In the vast wilds of California.

      by Hitoyasu

加州廣野古沼條に雁の行く

一休
159

91. Songs of the Immigrant Land

Snipe are calling
In the autumn reeds.
Snipe are calling,
While Hindus on the levee
Gaze up at the moon.

I crossed the ocean here,
Wrapped in a beautiful dream:
On the river delta
Talking with a western girl.

Once again:
Stories of divorce
On the river delta.
A woman is weeping,
Waiting for a boat.

Wait a little while
For the proper time;
The counterfeit child
Cannot talk about the past.

   by Okina-rokkei

「移民の歌」

しぎが啼く秋の蒲原しぎが啼くヒンヅー人は土手に月觀る。

美しき夢を包みて渡り來し西の女と語る川しも。

又しても離縁話に川下の女泣く泣く船をまつかな。

今しばし時機をまてよと偽りの子は苦げに過去を語らず。

翁六溪
160

The term "Hindu" was used broadly to refer to anyone of South Asian ancestry, when in fact most South Asian immigrants at the time were Sikhs from the Punjab.

The "counterfeit child" was presumably a paper son/paper daughter who immigrated using false documents.

92.

When the new bride
Arrives in camp,
The flowers bloom.

   by Tonkyo

93.

Married couples
Divide the room with sheets
Before sleep.

   by Kakumaru

94.

In a leaky tent
By lantern light
A woman makes sushi.

   by Nōdan

95.

An exile from Asia,
Beneath the moon in camp,
Sobbing.

    by Etsujin

大陸の流人キャンプの月に泣き

越人

164

96. Plowing

In her thoughts,
The plowing woman
Curses her fate.

    by Kitahira

「畑打」
耕し女運命を呪ふ心かな

北平

165

97. Pioneer

I cleared a hundred acres of land
   With just my own arms.
Under the 120 degree sun,
   Far removed from society,
The bounty wrought by the sweat of my skin
   Has come to nought.
The crop has rotted in the fields—
   It's another great failure.
From pennilessness, without help from anyone,
   I raised myself up.
Now to pennilessness I've returned—
   There's no mystery to it.
With my wife and children there are six of us—
   But after tomorrow How will we eat?
If we cannot eat,
   Then eat this flesh of mine.
Under the 120 degree sun,
   Having just my thin arms as my stake,
As a pioneer of our race
   In the field of brambles
   I made the flowers bloom.

           by Okusuke
           Imperial Valley

98.

Sorrow at the New Year
When I see the profile
Of my wife's face
Haggard with toil.

    by Tōbi

登美

労働にやつれし妻の横顔をながめてあれば初春悲し。

99.

The new bride's
Only worry
Is the gap in the wall.

    by Keimei

鷄鳴

板の隙許り新婦は氣にして居

100.

On Sundays
We go by train
To buy bean curd.

   by Etsujin

日曜は汽車で豆腐を買ひに行き
越人

101.

Even white people
Come to celebrate
At the sushi party.

   by Chahorin

鮨の座に白人も來て祝ひかな
茶布倫

102.

The colonists' success
Is a child's birth
In camp.

   by Unnunbō

殖民の實をキヤンプで産み落し
云々坊

103.

First tilling of the year—
Trying out
A steam-powered plow.

        by Sanshō

試みを鋤き初めけり蒸滊鋤

山椒 172

104.

Making rice cake soup
In the light of the Sierra Nevada
Coming through the window.

        by Fumio

雑煮つくる窓明け行くや山ネバタ

文男 173

105.

First letter of the New Year
To your parents in the old country—
Adding a picture
Of our newborn baby.

    by Kimyōan
    In Livingston

リビングストン　溟妙庵
174

産んだ子供の寫真も添えて故國の親御に初便り

106.

In the immigrants' schoolhouse,
Singing of the boundless spring
Of the imperial reign.

    by Rōi

浪衣
175

移民校舎歌洋々や御代の春

107.

Parents with rice cake soup,
Children with turkey,
We grow a year older.

          by Yakkodako

108.

The presence of the third generation
Makes grandfather
Into a speechless person.

          by Kimyōan
          Yamato Colony

109.

As host and guest pick up chopsticks
For rice cake soup,
The pros and cons of assimilation.

          by Yaji

110.

Gazing over our fields,
At New Year's first sunrise,
Both my thoughts
And my wife's thoughts
Are bright with hope.

   by Ruri Kimiko

所有畑に初日おろがむ
わが胸も妻が胸にも希望かがやく。

瑠璃公子
179

111.

In the bright New Year's dawn,
A broad stretch of fruit trees
And windmills.

   by Sekiki

初日朗ら果樹廣々と風車など

赤鬼
180

112.

The green pasture
In the setting sun
Shines brightly
In the radiance
Of Sierra Nevada snows.

   by Masaō Ikeda

落陽の緑の牧場あかあかとシエラネヴアタの雪のかがやき。

イケダ・マサオウ

On May 15, 1908, an eighteen-year-old "working student" by this name arrived in Seattle on the *Tosa Maru* from Yokohama. He was from Yokohama City in Kanagawa Prefecture. The manifest lists his next destination as San Francisco. The 1940 Census lists Masao Ikeda, born 1890, living in Los Angeles with his wife and four children. His occupation was fertilizer salesman.

113. The Yamato Colony: Winner of the Essay Competition (Round Four) on the Topic of "In Praise of Our Second Home" [1917]

> The first people who came to live and build this colony in the middle of Merced County heard the sad howls of coyotes carried by the biting, cold winter wind from Yosemite Valley. They endured many hardships to put order to this land: in order to draw fresh water, they had to bring it in

from many blocks away; wild grasses five feet high had to be cut and burned; and there was not enough food for their daily meals. Then they experienced a tragic event: sharp winds blew the dunes, which buried the crops into which they had put so much effort.

Now there remain twenty-two households, 72 men and women, and 39 children. These beautiful fields with a hundred ripening fruits are a result of many sacrifices, and show the traces of ten years of suffering history. When I think of the unexpected deaths of people such as Giichi Minejima and Mrs. Okuye, who are now part of the soil of the colony, I am so filled with sorrow I cannot even shed tears. Yet farmers can find consolation when looking at the Sierra snows in winter, and when the trees in the orchards blossom, all of our eyes are filled with the light of hope. I cannot help but be happy when I think of the irrigation supplied by gathering the crystal clear waters of the benevolent Merced River. It would be hard for city folk to imagine the pleasure of spending a summer's day on the riverbank, trailing a fishing line in the water, in the shade of a forest that has not seen an axe in a thousand years.

As the children are growing up immersed in the beauty of nature, school education, and the Christian teachings, the many future sacrifices and daily difficulties I may face are no hardship.

by a Farmer[182]

* * *

Giichi Minejima, born about 1869 in Japan, immigrated to California in 1902, and was one of the original directors of the Yamato Colony and its first *soncho* (village head). He was a native of Furusawa Village in Chiba Prefecture. He went back to Japan late in the decade, and returned in August 1909 aboard the *Siberia*, along with his new wife, twenty-three-year-old Kazuko (née Hayashi). He died at Lane Hospital on Clay Street in San Francisco only two years later, on July 4, 1911. *Nichibei* publisher and Yamato Colony founder Kyutaro Abiko paid his funeral expenses.

Mrs. Okuye was Take Okuye (née Morimoto), the wife of Yamato colonist Seinosuke Okuye. She died of cancer in March, 1910, at the age of fifty-one. In the 1910 Census, fifty-three-year-old Seinosuke is listed as a widower with three children, Haruko (age twenty-five), Kiyoshi (sixteen), and Kikuye (eleven). Take had traveled with her husband and two younger children from Japan only two years earlier, arriving in Seattle on September 2, 1908.[183]

History, the Law, and Discrimination

114.

Immigrants are forbidden—
Useless
Is the grove in summer.

    by Kashō

移民禁じて唯
　　徒らに夏木立
可笑
184

115.

After rising from my first dream of the year,
I wipe my eyes, only to see
An anti-Japanese newspaper.

    by Joun
    San Francisco

初夢の眼を擦って排日紙
桑港 如雲
185

116.

I'm spreading the news far and wide—
Eight hundred dollars
Will summon a wife this year!

    by Kōzuki

八百妻今年は呼ぶと振れ歩き
紘月
186

Beginning July 1, 1915, the Japanese government made laborers eligible to send for brides, as long as they could show they had $800 in savings. This rule was not enforced by the US Immigration Service; rather, Japanese Consulates in US territories required the proof before a picture bride was issued an exit visa from Japan.

117.

A harsh wind
Becomes a wind
Of Japanese exclusion.

  by Kagebenkei

空ツ風それが排日風に成り

影辯慶
187

118.

"Jap" it said
In the big headline
Of a Hearst newspaper—
Infuriating!

  by Nōdan
  Los Angeles

ジヤツプと云ふ字を大きく書たハースト新聞は面憎い

羅府

農男
188

In the 1920s, California newspapers owned by William Randolph Hearst included the *San Francisco Examiner* and the *Los Angeles Examiner*.

119.

The first three days of the New Year
I'll just sleep somewhere—
Prohibition law.

       by Shōichi
       San Jose

三ケ日何處かで寝てる禁酒法
サンノゼ　正一
189

The Eighteenth Amendment to the US Constitution prohibited the production, sale, and transport of "intoxicating liquors." The Volstead Act was the legal mechanism which enforced it. Prohibition remained the law of the land from January 1920 to December 1933.

120.

Wife, liquor, and land
All denied me.
What a celebration!

       by Kinsuishi
       Los Angeles

嫁や酒、土地封ぜられて「御慶」也
羅府　琴醉子
190

The first of the California Alien Land Laws was passed by the legislature in 1913. It prohibited "aliens ineligible for citizenship" from owning agricultural land or holding long-term leases on it. An even stricter law was passed by ballot initiative in 1920, and amended to remove loopholes in 1923. The Alien Land Laws were not invalidated until 1952.

121.

Even if our arms and legs
Have been ripped off,
There is still the Head Tax!

       by Gojōgen

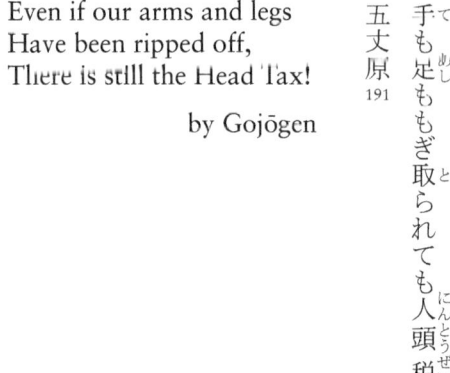

The governor of California signed the Alien Poll Tax into law in May 1921. It had been drawn up by the legislature in response to a constitutional amendment adopted by the people in November 1920. The law levied an annual tax of $10 on all alien male residents of the state between twenty-one and sixty years of age, excepting "paupers, idiots, and insane persons." Annual registration was also required of all aliens. The tax was immediately embroiled in litigation, and was ruled unconstitutional by the California Supreme Court in September 1921.

122.

In California
Tax is levied
On imported heads

      by Kureizumi

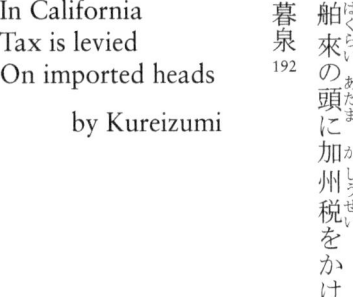

123.

From this house, too,
Brothers have left for war.
In the window
Two stars shine.

   by Shinroku

これも兄弟出征の家よ、窓に輝く星二つ。

新六
193

The practice of displaying banners with an embroidered blue star for every family member serving in the armed forces began in the First World War.

124.

For the sake of the country
We registered for the draft,
Yet we don't even have
The right to own land.

When we registered,
We were almost the same as whites.
With bitter smiles,
We return home as Japs.

Discriminatory treatment
Will only last awhile,
For the bent inchworm
Will stretch out again.

                  by Futaba

國のためとて登録すれど、所有權さへなき我等。

ホワイト並ぢやと登録すまし、歸りやヂヤップで苦笑ひ。

差別待遇もしばしの間、縮む尺取や延びるため。

二葉
194

At the outset of America's entry into First World War, the Selective Service Act was enacted, requiring registration for the draft. Aliens were not exempted. The first round of registrations took place on June 5, 1917.

2

Korean Inscriptions, 1910–1940

Homeland is my rivers and mountains

Korean immigration to the United States and its territories up to and during the period of the Angel Island Immigration Station's operation was on a very, very small scale, for both cultural and geopolitical reasons. Korea was deservedly called the Hermit Kingdom in the latter part of the nineteenth century. When King Gojong was crowned in 1864, he was only twelve years old, so his father the Daewongun (literally, "prince of the great court") assumed power and ruled in his stead. Though he attempted some positive reforms, Daewongun is most remembered for his radically isolationist approach to foreign relations and foreign influence. He ordered the eradication of Christianity in Korea, and the brutal campaign that followed resulted in the executions of nine French Catholic missionaries and approximately 8,000 Korean converts. In response, in late 1866 French naval forces and marines carried out a punitive raid on Ganghwa Island, which controls the river approach to Seoul. They held several fortifications for six weeks before withdrawing. Ganghwa Island was attacked again in 1871, this time by the United States. A diplomatic and trade mission had been dispatched to pursue treaty relations, supported by a naval escort of five warships. Korean batteries fired on the vessels, so the Americans raided the island, taking five garrisons and killing more than 200 Korean troops before withdrawing. Although the US dominated militarily, the diplomatic and trade mission was a failure as Korea refused to negotiate. The two attacks only confirmed the Korean court in its isolationism.[1]

The policy eventually led to disaster for Korea, yet not by agency of far-flung powers, but by those close to home. With the coronation of Prince Mutsuhito as Emperor Meiji in 1868, Japan embarked upon a campaign of rapid military and industrial modernization. Qing China also modernized, though to lesser effect. Russia commenced construction on the Far East segment of the Trans-Siberian Railway in 1890, and its leaders saw political and economic benefits to extending its influence into Manchuria. Korea was caught between three competing powers, and became a prize to be won.

Japan combined diplomacy and a threat of war (and yet another skirmish on Ganghwa Island) to force Korea to sign the Japan-Korea Treaty of 1876. By its terms, the Japanese gained special trading rights and privileges in Korea. Japan's rising influence alarmed China, and the two nations engaged in intense competition in Korea in the ensuing years. The Convention of Tientsin of 1885 stabilized the situation temporarily. Korea became a semi-protectorate of China from 1885 to 1894, while Japan bided its time. A flashpoint occurred in 1894, when the Korean government called for Chinese aid to quell a regional rebellion. The Chinese dispatched troops, and the Japanese did likewise. Japan made an escalating series of demands on the Korean government. In July, Japanese troops occupied Seoul, captured Kong Gojong, and established a pro-Japanese government. The Sino-Japanese War of 1894–1895 started in earnest the following month. It was fought primarily in Korea and surrounding waters. It ended with a humiliating defeat for China, which gave up any role in Korea's future, and also had to cede Taiwan to Japan.[2]

Meanwhile, in 1896 Russia gained a foothold in Manchuria under a concession from China to build the Chinese Eastern Railway. Harbin became a largely Russian city, and a major center for trade and transportation. In 1897, the Russian Navy occupied Port Arthur (Lüshun), and pressured China to lease the entire Liaodong Peninsula to Russia for a period of twenty-five years. Japan perceived a threat to its interests in Korea. This precipitated the Russo-Japanese War of 1904–1905. Japan's decisive victory stunned not only Russia but also the world. Russia was forced to withdraw from Manchuria, and to recognize that Korea was part of Japan's sphere of influence.

With its rivals eliminated, Japan wasted no time. It declared Korea a Japanese protectorate in 1905, and forced the king to abdicate and took over internal administration in 1907. In 1910, Japan formally annexed Korea. The country of Korea ceased to exist. August 29, the day the annexation was announced, was remembered by Koreans as "National Humiliation Day."

Between 1880 and 1902, just fifty Koreans entered the United States, mostly diplomats, students, and a few ginseng merchants. The first Korean immigration of any scale was to the Territory of Hawaii between 1903 and 1905, when approximately 7,400 laborers were recruited to work on the sugarcane plantations. The emigration of laborers from Korea was stopped almost entirely in 1905 when the Japanese protectorate was announced. Many of the Koreans remaining in Hawaii, especially those from non-agricultural backgrounds, found that backbreaking labor in the fields was not to their taste. By 1910, 65 percent of them had left the plantations. Some moved to the Hawaiian cities, others returned to Korea. About two thousand continued east, and landed in San Francisco and other West Coast ports. About 800 resided in California, mostly in small agricultural towns like Willows, Dinuba, Reedley, and Stockton. The rest settled in neighboring states, often working railroad construction.[3] Yet the window during which secondary migration of Korean laborers from Hawaii to the continental United States was possible was very short, as then President Theodore Roosevelt recognized Japan's authority over Korea in the Gentlemen's Agreement of 1907. His Executive Order No. 589 reads in part:

> I hereby order that such citizens of Japan or Korea, to-wit: Japanese or Korean laborers, skilled and unskilled, who have received passports to go to Mexico, Canada or Hawaii, and come therefrom, be refused permission to enter the continental territory of the United States.[4]

Subsequently, Korean immigration to the United States fell under the Gentleman's Agreement. Japan allowed about 1,000 Korean picture brides and a few family dependents to come in the next decade, but otherwise banned emigration from the Korean peninsula. Most of the picture brides joined husbands in Hawaii, while 115 came to the continental United States.[5]

In about 1905, pioneer Koreans in San Francisco formed the Korean Mutual Cooperation Association (KMCA) to unify laborers and students in California, and soon began to issue a handwritten weekly newsletter that quickly expanded to a widely circulated newspaper, *Kongnip Sinbo* [The United]. In 1907, soon after the Japanese forced the abdication of Korean Emperor Gojong, Koreans in Hawaii established the United Korean Association (UKA). The two organizations joined forces in 1909 as the Korean National Association (KNA).[6] The KMCA and the KNA provided vital assistance to another group of Korean arrivals in the period between 1906 and 1924: refugees fleeing Japanese rule. About 600 Korean refugees, many without passports, arrived at US continental ports in the period.[7] These immigrants included ex-government officials and intellectuals, but most were young people claiming student status. The first step for many, as it is today for those fleeing North Korea, was to cross the Tumen or Yalu rivers into northeast China. They then traveled to Shanghai or other Chinese ports to board passenger ships for America. Those who arrived in San Francisco found a protector in Reverend David Dae Wei Lee, a founding member of the KMCA and the KNA. Reverend Lee worked assiduously on their behalf, interceding with immigration authorities to gain their admission, posting bonds for them when necessary, paying for their medical treatment, and vouching for their student status.[8] The new arrivals received more of a welcome—relatively speaking—than other Asian immigrants to the United

States. Their status as refugees and students gained them a measure of approval. Moreover, many were Christians, and they benefited from the advocacy of American church communities.

The refugees formed the core of a Korean nationalist movement that was centered in San Francisco and Hawaii. *Kongnip Sinbo* in San Francisco was renamed *Sinhan Minbo* [New Korea]. It became the key independent mouthpiece for all Korean nationalist aspirations through the Second World War, as newspapers in Korea were subject to rigorous censorship by the Japanese. Reverend Lee was an early editor. It was published in San Francisco through 1941, then continued as a monthly in Los Angeles. *Sinhan Minbo* was in many respects a transnational newspaper. Its own circulation figures from 1908 (before the name change) estimated that for every 500 copies distributed in the continental US and 100 in Hawaii, approximately 3,000 reached the Korean peninsula. It was highly influential, so much so that the Japanese authorities considered it a dangerous source of unrest, and vigorously suppressed its importation.[9] Political activity in the Korean diaspora, and the importance of the *Sinhan Minbo* to nationalist efforts, surged following events in the peninsula in 1919. Following the sudden death of former Emperor Gojong on January 21, rumors began to circulate that he had been poisoned by the Japanese. (The suspicion is understandable, as Japan had orchestrated the assassination of Queen Min in 1895.) His funeral was scheduled for March 3. Amidst the discontent, on March 1 Korean nationalist activists took the opportunity to declare independence, touching off what later became known as the March 1st Movement. A wave of anti-Japanese demonstrations across the country ensued, with the participation of up to two million Koreans. The Japanese authorities cracked down violently, killing thousands and arresting many more.[10]

The Korean-American community currently numbers over 1.7 million, making it the fifth largest Asian-American group. Its growth to this magnitude has occurred extraordinarily rapidly, beginning with the Immigration Act of 1965, which abolished national quota barriers that had limited Asian immigration. About one million Korean Americans are immigrants themselves, and most of the rest are their US-born descendants.[11]

Although a considerable number of Korean arrivals were detained at Angel Island, to date only two Korean language inscriptions have been found on the barracks walls. These are described below. The remaining items in this chapter all come from the pages of *Sinhan Minbo*. Poetry was regularly published in the newspaper, and the sentiments of the compositions reflect the authors' refugee status. Their thoughts remain firmly tied to the old country, not new life in America.

WALL INSCRIPTIONS

1.

In-Bal Ryu
September 6
1927

류인발
구월륙일
一九二七
12

In Korean Hangul script and Chinese characters. Philip Lew, a twenty-seven-year-old U.S Army veteran, arrived in San Francisco aboard the US Army Transport ship *Thomas* on August 6, 1927. According to the passenger records, Philip was a Korean native who had enlisted in the US Army in Colorado, served his term, and then mustered out in Manila. He subsequently lived with his wife Mal Lew in Shanghai. His typed name and information first appears on the *Thomas* passenger manifest in the US citizens section—but the line is crossed out. He was then entered (by hand) in the alien passengers section; an accompanying note by immigration inspectors reads, "No. 2, Lew, ordered sent to Ang Island for examination by Oriental Division. Borden" (Fig. 2.1).

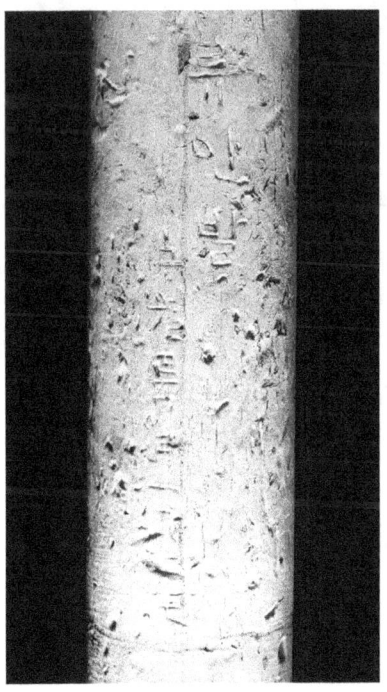

FIGURE 2.1 *In-Bal Ryu inscription. Photo: ARG and Daniel Quan.*

Clearly, the inspectors at the dock in San Francisco considered his citizenship in doubt. Fortunately, Lew's immigration case file still exists.[13]

The records suggest that he was an unfortunate victim of the immigration system. Born in 1900 in "Taiko, Korea" (Taiko is a Japanese pronunciation—as Korea was under Japanese occupation—and refers to the city of Daegu, 150 miles southeast of Seoul), Philip's Korean name was (in various records) spelled Yen-Bow Lew, In-Ho Lew, In-Ho Yoo, and In-Bial Yoo. All of these closely match "In-Bal Ryu," which is the way the name is spelled in contemporary transliteration. Although a native of Korea, much of Philip's childhood was spent in the US. His father, Gen-Yei Ryu, immigrated to Hawaii as early as 1902, and his mother Pil-La Kim Yoo (Ryu) followed in 1903. Philip's three sisters were born in Honolulu—and so were all US citizens. Philip had initially stayed behind in Korea, and then joined the family in Hawaii in 1912. The whole family then moved to the US mainland two years later. Philip became fluent in English. In 1919, he was working as a car driver in Denver.

On October 1, 1919 at Fort Logan, Colorado, Philip enlisted in the US Army for a three-year term. Within weeks he was ordered to overseas duty, first in Siberia and then in the Philippines. When he mustered out at the end of his term, on September 30, 1922, he was Private First Class in the 2nd Squadron of the Army Air Service, based at Fort Mills on Corregidor Island. He received an Honorable Discharge, and a good character reference. He spent about a year visiting family in Korea, and was married there. Then he and his wife moved to Shanghai, where he worked a steady job as parts manager at Bills Motors, an American-owned Ford dealership. They had a baby boy in Shanghai in 1925.

In the transcript of his immigration hearing, Philip said his reason for coming back to the US was to look for a better job, and that he had been recommended for a position with an import and export firm in Chicago. He was bewildered by his detainment at Angel Island, as revealed in letters he wrote to immigration and military authorities contained in his case file. He considered himself a US citizen. From the hearing transcript:

Q   Of what country do you now claim to be a citizen?
A   I claim to be an American citizen, because about three or four days prior to the time I enlisted in the American Army at Fort Logan, Colorado, on October 1, 1919, I filed my first papers, declaring my intention to become a citizen of the U.S. at Denver, Colorado. I was told by the Major, who commanded the Medical Department at Fort Logan, that I automatically became a citizen of the U.S. when I enlisted in the Army at that post, and he asked me several questions about the history of the U.S.
Q   Then in your opinion you have renounced your citizenship in Korea?
A   Yes, I do not think I am a citizen of Korea now.

Extant records corroborate his story, at least in part. His "Declaration of Intention" to naturalize was filed in US District Court in Denver on September 30, 1919, the day before his term of enlistment began. He apparently believed that his citizenship had been approved, for in the 1920 US Census record of his unit in the Philippines, he described himself as having naturalized in 1919. Members of the Special Board of Inquiry did not have those specific documents, but they did order investigators to check whether Philip's statements about the family's move to Hawaii and then the US mainland could be verified, and received reports in the affirmative. They also reviewed Philip's discharge papers, letters of recommendation from his employer and others in Shanghai, and a sheaf of correspondence from army staff approving his return to the US aboard military transport. Yet none of this made any difference:

> You are advised that it is the unanimous decision of this Board that you are inadmissible to this country because you are of a race ineligible to citizenship, not in possession of an immigration visa, your case coming under the provisions of Section 13(c) of the Immigration Act of 1924, and they have ordered your deportation to the country whence you came.

The rules for military naturalization were a subject of legal controversy in the period during and after the First World War, and confusion was perhaps inevitable. Laws designed to honor foreigners who served in the US armed forces with expedited citizenship came into conflict with those that institutionalized racial bias and exclusion. An Act of Congress on July 17, 1862 had authorized naturalization of any alien honorably discharged from military service who could demonstrate one year of residency, and a series of similar laws passed by Congress during and after the First World War all authorized military naturalization. A May 9, 1918 Act of Congress stipulated that "any alien serving the military during the war" had the right to expedited citizenship. Yet the judgments in numerous court cases held that those laws did not supersede existing bars to the naturalization of any person not of white or African ancestry. Though exceptions for Filipinos and Puerto Ricans were carved out, not until June 24, 1935 was military naturalization opened to all "aliens otherwise ineligible for citizenship." However, even that law would not have helped Philip Lew, as it applied narrowly to those who served between April 6, 1917 and November 11, 1918.[14]

Philip appealed the case, and though the decision was not reversed, he was allowed a temporary admission "for six months only" upon payment of a $500 bond. The inscription at the station is dated September 6, the day of his release. In December he wrote a letter to the Adjutant General of the Army asking for assistance: "I am still believing that I have some rights to fight for my steady residence in U.S.A." Yet none was forthcoming, and Philip returned to the Far East aboard the *Tenyo Maru* on March 8, 1928.

2.

In-Sik Lee   리
             인
             식
             15

The inscription was probably carved by nineteen-year-old student Hansik Lee, who spent two days on Angel Island from March 8–10, 1924 (Fig. 2.2).¹⁶ The attribution must remain tentative, however, as heavy paint overlays the Hangul syllables, particularly the third, and there is no additional text providing other identifying information.¹⁷

FIGURE 2.2 *George Hansik Lee's immigration file photo.*

On the 1924 passenger manifest, Hansik Lee claimed Korean ethnicity but he traveled with Chinese papers which said his birthplace was Fengtian, China (the city of Shenyang, not far from the Korean border). Yet in all other travel and government documents he gave his birthplace as Changwon (or nearby Masan), on the coast of present-day South Korea. His initial reluctance was probably due to his lack of a Korean (Japanese) passport. Lee adopted the English given name George, and after initial high school studies and stints in junior colleges in Sacramento and Modesto, studied civil engineering at the University of Southern California, where in 1931 he earned a master's of science degree, with a thesis on "Application of Irrigation Water to the Land." He soon relocated to Honolulu, where he worked as a draftsman for the Standard Oil Company (1940 Census and his immigration file), and for the Hawaiian Pineapple Company (Second World War draft registration). He enlisted as a private in the US Army on May 2, 1942, yet within a year was promoted to Lieutenant, probably due to his education and specialization. During the war he served on an airbase in Kunming, Yunnan Province, China, one of a system of such US bases that facilitated the airlift from India "over the Hump" of the Himalayas to China, to support units of the United States Army Air Forces (AAF) as well as resupply the war effort of the Chinese Nationalists. The laws prohibiting military naturalization by Asians that had denied Philip Lew the opportunity to become a US citizen were relaxed during the Second World War, by the Second War Powers Act in 1942 and the repeal of the Chinese Exclusion Act in 1943. First Lieutenant George Hansik Lee successfully petitioned for naturalization while in China. As he climbed the ranks, he was featured several times in laudatory articles in the *Honolulu Star-Bulletin* newspaper, like that headlined, "Once a Starving Korean Student, Captain Wins Success in Army."[18] After the war, Lee remained in the service, and worked for the United States Army Military Government of Korea, with the rank of Major. He died there in an accident on May 29, 1947. He was buried with military honors at the Schofield Barracks Post Cemetery in Honolulu.

KOREAN POETRY FROM
SINHAN MINBO[19]

Poems #3–10, #14–23 translated by Jikyung Hwang and Charles Egan

Poems #11–13 translated by Hyong-gyu Rhew

3. Farewell
by Jeong-Du Lee, Stockton

When my heart is in pain like this,
How can you be at ease?
A sorrowful twilight passes on Angel Island,
While a white gull wanders over the water.
My heart as I leave you,
Your heart as you go back, leaving me behind—
Ah, ah!
There is no use in crying;
The only thing we have is sorrow.
Can the death of a parent be compared to this?
Can the death of a friend be like this?
Our eyes welling with tears,
An indescribable heartrending farewell.
If we could stop the wheel of destiny,
You would remain in this land.

> Written on the day when for the last time I visited a brother who had come with me, but was forced to return to Korea—leaving Angel Island.
> July 22, 1927[20]

Jeong-Du Lee appears to be a pen name for twenty-four-year-old Korean student Han-Pyung Po, who arrived in San Francisco aboard the *President Taft* on July 14, 1927, and was landed after four days on Angel Island. Traveling with him was another twenty-four-year-old student, Wun-Chung Pak. Both were on their way to Stockton for studies at the College of the Pacific (now University of the Pacific). The two students had proper documents, yet Pak was diagnosed with clonorchiasis (liver fluke) and uncinariasis (hookworm). He was denied entry and deported on the *President Taft* on July 23—the day after this poem was written. Pak returned the following year aboard the *Taiyo Maru* with better results—he was admitted on September 7, 1928 and traveled on to Stockton. He later attended Huron College in Huron, South Dakota.[21] After studies in Stockton, Han-Pyung Po attended the College of Emporia in Emporia, Kansas, where he earned a degree in chemistry in 1932. See #14 below for another poem likely written by him.

4. Angel Island
   by Cloud

Angel Island, Angel Island, all the people said,
So I thought it would be like heaven.
Yet when the iron gate locks with a clang—

It feels like hell.
You, the masses of people
Who are wriggling in this steel-barred prison,
You have a home, you have a country.
So what is the reason for this sorrow?
It must be a hungry belly
That causes this Karma.[22]

「텬사도」 구름

텬사도, 텬사도, 하기에 텬당인줄알앗드니
쇠문을덜컥잠그니 지옥인듯십허라.
철창속에서우물그리는
수만흔사람들아 계나라, 계집두고
이어인슬흠인고? 아마도, 목구멍이
전성업원인가하노라.

5. A Night at the Immigration Station
by Gyeong-Sik Choi

This tired traveler
Has crossed a vast ocean—
Why must I sleep behind iron bars?
The rain cries out and wakes me up
Because it pities me.
Angel Island, sleeping tight,
No matter whether you hear this song or not,
It is the complaint of a foreign guest
Whose whole heart is burning.

Even though it's said America is wonderful,
How pathetic it has made me.
If my mother knew about this,
How shocked she would be.
This border created by rascals—
When can it be broken?
I hope people all over the world
Will become brothers soon.

April 3
Written on a rainy night at the
Immigration Station on Angel
Island, San Francisco, America.[23]

「이民局―야」 최경식

만리대양지튼손을 철창잠이웬일이며 소리니여우는비가
안타ㅅ가히쎄우단말가。 김히잠든텬사셤아 니노리를듯나마나
일쳔간장타오르는 이국고긱의푸념일셰。 아모리미국이조타기로
니쳐럼도구차한가 니어머님알고보면 얼마나놀나실가。
밍죵들이작란하는 국경이란언제부실고 셰계동포인류형데
하로밧비되고지고。
四月三日미국상항뎐사셤이민국에셔 비오는밤에

Gyeong-Sik Choi (Kyung Sik Choi or K.S. Choi in some records) was a native of Pyongwon County in South Pyongan Province (in present-day North Korea, to the north of the capital Pyongyang). He arrived in San Francisco aboard the *Taiyo Maru* from Kobe on April 3, 1925.[24] Twenty-year-old Choi had recently graduated from the Chosen Christian College in Seoul, where he had studied English, and was on his way to join the Class of 1929 at DePauw University in Greencastle, Indiana. At DePauw he studied English literature, and was a member of the Cosmopolitan Club, which was organized to facilitate meetings of international students with American students. He adopted the given name Philip. The 1926 university yearbook, *The Mirage*, includes a description of the club and a photograph of its members—Choi is identified as K.S. Choi in the text and P. Choi in the caption.[25] He stayed at DePauw for only one year, and then began graduate studies at Northwestern University in 1926. Philip Kyungsik Choi was awarded a master's in Sociology in 1930, with a thesis titled "The Urban Problem in Korea under the Japanese Regime."[26] He continued his education at the University of Chicago, where he had already begun taking classes in the spring of 1929.[27] Sadly, Choi died in Chicago on March 1, 1932, at the age of twenty-six. He had a heart condition that dated back to 1920 in Korea. The death record for "Phillip Choi" notes he was then a student of "U of C"—the University of Chicago. The cause of death was given as "chronic cardiac valvular disease," with associated kidney disease.[28]

6. Wandering
by Hae Il

Today east,
Tomorrow west.
This body of mine
Like floating duckweed.
Oh, how pitiful I am!
Mountain after mountain,
River after river,
The sun goes down and the road is far.
These tired legs
Shake even worse.
Oh, how pitiful I am!

Puppy, do not bark,
Lark, do not cry,
For this heart that longs for you
Burns even worse.
Oh, how pitiful I am!
Where is Eden?
Where should I go?
The spring of love and life flows on
To that Eden.
Oh, where should I go?

           In Delano
   Thinking about A.K.[29]

A. K. 사랑과 성명의 심흐르는 에덴이 어듸뇨
군을 성각하면서 딜네 노에셔
퍼피여 푸ㅣ지 마라
피곤한 이 다리 더옥 썰니도다
오오 가이 업서라
오오 가이 업서라
오늘은 동으로 닉일은 셔으로
표박하는 이 몸 비하면 부평이라 할가

오오 어듸로 가랴
어듸로 가랴
님 그린 이 가슴 더옥 타나니
오오 가이 업서라
오오 가이 업서라
산 넘어 쏘 산 강 건너 쏘 강 날져 물고 길은 머니

「류리」 히일

The agricultural town of Delano, California is approximately thirty miles north of Bakersfield. An enterprising Korean immigrant named Si-Dae Han moved there in the late 1910s and established a successful farm. Other Koreans moved to Delano, mostly to work for him. By 1930, the Korean enclave had grown large enough to support its own Christian church and pastor.[30]

7. The Fourth of July
by A Wanderer with No Country

Forty-eight stars shining,
Thirteen stripes intertwined,
Playing freely in the air of freedom,
Proudly boasting of prosperity,
The flag of the United States on the Fourth
 of July!
I envy and welcome such glory;
I admire and praise such honor.
The Spirit of Liberty nurtures you;
The Eagle dances for you.
Who is it who sees you and thinks this
 way?
The man with no country in the eastern
 peninsula.[31]

8. The Statue of Liberty in the New York Port
by Baek Han

In the sky above the New York Port,
Rising high,
A shining light on the shore of the Atlantic.

Statue of Liberty—
Let the torch in your hand
Shine all over the world
Without any shadow![32]

9. Hometown Thoughts
by Jin-Sil Son

Bright moonlight in late autumn
Colors the eastern sky.
A flying goose cries,
A blowing wind chills.
The faces of my loved ones vivid
   in my eyes;
The voices of my loved ones clear
   in my ear.

Picture my old mother standing
   at the gate
As if waiting for me.
See my little brother sitting alone
As if crying for me.
When I think of them, thoughts
   are endless;
When I miss them, I feel faint.
A lonely heart ten-thousand miles
   away;
All that fills my heart are
   thoughts of home.

When the sword of the enemy
   flashes,
My mother thinks of me.
When the arrow of the enemy
   flies,
My brother looks for me.
When will we meet again?
When will we see each other
   again?
On that day, at my mother's knee,
We'll pour out our sorrows.

   My prayer:
   An evil wind harshly blows;
   The waves of the world rise
      high.
   When wind and waves hinder
      my way,
   Oh Lord! Please save me!
   Please lead me by the hand,
   And hold my body.
   When agony comes upon me,
   Please guide me.

「본향생각」   손진실

느즌가울밝은달빗 동챵가울물드럿네
부난바람소슬한듸 눈에암암벗의얼골 귀에졍졍벗의소리
늙은부모문에셔셔 긔다리난그의모양 어린동생홀로안져 울며찻난그의형샹
싱각사록숫이업고 쯧할사록아득하다
원수칼이번듯할씨 나를싱각하난부모 원수살이날녀올씨 나를찻난우리동싱
맛날날이 그언졔며! 가득한것오직본향
차즐씨. 가어 니씨나! 만단신원다하리라
「나의긔도」 그씨부모무릅압헤
주여! 악한바람심히불어 세샹물결닐어나셔 나의압길막을씨에
나를구하소셔 나의손을실으시고 나의몸을품으소셔 몰녀드난고통속 나를인도하옵소셔!

[These lyrics were written and sung by Miss Jin-Sil Son, who came across from Shanghai, at the welcoming ceremony for Miss Maria Kim. Miss Son herself said the song was unsuitable for the occasion, but it was well-received by the general people.]³³

이샹은샹히에셔건너온 손신실녀사가뎌하야 김마리아녀사환영회셕에셔 독챵하면셔그시긔에난덕 합지안타고하며불너스나 (일반의호감샹을주엇슴)

Jin-Sil Son was from a prominent Korean family. Her father, the Reverend Jong-do Son (Jong-do Sohn, Jung-do Sohn), was an influential leader of the Korean independence movement and close associate of Syngman Rhee, later first president of the Republic of Korea (South Korea). While he was in exile in Manchuria, Reverend Son was also an early benefactor of Il-Sung Kim, founder of the Democratic People's Republic of Korea (North Korea). Jin-Sil Son herself was a dedicated member of a women's patriotic organization, and was actively engaged in the massive anti-Japanese demonstrations of 1919, known as the March 1st Movement. She arrived in San Francisco via Shanghai, and departed for studies at the University of Chicago in August 1923. In 1925, she married Chi-Chang Yun (Tchi-chang Yun, Chi-chang Yoon), the member of another prominent family. In 1948, he became the first ambassador of the Republic of Korea to Great Britain. Jin-Sil's brother Won-Il Son was the first commander of the ROK Navy. In retirement the couple settled in New York. All four of their children became US citizens.

Maria Kim (1892–1944) was a well-known Korean Christian leader and advocate for women's rights, as well as an ardent Korean nationalist. She was known to Korean students in the United States as "Korea's Joan of Arc." After studies in Japan, she returned home and engaged in a series of anti-Japanese demonstrations. In 1919, she was arrested and severely tortured, which devastated her mind and body. Released to seek medical treatment in 1920, she escaped to China the following year, and settled temporarily in Shanghai. She traveled to the United States in July 1923, and earned degrees at the University of Chicago and Columbia University Teachers College, before returning to Korea in 1932.³⁴

10. I Miss You, My Brother!
by Wun Ha

Who can stop rushing time?
It has been eight years I have not
   seen you.
A long eight years of suffering
   and trouble
Has covered my forehead in lines
   and wrinkles.
You are also a man—how could
   you not be changed?
On a dark night, in a cold wind,
   falling and tumbling on a
   sandy shore—
The memory of our crossing the
   Amnok still vivid in my eyes.
Unforgettable Shanghai,
   Shanghai of the bitter taste—
"You go first, and I'll follow after."
Every single sound of our
   farewell song still lingers in
   my ears.
It's been eight years since you
   crossed the Atlantic;
It's been four years since I
   crossed the Pacific.
You in the east, and me in the
   west—
How could I not miss you?

However . . .
Aren't we wanderers of
   destruction
And people of no freedom?
As I welcome the New Year, I
   wish you good health.
Pour all your blood and sweat
Into the success you have
   dreamed of.
For the measure of blood and
   sweat
Sends the world of painful tears
   away,
Welcomes the land of joyful
   laughter,
And is the shining jewel of
   humanity.

January 18, 1927, in
San Francisco[35]

「보고십다아우여!」

운하

스발리다라나는광음을누라서잡아미라 너를못본지발서 八년이다 八년이란기나긴세월에씨달리고부닥긴
나의이마살은주럼사리이리져가로노엿다 너도인간이여든엇지변함이업스랴 어두운밤、치운바람、
모리강변에업더지라잡바지라 압록강을거너오든그광경눈에삼삼 이즐수업고긔억이집흔상해입맛이 쓴
상히에서너는몬져가라나도가마하든— 그구실푼리별곡이아식도귀에남아잇다 너는틱셔양을거너온지 八년이되엿고
나는틱평양을거너온지 四년이되엿다 너는동에나는서에— 엇지보고십지안으랴!
우리는파멸을당한방랑쟈— 자유가업는인간이안이냐? 시히를마지면서너의건강을빈다 . . . . 그러나. . . . .
너의피와쌈을힘끗소다라 피와쌈의갑은— 괴로운눈물세상을먼곳으로보닉고 힝복시런우슴나라를마자드리는
인간의빗난보비란다

一九二七一월十八일 상항

Amnok is the Korean name for the Yalu River that separates North Korea and China.

11. Longing for the Homeland by a Student Refugee
by Young Refugee Lip

1. The autumn moon is bright,
   And from the myriad trees
   Blows the wind—
   It's surely the wind of autumn.

   [Refrain] Splendid rivers and
              mountains at home
              And my parents and
              siblings—
              Are they all well?
              I wish I knew.

2. Leaving behind the mountains and
     rivers of home
   To go to the land of a different
     tongue
   I come, and my heart
   Is beyond description.

3. Since I departed from parents and
     siblings
   I have heard nothing from them—
   In the middle of an expansive ocean
   I am sitting alone.

4. Dear moon, allow me to ask you,
   For you can see
   My parents and siblings at home—
   Are they all in peace?

5. A man who has lost his country
   Has nowhere to turn.
   Miserable and pitiable I am,
   Oh, August Heaven, watch over me.

KOREAN INSCRIPTIONS, 1910–1940

6. Wherever I go,
   I have no one to welcome me.
   Whatever misfortunes I face,
   I have no one to appeal to.

7. I am adrift here and there
   With no one to turn to,
   But the resolution in me,
   I will achieve in the end.

8. I left the peninsula
   Empty-handed,
   But when I return home
   I know what will be in my hands.

9. Whatever hardships I face,
   I will endure.
   On the day I achieve my goals
   Oh, those enemies . . .

10. I pray you, dear Lord,
    Help me:
    The wishes deep in my heart,
    Pray you I achieve them.[36]

六 엇던곳을가더린도
  반길즈도업고
  아모련환란당ᄒᆞ여도
  호소홀곳업네

七 엇던곤란당ᄒᆞ든지
  류리ᄒᆞᄂᆞᆫ
  의지업ᄂᆞᆫ내가
  일편단심쇽먹은맘을
  셩취히노ᄉ코야

八 덩쳐업시
  내가반도ᄯᅥ날찌ᄂᆞᆫ
  공슈로왓지만
  이후에본국갈씨에ᄂᆞᆫ
  가져갈것잇지

九 내가반도도ᄯᅥ날찌ᄂᆞᆫ
  참고견대여셔
  내목뎍셩취ᄒᆞᄂᆞᆫ날에
  뎌원수들을

十 원ᄒᆞ오니하ᄂᆞ님은
  나를도와쥬샤
  나의깁히원ᄒᆞᄂᆞᆫ바를
  셩취케ᄒᆞ소셔

12. There's a Long Way Ahead [to the tune of "It's a Long Way to Tipperary"][37]
by Jangbaek Mountain Recluse

Carrying four thousand years of history
   on the shoulder,
Leading the big family of twenty million
   people by the hand,
Resolutely we take the road, in search of
   a place of life—
Even treading on boiling waters and into
   the blaze, we won't dodge.

[Refrain]   There's a long way ahead,
            But keeping on without stops,
            Even the deep sea and the high
               mountains
            We will reach someday.
            From the fog-covered
               peninsula
            Stands out the Chayu Peak—
            Fellow young men,
            Let's go forward with courage.

As we the valiant men go forth
There are no Alps we cannot traverse.
Let's pluck up the adventurous spirit
And advance on through the hardships
   and torments.[38]

「우리갈길이멀고나」 (곡됴는 티퍼딍이와갓흠) 댱빅산인

사천여년긴력사를질머지고서
이천만인만흔가족손을잇글어
최후결심살곳차져나션길이니
도탕부화할지라도피치안켓네

(후렴) 우리갈길고머나
쉬임업시가면
깁흔바다높흔산도
장차달하리로다

반도운무중에
차유봉놉도다
청년들아일성용감으로
압흐로나아가자

우리들은대댱부라압헤나갈쎄
못넘어갈「알프」산이어듸잇스랴

모험뭥진한난우리경신발휘하여셔
괴로우나어려우나나아갑셰다

Though Jangbaek Mountain Recluse is one of the pen names used by Korean writer, poet, and independence activist Kwang-su Yi (1892–1950), perhaps best known for writing the novel *Mujong* [The Heartless], this poem is not very likely to have been written by him. In any case, the name leads our attention to the China-Korea border. Jangbaek Mountain, which is generally known as Baekdu Mountain, is the highest mountain in Korea, located on the border between China and Korea in Yanggang Province. Chayu Peak is another mountain near the border in the northeast. Located in North Hamgyeong Province, it is the highest of the mountains there that stand on the route leading to the Tumen River. The Tumen River was then and is now the preferred border crossing, as its waters are shallower and narrower than those of the Yalu River. Thus this song is likely associated with feelings of Koreans who were crossing the northern border to China to seek refuge.

13. Disembarking at San Francisco Bay
by S.

1. Oh, San Francisco Bay and Golden Gate Park,
   How have you been?
   On the nineteenth of September last year,
   When I bade farewell to you,
   It was a separation
   With no promise of reunion.
   Seeing your faces again today
   Is an immeasurable joy.

2. With the sound of a steam whistle
   I departed San Francisco Bay in misty cloud;
   In tattered clothes and a crumpled hat
   I returned to my old homeland as a single-celled spore.
   The mountains and streams remained the same,
   But the people's hearts were utterly different.
   The tiny thatched hut was overgrown with weeds,
   And there was no one living in it.

3. After the sun set over the west mountain
   I climbed the Floating Jade Tower.
   It was indeed where I'd sauntered
   But the love I had was nowhere to be found.
   The willow trees on the Brocade Islet
   Were barren on every branch,
   Without even a trace of
   Orioles which once flew in and out.

「상항만에나리면서」 에쏘싱

一 상항만금문공원아 그간네잘잇엇더냐 작년구월십구일에 너와나와쟉별할씨 긔약업시 니별을맛기엿더니 오날네얼골다시보니 깃부기측량업다

二 상항만긔뎍일셩에 운무중에작별하고 페의파립단표자로 고국강산돌아가니

산천은의구한데 세상인심다변하고 삼간초옥풀밧이오 쥬인은간곳업다

三 일락셔산지난히애 부벽류에올나보니 노든자최분명컨만 노든임은간곳업고

능라도에쇠한버들 가지가지심겨잇고 ᄉ괴꼬리의드나들던 그쟈최도전혀업다

4. Heaven and earth were bleak,
   The people were nowhere to be seen,
   And half-naked creatures with shaven heads
   Scuttled around at whim.
   My eyes could not bear to see that,
   And my heart was scarred with pain.
   So I turned around
   And returned to North America.

5. Oh, San Francisco Bay and Golden Gate Park,
   From past to present you remain the same.
   In all seasons of spring and summer, autumn and winter,
   You've welcomed myriad travelers
   And seen off thousands of guests—
   You're rich in experience of human feelings.
   The world may change,
   But you, I know, will not.

6. You greet me with joy, and so I say
   You alone do not change
   You alone are my love.
   I wonder how I would live without you;
   I wonder what you would do without me.
   I will forever and ever
   Sing in praise of you—
   Oh, Golden Gate Port, my love![39]

四 텬디는 적막한데 녯쥬인볼수업고
  목불인견볼수업고 심쟝샹히못견디셔
  옷발벗은종다리가 제멋디로노라나니
  니갈길을다시돌녀 북미쥬에다시왓네

五 상항만금문공원아 너난고왕금리로
  춘하츄동물론하고 만긱을환영하고
  너하나영원불변

六 네가나를반겨하니 너밧곈변함업고
  너밧겐사량업다
  너업든덜나엇지살며
  아—나의사량금문항

나업든덜네엇지하랴
니너를영원토록
기리찬숑하리로다

Floating Jade Tower (Bubyeongnu) is in the North Korean capital of Pyongyang. Originally built in 393 (and reconstructed multiple times), it was so named for the beauty of the blue-green waters of the nearby Daedong River. Brocade Islet (Neungnado) is between the banks of the Daedong River, also in Pyongyang.

14. Four Poems on Parting: Leaving Stockton
by Jeong-Dae Lee

1. On the day I came,
   Summer was at its height.
   This strange western world—
   Secretly I admired it.

2. Solitary was I when I stepped on this shore.
   Yet poverty, hardship, pent up thoughts
   Released me as I spoke with you.
   Truly we must have ties of destiny.

3. After all, I grew fond
   Of this, my second hometown.
   Sadly now, I bid farewell—
   The more I think of it, the sadder I become.

4. Today is a day for parting,
   Another year of hard battles begins.
   Yet as we vow to rush towards them
   All our sorrows disappear.

    This poem is dedicated to my dear friend
    Yang-Rae Bak, and his wife and family.
                       January 21, 1929[10]

「별리四곡」

一 이 몸이 오던 날은 무러 녹던 여름 하는 낫설다는 서반구에 남몰니도 동경하엿어라。

二 쓸쓸히도 이 짱 밟어 간난신산 풀어니여 묵은 회포 원정터니 그야말로 인연이엿던가。

三 그만히도 정들다는 제이고향 간난신산 안타갑게 하직하는 이 니 몸엔 싱각사록 더욱서러워라。

四 이쩌나가는 오늘날은 히를밧권 힘한전선 돌진키로 밍약하니 섭섭한 맘 다 살아지도다。

이시는니가 가쟝친밀한 박양리씨와 동부인쪼한 그의 가족의게 드림。

一九二九년 一월 二十一일

This poem is likely also by Han-Pyung Po, though the pseudonym differs very slightly from that for #3 above, Jeong-Du Lee. Note that in the first stanza the poet states he arrived in high summer, just as Po did in July 1927. And departure from Stockton in early 1929 is a reasonable match for the start of Po's baccalaureate program at the College of Emporia, where he graduated in 1932.

Yang-Rae Bak is probably Yang N. Park, a forty-nine-year-old farmer who lived with his wife and four children in Stockton (1930 Census).

15. Dream
by Yeo-Sim Ju

I see my hometown in a
  dream. I see my beloved.
What bitter fate, such jarring
  thoughts.
Racked with sobs, I share my
  grief.
But when morning comes, and
  I wake up,
The empty feeling deep in my
  heart grows.
In dreams I fly free.
I say what I want to say.
I eat what I want to eat.
Longed for land, longed for
  face.
Yet the dream is brief,
And sleep but a moment.
Even before departing the
  dream, I go out with a broom
And cry with the fog of dawn
  in my sorrow.

November 11, 1927[41]

「쑴」 쥬여심

쑴에는 고향을 봄니다。 님을 봄니다。 서른사정긔믹힌싱각,
나는 몸부림하며 움니다。 하소연함니다。
그러나 아츰이 되여 잠씰 때에는
허수— 한 가긔는 비, 나 더함니다。 쑴에는 날아 봄니다,훨훨、
하고 싶흔 말도 하고 먹고 싶흔 것도 먹기도 함니다。
그립은 강산 그립은 얼골 그러나 쑴은 잠간 임니다。
잠은 잠간 임니다。 쑴이 치씨기도 젼에 비들고 나서면、
섭은 싱각은 시벽안기 와 함씌 움니다。

一九二七、十一、十一

Yeo-Sim Ju was one of a number of pen names used by prominent writer, scholar, and editor Yeo-Sop Ju (Yo-Sop Chu, Yoseop Joo) (1902–1972). After receiving part of his early education in Japan, he returned home in 1919 to participate in the independence movement, and was consequently jailed for ten months by the Japanese authorities. He moved to Shanghai to complete his high school and undergraduate studies, and then spent 1927–1929 in California, earning a master's in Education at Stanford University. Ju later worked as chief editor of *The Korea Times*, and served as chairman of the Korean chapter of International PEN.

16. Hometown Thoughts
by Yeo-Sam Ju

The room in which I live is filthy,
Yet my life is cleaning others' houses.
Arms numb, legs painful, stomach starved.
Exhausted body, exhausted mind.
Light fades on the road at dusk,
As I travel home, gasping for breath.
Ah! In the eastern sky, dimly,
Twinkle, twinkle, shining star.
Hometown is a beautiful country;
Homeland is my rivers and mountains.
Leaning against a twig gate,
Waiting with a sigh—
It seems as if I see my mother's face.

How sad is the sound of the wind;
Even the wild geese fly crying.
Could I see my hometown in a dream?
Yet tossing and turning, I cannot sleep.
Why is the moon so bright?
Or to become the moon myself?
Quietly shining down
Below the window, where my beloved sleeps.

How plaintive the sound of crickets;
The sound of falling leaves brings tears.
Hoping to lighten my heavy heart,
Brush in hand, I sit down under the cold lamp.
Though my thoughts are huge as mountains, I cannot write them out.

「고향싱각」 주여삼짓음

나있을방은이리도더럽은지고、그리도남있을집이나쓸어주는신셰를 팔은져리고다리는앞허
빗좃차곫아드니 피곤한몸、피곤한마음 어둡어가는황혼길을 허덕이어돌아올씨
아！져동쪽하늘희미하게도 반ㅅ작〳빗나는별。고향은아름답은나라、본집은그립은강산。
싸리문지대서서 한숨지며기다리는 어머님얼골마주뵈오듯
바람소리는구슬피도 기럭이쏫차울고가네 쉼에나마그립은고향볼가？
달은웨져리도밝은지고、에라이니몸져달이되여 님줌으시는창문밑에 조요히빛의여나볼거나。
귀쏘람이소리쳐랑히라。락엽소리―눈물지네。하답답한가슴풀어볼가하여 붓들고찬등밑에주져안즈니
싱각은틱산같아도써지진안네。

(Why is the moon so cold?)
Even though the letter is of only a
   few words,
It is written with my true heart—
My beloved should understand.
           September 29, 1927[42]

편지야 몇 자 안 되지만
정성들이 쓴 것인줄
님이야 알아주시련만!
一九二七、九、二九
（달빛은에져리도 싸늘한고!）

Yeo-Sam differs from Yeo-Sim only by the addition of one short Hangul stroke. Considering the style and format of this poem, it is almost certain it is also by Yeo-Sop Ju.

17. Send Off
by D. W.

1. As the guest is about to leave,
   Even the falling rain stops.
   Warm sunlight
   Shines down—though
   In my heartbreak,
   A rain of tears falls.

2. The guest is going
   To the sweet homeland.
   My parents have gotten older.
   Whether waking or sleeping,
   I want to see them.
   Yet I cannot leave,
   And my heart is sorrowful beyond measure.

3. The guest is leaving
   On a huge ship,
   Readying for the journey—
   That ship,
   Amid the sound of bells
   And shouts of goodbye,
   And the ebb, and the flow,
   Leaps forward and through the waves,
   While multicolored streamers
   Lightly float—
   It is farewell indeed.

4. The face of the guest
   Gradually edges away,
   A white handkerchief waves
   In and out of sight,
   Oh capricious human world!
   I wish you a smooth journey
   As you traverse
   The far, far hills of water.

   At the port of San Francisco,
   September 12, 1928[43]

「견별」

D. W.

一 손님이 가시란잇가 오던비도안이오고 싸덧한힛빗이 니리쏘이것만
섭섭한나의 마음 눈물의비 가나림니다

二 손님이 가시는곳은 졍깁흔고향의나라 늙어진나의부모님
자나쎄나보고지고 갈수업는나의마음 구슬프기ㅅ쟉이업소

三 손님은 감니다 크나큰윤션을타고요 갈길에분주한져윤션
이리굼실져리굼실 물ㅅ결싸라압흐로 ㅅ 힘업시쎠러지는 오식죵이의줄! ㅅ쾡멩이소리에 쌋바이고함을치면서
참견별인가함니다

四 손님의올골은 졈졈머러지고 휘둘니는하얀수건 보일덧말덧!
인간의셰샹! 부대평안히가소셔 멀고먼물고기를 넘고넘어셔! 오—변화만흔

九、十二日 (상항부두에서)

18. Before Sleep
by Wun Ha

I lie down on the bed exhausted
After a hard day's work.
How lonely it is
In this cold, cold blanket.
Sleep won't come to my tired body,
My eyes just blink.
The sounds of sky, earth, and man
All sleep in the silent night.
All I can hear
Is the melancholy train whistle.[44]

19. The Laugh [excerpt]

1. Our black hair,
   Flat noses, yellow faces,
   When we are ridiculed—
   Laugh! Never stop laughing.

2. When you lay down
   Your aching heart and tired body
   On that cold and ruthless bed—
   Laugh! Never stop laughing.[45]

20. Leaving San Francisco
by Wun Ha

1. How ruthless you are, San Francisco!
   My heart ached
   As if a sweet lover had said goodbye to me.
   Like a mother seeing the grave of her only son,
   How lonely it was
   When you pushed me away.

2. How ruthless you are, San Francisco!
   My sorrow is that I do not have a country
   And float like duckweed without a place to go.
   I was like a starving child crying for food
   When you pushed me away,
   Or a beggar who shivers in brutal winter
   And has no road to follow.
   I was suffocated
   As if black clouds had covered the sun
   When you pushed me away.

   In the Siskiyou Mountains,
   March 19, 1925[46]

「桑港을쩌날씨」 운하

一 상항아 무정하더라 다 정한이인의 쟉별을당한것갓치 마음이쓰리고앞파
독자의무덤을보는어머니와갓치 엇지그리고격할가!
네가나를쩌미러니를씨

二 상항아 무정하더라 방향업시흘너가는부평초와갓치
네가나를쩌미러니를씨 나라업난설분마음
어린아히비곱하밥찻는것과갓치 져틔양의빗을흑운이가리운것갓치
갈길이망연하도다 나외가삼은답답히!
네가나를쩌미러니를씨 언동설한에벌벌쩌난걸인과갓치

三月十九日스큐야마운텐에셔

21. Crossing the Sierra Mountains
by a Man of Yaksan Mountain

On this winding road
Where Indians used to come and go,
Trees grew tall
And trunks grew broad.
The people's traces are gone in the vastness;
Only the trees tell their history.

Going through tunnels,
The train is like a thunderbolt.
It rounds curve after curve,
And in the blink of an eye rises up the mountain.
When everywhere is darkness,
It runs through walls of earth.

Once red men were masters
Of these rivers and hills—
Yet where did they go?
I ask the Sierra Mountains.
In the sound of a flowing stream
I hear weeping for the past.

Ah! The people are gone now,
Yet how could they rise
And then fall so far?
When the transcontinental train
Blew its whistle on the pass,
Red men had no place to go.[47]

Yaksan Mountain is located in North Pyeongan Province in North Korea.

22. Eighteen Years in the United States
by One Who Laments the Times

It's been eighteen years since I
   came to America—
Why have I spent so long
Floating like duckweed on the
   water?
Looking back
At my windblown footprints—
What traces are left?

From the ship I first saw San
   Francisco in ruins,
Eighteen years later I see
Only traces of fire and collapse—
Where is the devastation?
When I see the glamorous
   buildings everywhere,
I know how they have spent
   eighteen years,
Yet what have we done during
   that time?

I left an independent country,
But now I have no country.
I'm a man with no place to go.
Gazing at the setting sun,
Thinking of my home country,
A sad song sung endlessly,
Makes me grieved and resentful.

My precious youth was spent in
   study,
But somehow I frittered it away.
Look at the ruthless frost on my
   temples—
Oh Creator! Why so heartless?
As I look east and west, present
   and past,
Where is the man who can take
   back Baekdu Mountain?

「미국에十八年」   悼世生

미국온지열여듭히 물우헤쓴평초갓흔이니 무엇히셔이긴세월보니
머리들어뒤도라보미 바람몰이에발자최갓히 지난간흔적어디〈

볏머리셔보든진진후상항시니 열여듭히후오날에보미
화려한건륙만여긔져긔볼씨 불타고집문허진자리군디〈
독립국빅셩을써러낫든이니 우리의그동안은무엇하고보니
셕양져문날써러져가는히 지금에는나라업난사람되미 갈어도갈곳이업난一남이
조흔청춘시절치〈샹아리 바라보며고국싱ㅇ각할씨 히염업시부르는슬픈노리 엇졀수업시비분강기!
조물주여웨그리무졍히! 이럭저럭쓰업시다보니 귓미혜사졍업는서리ㅅ발보미
동셔고금을다도라보미 이비ㄱ두산ㅅ비일쟈그어디?

Ah! Ah! Heartless eighteen years!
I followed the road you made,
Yet my traces grow fainter and fainter.
Nor will we ever meet again
The patriots of the past who followed you.
When we think of them,
Our hearts indeed are resentful.

In this world I will not meet the mountain again;
The past was nothing but failure.
The country was lost, and houses collapsed,
Leaving only hope for the future,
A distant future like a dream.
In that future, hard to reach,
We'll accomplish the dream—
Great ventures will bear fruits of success,
Wealth and honor will shine in the light of history.
So let's forget the pain and step forward![48]

For Baekdu Mountain, see the note to #12.

KOREAN INSCRIPTIONS, 1910–1940   145

23. Let's Go Home
by Pyeongnim Ui-Seok Cha

1. Even though America is wonderful,
   It's not a place to live long.
      Asian peoples—
      Let's go back to Asia!

2. Even though this is not a barbarian
      land,
   When spring comes, it doesn't feel like
      spring.
      Though I've lived here half my life,
      I haven't seen a single flower.

3. The yellow-haired alone
   Are the masters here.
      Even if I live here forever,
      I'll always feel the sorrow of a
         foreign land.

4. Though making a living is easy,
   Life is more than eating.
      I won't allow discrimination and
         contempt
      To make me live like an exile.

5. Though everywhere in Asia is poor,
   There too are sources of wealth.
      Let's take up hoes
      And dig the ground with our own
         hands.

6. The Philippines is hot, but
   For poor people the living is easy,
      And on the vast fertile plain of
         China,
      One can live for long.

「불여귀」 평림차의셔

一 미국싸가죠타지만
   오리살곳못되나니
   동양사람동양으로
   도라가서살아보세

二 오랑키쌍이아니언만
   봄이와도봄철인지
   반싱남아살앗셔도
   화초구경못하엿네

三 노랑머리져히들만
   주인자셰혼자하니
   종신도록살더라도
   긱회면치못하겠네

四 벌어먹기쉽다지만
   먹고만은못사나니
   구별심한천대밧고
   장류지게말게

五 동양텬디가난치만
   부원부고다잇나니
   곡광이를갈아쥐고
   니손으로가서키세

六 필립핀이덥다지만
   빈민살기용이하리
   옥야쳔리즁원쌍도
   장구하게살만하네

7. Though the oppression of foes is terrible,
   The hills and rivers of my country are mine.
      Koreans to Korea!
      Let's go home and live.

8. Even though America is wonderful,
   It's not a place to live long.
      Let's quickly pack our bags,
      And cross the Pacific.⁴⁹

七 원수압박 심하지만 고국강산 니 땅이지

대한사람 대한으로 환향하여 살아보세

八 미국사가 죠타지만 오리살곳 못되나니

어서밧비 짐싸들고 틱평양을 건너가세

The Korean nationalist sentiments of the author are clear, but though he calls for Asians to return to Asia, he himself never did. In 1905, ten-year-old Ui-Seok Cha (1895–1986) left his parents behind and immigrated to America, first to Hawaii and soon after to San Francisco. With only an older cousin to turn to for assistance, he lived a hardscrabble existence for the next eight years. One of the jobs he took to keep body and soul together was as typesetter for the *Sinhan Minbo*. It was his great good fortune to meet patrons who helped guide his development. One of them, Presbyterian missionary George Shannon McCune, arranged for him to attend the high school attached to Park College, near Kansas City, Missouri. He took the English given name Emsen, and enrolled as Easurk Emsen Charr. He excelled in his studies, and upon graduation prepared to begin undergraduate studies at Park College. Yet the United States had just entered the hostilities of the First World War, and wishing to demonstrate his loyalty to his new country, he volunteered, serving eight months in a medical unit near Washington. He then returned to Park College and completed his degree. After trying medical school for one semester at the University of Kansas, and pharmacy school in Chicago, he married a nursing student, Evelyn Nien-wha Kim, and started a family. The Depression years were difficult for him, and he lost his job at the mapmaker Rand McNally in Chicago. It was about this time that he wrote this poem. He took his family back to San Francisco, where for much of the 1930s he worked in his nephew's Chinatown barbershop. Charr has a permanent place in the history of US naturalization law. In 1921, he sought military naturalization from a Circuit Court in Missouri, based on his service in the First World War. The decision went against him, and came not from the Circuit Court but direct from the Federal District Court in Kansas City. The denial of Charr's petition was used as a precedent by the US

Supreme Court for denying all naturalization to Asians, in decisions like Ozawa vs. the United States (1922) and United States vs. Thind (1923). Charr continued to press his case in subsequent years, and his citizenship was finally granted in 1936, following the 1935 act of Congress that permitted naturalization to all First World War veterans who had served honorably, regardless of race or ethnicity. Citizenship allowed Charr to undertake government employment, and he spent the remainder of his career in the civil service. In 1961, he self-published his autobiography, which has since been reprinted as *The Golden Mountain: The Autobiography of a Korean Immigrant, 1905–1960*.[50]

Even though Charr arrived in San Francisco well before the opening of the Angel Island Immigration Station, he still had a personal connection to the place. Evelyn had long outstayed her student visa, and in 1932 the Immigration Service detained her on the island pending deportation. Charr mounted a vigorous campaign to have the order stayed, and received support from the American Legion, administrators and alumni of Park College, and the Presbyterian Church. The effort was ultimately successful, and she was released.

3

Chinese Inscriptions, 1910–1940

Our families are poor, so we cross the foreign seas

The experience of arriving Chinese travelers during the years when the Angel Island Immigration Station was in operation was dictated by the terms of the Chinese Exclusion Act, which by 1910 had already been in force for almost three decades. In the mid-nineteenth century, immigration from China had been relatively open, and even encouraged—at least on a national level. The Burlingame-Seward Treaty of 1868 (which amended an earlier US-China treaty) affirmed friendly relations between the two countries, gave China most favored nation trading status, and eased immigration rules. The vast majority of early Chinese immigrants came from a very small region in China: five counties in the Pearl River Delta southwest of Guangzhou. Up until the Second World War, immigrants mostly came from these same places: the "Four Counties" (Cantonese "Sei Yahp"; Mandarin "Siyi"), Taishan (formerly Xinning), Kaiping, Enping, and Xinhui; and nearby Xiangshan (now Zhongshan) County.

Yet there was pushback from the West. The Gold Rush brought a sudden influx of Chinese laborers to California: while 450 Chinese arrived in 1850, and 2,716 are recorded for 1851, 1852 brought 20,026. By 1860, Chinese comprised from 12 to 23 percent of the population of various mining counties. The immigrants faced racism, unequal treatment in law, and even mob violence in the gold fields. In 1852, California instituted a monthly "foreign miners' tax" aimed at the Chinese to discourage their participation, and in ensuing years the amount was increased multiple times.[1]

As the Gold Rush wound down, Chinese laborers found employment building the railroads, most importantly the Central Pacific Railroad, which was the western half of the Transcontinental Railroad (constructed 1863–1869), but also other lines before and after that period.[2] Charles Crocker, an original director of the Central Pacific Railroad and its construction supervisor, strongly advocated hiring Chinese workers, not because of any broad-minded or progressive inclinations, but because he faced a labor shortage and Chinese could be paid less than white workers. When the Chinese labor pool in California proved insufficient, the railroad contracted to recruit laborers directly from China. Estimates are that at any one time, 10,000 to 15,000 Chinese worked on the project. It was hazardous work, and Chinese workers were often assigned the most hazardous tasks. In June 1867, after a horrific tunnel explosion north of Cisco in the Sierra Nevada killed six men, including five Chinese, thousands of Chinese workers went out on strike for better pay and working conditions. Crocker responded by cutting off food and supplies to their camps, and offered no concessions. Eight days later, the workers ended the strike. Even so, the solidarity of the Chinese workers did have an effect: in ensuing months the company quietly increased their pay.[3]

After the rail line was completed, some Chinese workers returned to China, and some turned to other construction activities and farming. Many eventually settled in the cities and towns and opened small businesses—laundries were the most common—worked in small manufacturing of products like cigars and shoes, or engaged in miscellaneous occupations.[4] Yet anti-Chinese sentiment only increased among white laborers, and the California state government responded. Most notable among a series of anti-Chinese laws in California was the "Anti-Coolie Act of 1862," designed to "Protect Free White Labor against Competition with Chinese Coolie Labor, and to Discourage the Immigration of the Chinese into the State of California." The Act imposed a general head tax on Chinese laborers and merchants. The economic downturn of the 1870s sparked widespread dissatisfaction, and politicians like Senator James Blaine and labor leaders like Denis Kearney of the Workingmen's Party of California blamed the Chinese for depressing wages and creating unemployment, and fanned the flames against them. Given this climate, it is not surprising that violence followed. A large mob attacked and murdered between seventeen and twenty Chinese men in Los Angeles in 1871, and ransacked Chinese-occupied buildings and robbed residents. In 1877, in San Francisco, mobs attacked Chinatown over a two-day period, killing four and burning many Chinese businesses.

At the federal level, there was support for restricting Chinese immigration, but also for maintaining diplomatic channels and international trading opportunities. The US government responded with what were considered half measures by the radicals in the West. In 1875, Congress passed the "Page Act," which "forbade the entry of Chinese, Japanese, and other Asian laborers brought to the United States involuntarily and Asian women brought for the purpose of prostitution."[5] This was the first time immigration had been restricted as a matter of national policy.[6] The most lasting impact was on the immigration of women. The Act targeted prostitution, but also included language that required *all* Asian women "to obtain certificates of immigration demonstrating they were not emigrating for lewd or immoral purposes."[7] This put consuls abroad and immigration authorities at home in the position of policing sexuality, and "resulted in the virtually complete exclusion of Chinese women from the United States."[8] A revision of the Burlingame-Seward Treaty with the Chinese government was also negotiated; the resulting Angell Treaty was signed by the two powers in 1880, and ratified in the US the following year. By its terms travel by all Chinese laborers to the United States was temporarily suspended. Congress went further in 1882, and passed the landmark Chinese Exclusion Act, the first anti-immigration law ever directed at a single ethnic group. The Act stated that "in the opinion of the Government of the United States the coming of Chinese laborers to this country endangers the good order of certain localities within the territory thereof." It excluded Chinese skilled and unskilled laborers and Chinese employed in mining from entering the country. Only a few classes of people were exempt: government officials, merchants, teachers, students, visitors, and family members of US citizens. There were even penalties for masters of ships who brought Chinese laborers to this country for immigration purposes. The Act was initially for a period of ten years; it was renewed for another ten years in 1892 (the Geary Act), and made permanent in 1902. During those two decades, amendments and additional laws were passed which made the terms even more restrictive for Chinese travelers and immigrants, and more onerous for Chinese residents. The Chinese Exclusion Act and related laws were not rescinded until the Magnuson Act of 1943, when China was an ally of the US in the Second World War. Even then Chinese immigrants were limited to the extraordinarily low annual quota of 105. It was not until the Immigration Act of 1965 that significant Chinese immigration to the United States was again permitted.[9]

However, as historian Beth Lew-Williams points out, the law as instituted in 1882 was a watered-down version of a bill vetoed by President Chester Arthur, and was in practice not very effective as there were few enforcement mechanisms. She distinguishes a Chinese "Restriction Period" from 1882 to 1888 from a harsher "Exclusion Period" from 1888 to 1943. Indeed, the 1882 legislation did not noticeably slow Chinese immigration, only transformed it into illicit streams crossing the borders of Canada and Mexico, and entering fraudulently through US ports. A new wave of anti-Chinese violence ensued, which peaked in the middle of the decade. From 1885 to 1886, vigilantes in 168 separate communities in Western states drove Chinese residents out. Some of these locations were large cities, like Seattle, Tacoma, and Portland. Eighty-five Chinese were killed, sixty-two of them in large massacres in Rock Springs, Wyoming Territory, and Hells Canyon, Oregon.[10]

The Scott Act of 1888 tightened the 1882 law. It called for total exclusion, including rejection of the "return certificates" routinely given to Chinese residents in the US who had returned temporarily to China. It was upheld by the Supreme Court, and created a precedent giving the federal government unilateral authority to set immigration policy, even when it violated prior diplomatic agreements. The Geary Act of 1892 added a requirement that all Chinese must register and carry residence permits at all times to prove they were lawful residents. Failure to comply could result in imprisonment and deportation. Thus exclusion, which previously had governed entry at the border, was expanded to the nation's interior.[11]

Before the Civil War, the federal government had not often inserted itself into immigration guidelines and enforcement, leaving such matters to the states. Nor had citizenship been clearly defined. The Fourteenth Amendment of 1868 changed all that; it "defined a singular form of national citizenship, granted citizens certain rights and immunities, and pledged federal protection of these civil rights."[12] Judicial decisions in the following years found that "states had little right to police the movement of citizens and aliens,"[13] in accordance with the due process and equal protection clauses of the amendment. Citizenship was guaranteed to "all persons born or naturalized in the United States" language which constituted the first affirmation of birthright citizenship, and the extension of citizenship to freed slaves. As for naturalization, the picture was muddier. The Naturalization Act of 1790 limited the right to "any alien, being a free white person" who had been in the US for two years. Mexican Americans gained the right pursuant to the 1848 Treaty of Guadalupe Hidalgo (making them legally "white"). Native Americans gained citizenship piecemeal, until the Indian Citizenship Act of 1924 made it universal. In 1870, Congress renegotiated the terms of the Naturalization Act, and extended the right to "aliens of African nativity and to persons of African descent." Yet the 1870 legislation specifically denied Chinese the right to naturalize because of their "undesirable qualities."[14] They did not gain the right to naturalization until the 1943 Magnuson Act.

Chinese were the first ethnic group to be targeted by the federal government for immigration restriction, and the criminalization of their experience "produced the category of the illegal alien."[15]

> Once the federal government began to fashion the national citizenry, it was only a matter of time until it defined who would stand outside those ranks. The existence of the citizen demanded the concept of alien—and they developed in tandem.[16]

Once the exclusion of Chinese became national policy, the bureaucracy to enforce it gradually developed; the Chinese model was then extended to other groups. Today's immigration system is a massive undertaking and use of American power: hundreds of thousands of people serve as gatekeepers in embassies and consulates abroad, enforce border controls at home, administer detention camps, perform judicial and extra-judicial reviews of immigration cases, execute deportations, and police workplaces in search of "illegal aliens." Arguments over immigration policy are both a symptom of and a cause for political paralysis in the United States. Yet it should be remembered that the modern concept of the "illegal alien" is a construct based in historical decision-making.

Thus throughout the period from 1910 to 1940, Chinese arrivals at San Francisco needed to qualify as members of the exempt classes to gain admission. Government officials, teachers, students, and visitors were a tiny minority of the total. More claimed merchant status, for example by providing documentation and witness testimony of partnerships—fictional or otherwise—in businesses in the United States.[17] Yet most Chinese would-be-immigrants attempted to prove they were family dependents of US citizens.[18] As naturalization was barred to Asians until the Magnuson Act, for anyone of Chinese extraction to be a citizen required native birth in the United States.

The Exclusion Act stacked the deck against would-be Chinese immigrants. Yet they had substantial resources as well, based in the solid transnational networks tying Chinese communities in the United States with the home counties in Guangdong. Money, information, and personal relationships freely crossed the Pacific, and powerful Chinese benevolent associations maintained footholds in both countries.[19]

The 1906 Earthquake was a tragedy for the city of San Francisco, but it also created an opportunity for the Chinese community. The catastrophic fire which followed the quake destroyed most government records, including those concerning birth and residency. To build a new records base, the authorities perforce had to rely on oral testimony. After the disaster, large numbers of Chinese—including many immigrants from China—claimed citizenship based on birth in the US. All that the Chinese applicant required was the testimony of two citizens that he or she was in fact born in the US. (While legally the testimony of US-born Chinese citizens was acceptable, in practice only that of white citizens was viewed as relevant.) The result was a sudden increase in the number of new citizens, often claiming they had children born in China.[20]

Most of the Chinese detained at Angel Island applied for entry as children of US citizen fathers, who had the constitutional right to call for their dependents still abroad. Those without true fathers in the United States often became "paper sons" or "paper daughters." They were provided—or purchased—false papers identifying them as children of Chinese men who were US citizens. Because official records were so scarce, the immigration authorities had to rely on an interrogation system to match the stories of the applicants with those of the supposed fathers and supporting witnesses. To pass the hearings to the authorities' satisfaction, applicants had to flawlessly relate minute details about family genealogy and village life. As described by the authors of *Island*, regardless of the validity of the Chinese arrival's claim for entry, he or she prepared by memorizing detailed coaching books. The Exclusion Act and related laws placed immigration officials and would-be Chinese immigrants in diametrical opposition. The relationship was complex: although the officials had the power of decision, they also had procedural limitations and a great lack of information. Their judgments could be very subjective, but were usually made within the parameters of professional guidelines. There was a "system" for adjudicating cases, and Chinese immigrants learned to work it. The testimony and support of community networks (both in the US and China), benevolent associations, and professional immigration handlers prepared applicants for the ordeal.[21] By the time the Angel Island Immigration Station opened in 1910, exclusion had been a fact for over a quarter century, and investigations took place in an atmosphere of mutual suspicion. It is undeniable that a great majority of the Chinese arrivals applied for exempt status under fraudulent pretenses, but the actual proportion is unknown.[22] From the immigrants' perspective, fleeing the grinding poverty and chaos of South China of the time was an extraordinarily strong motivator, and certainly the exclusion laws were unjust and unreasonable. In any case, although many were turned back, many others were successful in their requests for entry. Erika Lee notes, "Some were unfairly excluded from the United States, while others gained admission through evading and circumventing the law."[23]

Although large numbers of people of other ethnicities were held at Angel Island, at any given time Chinese detainees were by far the majority, as the Chinese Exclusion Act caused a high proportion of Chinese arrivals to be transported to Angel Island, and the interview process could take weeks or months. Statistics concerning the length of stay of Chinese detainees, the number deported, and the deportation rate have varied widely over the last three decades. The second edition of *Island* has brought more clarity. The authors and many volunteers spent a thousand hours poring over handwritten case information for 95,687 persons on "Lists of Chinese Applying for Admission to the United States through the Port of San Francisco, California, 1903–1947." They found that 49 percent of Chinese were admitted upon the day of their arrival, and did not spend time on Angel Island. Of those who were detained, the median length of stay at Angel Island varied from a low of 7 days in 1918 to a high of 42 days in 1940, with a median stay of 16 days for the entire 1910–1940 period. There were outliers: close to two hundred people were detained for more than one year, and three people were held more than two years. Inspectors denied admission to 9 percent of applicants, but many cases were successfully appealed, bringing the actual deportation rate to 5 percent.[24]

The Chinese Exclusion Act and related laws were a constant during the period of the station's operation, and the nature of the applications from

Chinese immigrants, and the system used to process them, also remained relatively stable throughout the thirty years. The authorities needed no other instruments to exclude Chinese. For Japanese and other Asians, and even for Europeans, changing US laws and policies affected immigration trends and practices, and a variety of instruments was brought to bear to limit entry.

The items in this chapter include poems and parallel couplets, miscellaneous prose, and even illustrations with text. The themes of the poems and couplets are similar to those in the *Island* collection—homesickness and sadness, indignation about detention, trepidation about possible deportation, expressions of patriotism to China and despair at China's weakness, and the desire for revenge. One new type can best be described as "advice for compatriots"; examples provide cautionary information about barracks life and immigration regulations. Several miscellaneous prose inscriptions are political in nature, and illustrations with text are appeals for good fortune. The last item below—a 1982 memoir of an immigrant's 1912 detention at Angel Island—is not from the station walls, yet is consistent with the content of the rest.

WALL INSCRIPTIONS

1.

Clouds and hills all around,
   a single fresh color;
Time slips away and cannot be recaptured.
Although the feeling of spring is everywhere,
How can we fulfill our heartfelt wish?

    Inscribed by a Traveler from the City of Iron
                           in Xiangshan

香山鐵城行〔旅〕人題
吾人何遂心中德
隨處皆然顯春意
光陰去卻復難得
四面雲山清一色

25

The City of Iron was another name for Shiqi, the administrative center for Xiangshan County in Guangdong Province. Xiangshan was renamed Zhongshan in 1925, in honor of former President of the Republic of China Dr. Sun Yat-sen, who was a native of the area. Dr. Sun was posthumously known as Sun Zhongshan. Zhongshan County was elevated to a prefecture-level city in 1983.

FIGURE 3.1 *"Clouds and hills all around."* Photo: ARG and Daniel Quan.

2.

I begged my friends and neighbors,
And thought of a thousand plans,
In order to borrow several hundred dollars,
Because I wanted to do business in Mexico.

It seems like I'm being punished for some transgression.
Three times I've asked the governor—
Why am I imprisoned on this island?

      Written by a passenger from the Steamship China

勞盡鄉鄰憶想千計週貸數百餘圓
只願經營墨國
儼如為取報應一般日求三次令尹
為何留困埃崙
搭差「拿」「火」船客作
26

Transients on their way to Mexico and other parts of Latin America were also subject to detainment at Angel Island.

3.

The Manchu have lost;
The Han have risen.

滿既亡矣
漢已興矣
27

The Chinese Revolution of 1911 was sparked by a military uprising at Wuchang in Hubei Province on October 10, and culminated with the abdication of the emperor of the Qing dynasty on February 12, 1912. A rallying cry of the revolutionaries had been to overthrow the Manchu and restore Han rule. The Qing rulers were Manchu, a Tungusic people from northeast Asia who led a confederation of other peoples of the steppes which conquered China in 1644. The Han people constitute the overwhelming majority of Chinese inhabitants, and are so-called to commemorate the great Han dynasty (206 BCE–220 CE). After the establishment of the new Republic of China, its leaders quickly adopted a policy of inclusion, in recognition of the vast numbers of non-Han peoples living within the borders they claimed. The two lines here are an exact quote from the conclusion of an essay by the Confucian scholar and political reformer Kang Youwei in which he calls for unity, written in January 1912.[28]

4.

Barbering Place 剪髮處[29]

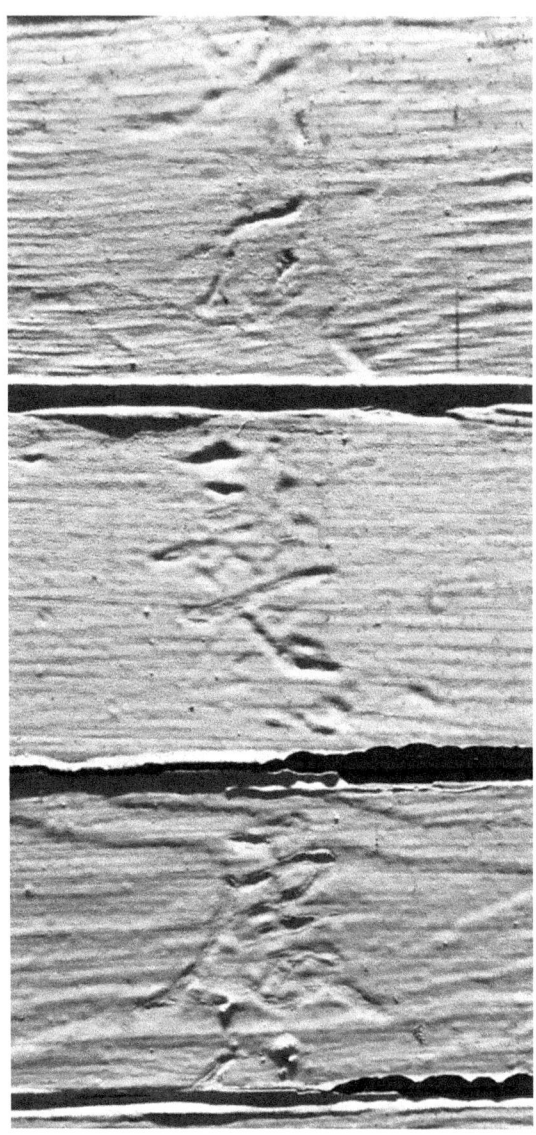

FIGURE 3.2 *"Barbering place."*

It is attractive to imagine some enterprising tradesman setting up shop in front of this wall inscription to spruce up his fellows for their immigration interviews, but there was likely a much more serious purpose (Fig. 3.2). When the Manchus established the Qing dynasty in 1644, they decreed that all Chinese male subjects must adopt the queue—a Manchu hairstyle in which the front of the head was shaved, and the hair in the back was braided. Non-compliance was a reason for execution. In the last years of the dynasty, and especially during the revolutionary fervor of 1911, a movement to cut off this symbol of subjugation became widespread. For example, on January 15, 1911, a major queue-cutting event was held in Shanghai. To the sides of a raised stage, ten or more barbers set up "Patriotic Barbering Places" (義務剪髮處), and cut the queues of more than a thousand attendees. "All that could be heard was the sound of applause, cries of "Bravo!," the snip of scissors, and the exchange of congratulations of newly bald-headed men."[30] Contemporaneous with the queue-cutting movement was a campaign to end foot binding for women, though the practice continued in some regions for years after the Revolution.

FIGURE 3.3 *Two birds*.

5.

It's been a long time since
   I left my home village;
Who could know I'd end up imprisoned in a
   wooden building?
I'm heartsick when I see my reflection, my
   handkerchief is soaked in tears;
I ask you, what crime did I commit to deserve
   this?

Inscribed by Li Hai
South Village, Taishan

離別鄉井許已久
誰知流落木樓囚
顧影痛憐淚滿巾
試問罪何執我咎
李海題[31]

FIGURE 3.4 *Li Hai poem*. Photo: ARG and Daniel Quan.

Li Hai has not been identified (Fig. 3.4). There are two possible locations for "South Village" (Nancun) in Taishan County, Guangdong Province. One is in Sijiu Township, not far from the county center at Taicheng. There is also a Nancun near Duhu in the southern part of the county, near the Huangmao Sea.

The first couplet, but not the second or the signature, is also recorded in the Tet Yee manuscript.

FIGURE 3.5 *Sailing ship*.

6.

The Republic of China   中華民國 [32]

These words are inscribed on an exterior wall of the barracks, and next to them is a rough representation of a Chinese flag with a plain field and a sun with pointed rays. This is not the well-known Republic of China flag still used in Taiwan, which was not adopted formally in China until 1928, but an emblem designed in 1895 by revolutionary martyr Lu Haodong, called the "Blue Sky with a White Sun." This flag was never the national flag, but was used after the 1911 uprising by revolutionary armies in Guangdong and other southern provinces, which suggests this inscription is very early.

7.

Great Blessings to Those Who Enter This House   進伙大吉 [33]

This common expression of good fortune is very likely tongue-in-cheek here. Traditionally posted by the front door when people move into a new house, it is—at the very least—ironic that the words are inscribed on prison walls.

8.

It's useless to become friends with those of narrow mind;
It's useless to have wealth if one disdains the poor;
It's useless to show off one's cleverness in daily affairs;
Understanding human nature all comes from learning;
Attention to details leads one to the proper way.

量度淺狹交友無益
遇貧驕傲雖富無益
作事乖張聰明無益
動達人情皆由學問
深明細務即為經綸
南海一題一口 [34]

Inscribed by Nanhai

The Confucian sentiments of this prose inscription are very clear. Compare the canonical text "The Great Learning," which reads in part,

The ancients who wished to manifest bright virtue in the world first brought order to their states. Wishing to bring order to their states, they first harmonized their families. Wishing to harmonize their families, they first cultivated themselves. Wishing to cultivate themselves, they first rectified their minds. Wishing to rectify their minds, they first made their wills sincere. Wishing to make their wills sincere, they first extended their knowledge. Extension of knowledge lies in the investigation of things . . . From the Son of Heaven down to the common person it is the same: all must take the cultivation of the self as the basis.

Nanhai (South Sea) is the name of a district under the administration of Foshan Prefecture in Guangdong Province.

9.

The season is changing;
Return me my freedom!
Oppressive government and cruel treatment—
One day there will be revenge.

口化季節
還我自由
專政苛虐
來日報仇³⁵

10.

I heard that in the land of the Flowery Flag,
　a new city was rising;
I stood up, jumped for joy, and began my
　journey.
Dwelling in the wooden building, I've heard
　news,
And now I don't know when I'll be able to
　help it grow.
In the beginning, Zeng Yuan raised Master
　Zeng;
Who could have known that Yan Lu would
　cry for Yan Hui?
When I was interrogated, I didn't say a word,
And now I'm packing up and being deported.
This wanderer doesn't have funds for
　another ship passage now,
So I'll bide my time, like the Grand Duke on
　the fishing pier.

聞得花旗新埠開
故起踴躍動程來
在處木樓聽消息
未知何日得栽培
當初曾元養曾子
誰知顏路哭顏回
審查之時無一語
故〔去〕收拾撥返來
〔遊〕子船費日烏有
恰似太公坐釣台³⁶

The Land of the Flowery Flag is a Cantonese colloquial term for the United States.

The third couplet alludes to two disciples of Confucius. Master Zeng is Zeng Shen, a philosopher who was particularly renowned for his filial piety; he is often credited with the authorship of "The Great Learning." His father was Zeng Yuan. Yan Hui was Confucius' favorite, yet he tragically died in poverty before the age of thirty, leaving his father Yan Lu to grieve. The Angel Island author uses the allusions to these two pairs of fathers and sons to describe his relationship with his own father. He suggests that Master Zeng became a moral paragon because his father Zeng Yuan raised him properly, and thus implicitly praises his own father. Yet now, he suggests, his failure to immigrate to the United States will be a shock and disappointment to his father, just as Yan Hui's death was to Yan Lu. The author's failure, in his mind, is an unfilial act.

The Grand Duke is the semi-mythological Jiang Ziya (a.k.a. Jiang Shang, Lü Shang, or Lü Ziya), who was enfeoffed as Taigong (Grand Duke) for his services to the founders of the Zhou dynasty. In the last days of the Shang dynasty in the eleventh century BCE, it was said that Jiang resided near the Wei River in the fief of Ji Chang, future King Wen of Zhou. There he would engage in fishing, yet his hook had no barb, and was suspended three feet above the water. Ji Chang was intrigued, and invited Jiang to discuss strategy. Thus Jiang Ziya "hooked" a patron by fishing. The Angel Island author hopes that he too will find a patron to finance another trip to the United States. Another allusion to Jiang Ziya is found in Poem #123 of *Island*.

11.

I wandered on a long journey of 70,000 miles,
All from a desire to reach the land of the Flowery Flag.
I hoped that one day when my business was successful,
I'd return in glory to my hometown.
I've exhausted my mind and body for twenty years—
How much longer must I stay on this island?
When somewhere I find a place and settle down,
My beautiful dream will be consigned to the vast sea.

12.

I became a prisoner—tears wet my handkerchief;
To become a man of wealth—bitterness and hardship.

立囚身沾巾

作富人苦難
₃₈

13.

There are six Chinese poems by a single detainee in the European Sitting Room on the second floor. Four are on the north wall, and two are on the south wall. Each poem group bears the detainee's full signature. The signatures are very faint, but comparison of one with the other suggests the name is 黃祖名 (Mandarin Huang Zuming, Cantonese Wong Zou-meng, Taishan dialect Wong Dou-men). The calligraphy of the six poems is some of the most artistic and individualized in the building. The writer employs a semi-cursive "running script." The strokes within characters run together in a graceful, organic, and dynamic way without losing the legibility of standard script.

CHINESE INSCRIPTIONS, 1910–1940

Dwelling in the Wooden Building, I give in to despair;
Between high hills and the ferry pier, my brows furrow in pain.
Letters do not arrive, my thoughts hopeless;
In bitterness and sadness, I watch for my early release.

Viewing the landscape arouses deep feelings;
Sadness strikes the prisoner in the wooden building.
Harsh treatment is hard to bear, and my heart is breaking;
After more than a month of wandering, tears wet my cheeks.

The ancestral land is in chaos, and vile practices remain;
More and more each day, diehards exert their tyrannical power.
Who can unify the affairs of the Han people?
All compatriots overseas should build a bridge home.

Experiencing parting is the saddest thing;
When holidays come, I remember my family even more.
From afar, I know my brothers are climbing to a high place,
Dogwood sprays in their clothes, short one man.

           Inscribed by Huang Zuming
           A passenger on the SS *China*

FIGURE 3.6 *Huang Zuming poem—"Dwelling in the Wooden Building."*

The terms "diehard" (short for "diehard traditionalist," 頑錮守舊) and "vile practices" in the third poem were common in early-Republican discourse. The revolutionaries argued that those who held onto old Chinese ideas perpetuated authoritarianism and held back progress. Both terms are used, for example, in the scholar, journalist, and reformer Liang Qichao's (1873–1929) "On the New People" (新民說), published serially between 1902 and 1906.

The first line of the fourth poem is original, while the final three lines follow the Tang dynasty poet Wang Wei's (701–761) "Remembering My

Brothers in Shandong on the Ninth Day of the Ninth Month." The day commemorated in Wang's poem—and here—is the Double Ninth (Chongyang) Festival. The custom was to climb hills in the countryside, and picnic with family and friends. Carrying or wearing twigs of dogwood and drinking wine in which chrysanthemum petals floated were believed to protect against illness.

14.

I'm distressed our ancestral land is in such peril—
Slashed and gouged for over two hundred years.
Compatriots must renew their will to strengthen the country;
Chinese from then on will have no sadness.

The national shame is hard to forget, and we became prisoners;
What joy is here for heroes?—we must soon unite!
In years to come, when there is a gathering of warriors,
I wish to go back, strap on my armor, and take my vengeance.

祖國危亡甚可憂
二百餘年歷劍剖
同胞早復國強志
漢家從此後無愁

國恥難忘〔囚〕生
英雄何乐早列盟
他年若得風雲會
願歸展盔自縱橫

黃祖名題40

Inscribed by Huang Zuming

"Slashed and gouged" is a reference to incursions and colonization by imperialist powers.

The third line of the first verse, in both language and spirit, harks back to the Self Strengthening Movement (自強運動) of the late-nineteenth century, when the Qing court attempted a series of reforms to bring China to parity with foreign powers.

15.

I set out, and one day was locked up;
In a wild place, half a year idle.
Coming here was so easy,
Yet this place is bitter and hard.

〔動〕程一天關
僻野半年閒
來時容乜易
此處甚艱難41

16.

Before my bed, the bright moonlight.
I thought it was frost on the ground.
Raising my head, I stare at the bright moon;
Lowering my head, I think of home.

床前看月光
疑是地上霜
舉頭望明月
低頭思故鄉

This is perhaps the most famous poem in the Chinese language, "Quiet Night Thoughts" (靜夜思) by the Tang dynasty poet Li Bo (701–762). The full moon is a symbol of family unity in Chinese culture, yet to the traveler is only a sad reminder of what he is missing. It seems the Chinese detainee who carved this poem on the wall was unable to compose an original poem, and instead turned to this time-honored expression of homesickness.

17.

Our country is now a nationalist dictatorship;
In future the empire will belong to Yuan Shikai!

我國現下民國專制
將來袁世凱天下也

Yuan Shikai was a shrewd military commander and politician of the late Qing and early Republican periods. He supplanted Dr. Sun Yat-sen as President of the Republic of China in 1912, and attempted to have himself named emperor in 1915. Yet provincial governors rebelled, and Yuan failed. He died in 1916, a broken man.

18.

While on ship, the waves filled the sky;
I endured bitterness and sorrow.
Upon arrival, I met with cruelty,
And was imprisoned in a jail.
I've drifted into Youli,
And recall sorrow on top of sorrow.
The family at home leans on the gate and stares.
Broken-hearted, they long for one far away.
My hard life and my family poverty
Bring two streams of tears.
If one day I can land on this shore,
Then I'll attain my heart's desire.

提起淚雙流
家人依閭望
囚困在監牢
船中浪滔天

若得上阜日
斷腸空悠悠
羑里飄零到
捱盡苦及愁

方遂我心頭
身世及家境
回憶愁加愁
到此遭苛待
44

This poem appears in both the Tet Yee and Smiley Jann manuscripts, with minor differences, so was certainly on the walls in the 1930s. The text here follows Tet Yee. See the Appendices for suggestions of where it may have been located.

Youli was where King Wen (*c.* twelfth century BCE) of the pre-dynastic state of Zhou was imprisoned by King Di Xin, the cruel last ruler of the Shang dynasty. King Wen was idealized by writers such as Mencius as a paragon of moral leadership, so his imprisonment has traditionally been considered a foul and unjust act. Later, King Wen's son King Wu succeeded in overthrowing Shang and establishing the Zhou dynasty. Allusions to Youli appear in two *Island* poems as well, which suggests that the poem writers were inspired by and responded to each other, and formed a literary community with a recognizable "Angel Island style."

19. Random Thoughts

Unbidden, my homesick heart
Feels the sting of parting.
Sadly, the moon this night
Shines only on a foreign land.

4th [??] Day [??], 9th Month,
1st Year of the Republic
of China (1912)
Inscribed by Li Jingbo of
[??] Village, Taishan
Tenyō Maru

天洋丸
45
李鏡波題
台邑口口村人
民國初年九月[四]口[日]
可憐今夜　獨照他鄉
無賴鄉心　偶感離情
偶感七絕

While the general meaning of this poem is clear, it is in fact a fragment. It is side by side on a second floor wall with another four-line quadrisyllabic poem, published as *Island* #109. It, too, is a fragment. To the right of the pair is the title, which reads in full "Heptasyllabic Quatrains on Random Thoughts." The addition of a window at the location resulted in the loss of the final three characters of every line. The signature lines are intact, but faint and partially illegible.

20.

My house had nothing but bare walls, so I left my native place,
Abandoned wife and parents, and took ship across the sea.
After cleaving the waves and riding the wind, we arrived in Mexico;
As I gazed at the moon, my lonely heart wandered back home.

家徒壁立棄鄉留
捨別妻親〔上〕洋舟
破浪乘風登墨處
望月鄉心敖家流
46

This quatrain precedes another six lines on the wall that are transcribed and translated in *Island* #133. A fragmentary version of the four lines here is included in the Chinese text there, but not translated. While *Island* suggests the two parts are a single poem, I conclude they are two separate poems because of a rhyme scheme change.[47] The quatrain describes how the author traveled to Mexico. The six-line poem tells how he left Mexico and was detained at Angel Island.

21.

My ambition as grand as the four directions;
This bitterness is hard to bear.
What problem was it
That put me in a hospital room?
I am loyal and principled,
But now shamed and wounded.
I had departed my ancestral country,
But am now deported back to Tang.

志四方苦難當
何有碍入醫房
口忠節口污傷
〔出〕祖國口返唐
48

Failure to pass the medical examination was grounds for deportation.
    Tang is China, and is so called in reference to the great Tang dynasty (618–907).

22.

When leaving home, don't show your wealth to prying eyes!
In my pants I also had silver dollars.
I hung the pants on the bed, without a care—
In a flash they were stolen, and I'm so angry I cannot speak.
I'm heartsick for my mother, who sold everything for me;
That bastard son of a turtle is so barbaric!

出門尔財勿露眼
鄙人袱袋亦元銀
掛在床中心不關
瞬息被偷啞自恨
感者母親常賣散
雜種龜仔有咁蠻[49]

23.

When you go downstairs for meals,
You should beware of thieves.
Take your money with you
To avoid big loss of wealth.

Although there are thieves among us,
Carefully follow this rule.
To be prepared is to avoid disaster,
And in due time you can leave here.

食飯下樓地　提防有盜主
錢銀隨［身］去　免失大財利
雖有賊兄　謹慎規矩
有備無患　以次別離[50]

The dining halls were located down a covered stairway from the barracks building.

FIGURE 3.7 *"When you go downstairs for meals."* Photo: Michael Nelsen.

24.

Compatriots who come to America should keep memories clear;
When under interrogation or giving testimony, don't ruin your luck.

同胞來美須記緊
審問口供勿倒運
51

25.

I wandered across the world, and endured much hardship;
Now I dwell in a wooden building, and suffer coercion and abuse.
Compatriots should know that our race is despised;
Let it be others who labor like oxen and horses.

Inscribed by Zou Xiwen

又題七絕一首
天涯漂泊悔風塵
口口樓「居」一屈劫身
口口應知民族賤
口口牛馬任他人
西文鄒題 52

Although there is little trace of the first two characters of lines 2–4, the basic message of the poem is clear. The language in the last two lines echoes sentiments expressed by Sun Yat-sen's revolutionary alliance, the Tongmenghui. For example, the editorial mission statement published on August 19, 1910 in the first issue of the San Francisco *Shaonian Zhongguo chenbao* (少年中國晨報) [Young China Morning News], a Tongmenghui mouthpiece, contained the following:

> Our compatriots who these days come searching for food across the seas suffer all types of abuse by foreigners. They are like slaves, like oxen and horses, like worthless weeds ... There is no place that the blood and tears of overseas Chinese does not flow ...[53]

26.

My family was poor and landless; it was hard to find food;
Yet no one willingly becomes a failure.
My father advised me to come to America;
With a single word I ruined my chance.

Inscribed and carved
by Shi Ning

家窮無地難覓食
無人肆意不成器
老父提攜欲美來
因為一言自喪氣
石寧題勒 54

This is the first of three heptasyllabic quatrains by the same author; the other two are only partially deciphered.

27.

I tended [house and home] for more than thirty autumns;
Rushing about in search of food, I wandered abroad.
After a swift thousand-mile journey, I reached American lands—
And was locked in a jail, where there are ten-thousand kinds of cruelty.

人[守]口[庭]卅餘秋
覓食奔波出外遊
千里馳驅到美境
萬般苛待禁監樓
₅₅

This is the first half of an eight-line poem. The second half is only partially visible.

28.

It's hard for Chinese to come to America;
There is so much sadness in this place.
The foreign slaves have always bullied and cheated our country;
When the people are rich and strong, we'll destroy the foreign lands.

      Inscribed by Liu XX
      Ning County, Ling Village
      2nd Month, 2nd Year of the
      Xuantong Reign (1910)

華人往美甚艱難
愁盡幾多在此方
番奴特強欺我國
民為富強滅番邦
宣統[二]年二月
寧邑靈[村]人[題]
劉口口
₅₆

This is the first of two heptasyllabic quatrains by the same author; the other is only partially deciphered. Although the number carved below "Xuantong" is difficult to see, it can only be a 2 (二) or a 3 (三), as the reign period only lasted from 1909 to late 1911 when the revolution occurred. Either way, this is the earliest dated inscription anywhere at the Immigration Station.

"Slave" is a traditional pejorative term used for foreigners, and is not used in its literal sense. It was commonly held by Chinese of the early twentieth century that exploitation by imperialist powers had kept China weak and unable to take its rightful place on the world stage.

Ning County is Xinning. The name was changed to Taishan in 1914.

CHINESE INSCRIPTIONS, 1910–1940

FIGURE 3.8 *Detail of "It's hard for Chinese."*

29.

Misery and travail for so many long years;
Swept along hard roads, bitterness hard to express.
We must strive together to turn back the wild waves;
China from then on will show its great power.

Careworn is the wanderer in the wooden building;
How to bear harsh laws and confinement?
Cruel doctors found I have parasites;
My heart is pure, my words confused.

辛苦風塵多歷年　漂浮險阻苦難宣
［力］［挽］狂瀾念齊力　中國從此逞強勸
木樓遊子心忉忉　苛例受拘意若何
狼醫驗明蟲疾有　［清］［清］白白話糊塗

57

30.

Those who have not endured hardship
    Cannot be said to have hot blood;
Those who have experienced imprisonment
    Never have cold hearts.
          Composed by Yuqing from Tangxi,
                  Taishan

非被困難云無熱血
若因囚仇謂不寒心
玉清氏作
台山唐溪58

Tangxi Village is in Hetang Township, in the Pengjiang District of Jiangmen City. Jiangmen is presently the prefectural capital for the Siyi (Sei Yahp) region, which includes the county of Taishan.

31.

I floated ten thousand miles across the Pacific Sea,
Yet before the waves were stilled, I was detained in prison grounds.
For the sake of my studies, I never complained of hardship,
But who knew there would be such high debts to pay?
For three months I have been continuously imprisoned,
This year has everyday brought me nine rounds of sorrow.
Heaven has eyes, and molds heroes' bones through suffering,
But now I'm at a dead end, and wipe the tracks of my tears.

漂浮萬里涉平洋　海［浪］未消候質場
只因學業休云苦　誰道銷出負債償
繼續牢期三個月　來年一日九回腸
蒼天有［眼］磨英骨　流落窮途揮淚傷59

32.

A cold moon shines on the plum blossoms

寒月照梅花60

33.

Surrounded by mountains and tidal shores.
Inscribed by a passenger who arrived on the SS *Nanking*
24th day of the 3rd month, Year 10 of the Republic [1922]

環山河塗
民國十年三月二十四日搭南京到刻

The short-lived China Mail Steamship Company was founded by a group of San Francisco Chinese businessmen in 1915. The group purchased three ships, of which the SS *Nanking* was the second. Built in 1913, it was operated by the Pacific Coast Steamship Company as the SS *Congress* until it was damaged by fire in 1917. The China Mail purchased, refitted, and renamed it. It plied the Pacific routes from 1918 to 1923, when the company went bankrupt.

34.

Although the Five Nationalities have united as one family,
Yet the great powers still despise our China.
It's all because our country has risen up in arms
That compatriots here are bullied by white devils.

五族雖云合一家
列強輕視我中華
皆因國內干戈起
僑胞也自受鬼蝦

This poem is recorded by both Tet Yee and Smiley Jann, with slight variations, thus it was certainly on the walls in the 1930s. The text here follows Jann's version. The first couplet is a close match with *Island* #68 still visible on the north wall of the first floor Chinese dormitory—Yee's version is almost identical with the published text. Yet the second couplet in the manuscripts differs from that on the wall. The content of both the wall poem and this one refers to the 1911 Revolution and the founding of the Republic of China, so they must have been early Angel Island compositions.

The Five Nationalities are the five major ethnic groups in China as recognized at the time of the 1911 Revolution: Han (the dominant ethnic group in China), Manchu, Mongol, Hui (Muslims), and Tibetan. The harmonious union of the Five Nationalities was an important rallying cry of the revolutionaries. When the Republic of China was founded, its first national flag comprised five horizontal stripes of different colors, each representing one of the five groups.

35.

The island's name is "Isle of Immortals,"
Yet in fact this place is a prison.
Why are we detained in such a place?
Only because home and country are poor and miserable.

埃崙名目云仙島
此地原來是監牢
吾輩因何留此地
無非家國兩貧愁
63

This poem was recorded in the Smiley Jann manuscript. The first couplet is very similar to that in *Island* #34, yet the second couplet differs.

36.

It was easy to land at the port here,
But upon arrival, I was thrown in prison.
Though it's hard for compatriots to work together,
We must soon unite to destroy the barbarians.

來〔此〕登埠易
口口困監牢
同胞難同志
早合滅蠻夷
64

"Barbarian"—similar to *yidi* in #27, the compound *manyi* referred to non-Chinese groups to the south (*man*) and east (*yi*), and was used pejoratively for any non-Chinese group.

37.

Overthrow Japanese imperialism!

打倒日本帝國主義
65

Japanese territorial expansion began in the 1870s in Korea, which was officially annexed in 1910. Occupation of Chinese territories dates to the First Sino-Japanese War (1894–1895), when the decisive Japanese victory forced the Qing government to cede Taiwan. With its victory in the Russo-Japanese War (1904–1905), Japan gained control over southern Manchuria, including the important Liaodong Peninsula. Then, following the First World War, Chinese were shocked to learn that Germany's former sphere of influence in Shandong Province was given to Japan by the terms of the Treaty of Versailles. Chinese outrage led to demonstrations in the street on May 4, 1919, and sparked the May Fourth Movement. This movement constituted a comprehensive questioning of traditional literature, culture, and politics, and had massive implications for China's future.

38. General Zhao Zilong's Whole Body was Courage

I first asked the innkeeper, to get to Mexico,
Need I borrow many silver taels?
Is it true what I heard then? I think not!
He said I could go to America without any money.
Cruel barbarian doctors give us smallpox shots;
Nasty cow thistles are served three meals a day.
Everyone has seen this—how pitiful it is.
Yet our families are poor, so we cross the foreign seas.

      By a Wanderer from the City of Iron
                        March 2, 1921

趙子龍一身是膽
先問客棧往墨方
真否時聞應是假　可到美國又﹝無﹞銀
強蠻醫生又種痘　惡種牛﹝菜﹞食三﹝餐﹞
眾人看過真可惜　仍係家貧出外洋
民國拾年三月初二鐵城﹝流﹞口口口 66
任揭銀兩若如何

General Zhao Zilong (c. 168–229 CE), whose formal name was Zhao Yun, was one of the Five Tiger Generals who served Liu Bei, ruler of Shu-Han during the Three Kingdoms period. His exploits were highly dramatized in the popular sixteenth-century novel *The Romance of the Three Kingdoms*. After General Zhao heroically saved Liu Bei's infant son from captivity, the novel recounts, Liu Bei lauded him saying, "His whole body is courage." The Angel Island author cites General Zhao in the title to encourage other Chinese immigrants to be brave in the face of the detainment ordeal.

The term for "innkeeper" here suggests more than simply the manager of a hostel. In traditional times, innkeepers also carried out a range of business services for clients—including, it appears, arranging passage to America.

Mexico followed the lead of the United States and began to enact anti Chinese laws and limits on immigration in the early-twentieth century. In 1921, almost all Chinese immigration was banned—only those with capital to purchase land for farming were permitted to enter the country. This poem is dated 1921, and so it appears the author was unexpectedly stopped at Angel Island due to the new law. The following two poems also refer to the need for money to enter Mexico, and so were likely written in the same year or later.

From a modern perspective, vaccinations are generally welcomed as a means to avoid disease, yet to early-twentieth-century immigrants from Chinese villages, needle injections were invasive and counter to traditional concepts of health. "Cow thistle" is a loose rendering of the Chinese term *niucai* (牛菜) (a.k.a. *niubang*, 牛蒡), which refers to Burdock, a wild plant of the thistle family. The broad leaves and roots of Burdock can either be eaten or made into medicine.

39.

I tended house and home for dozens of years;
After thinking it over a thousand times, I began this journey.
When I arrived at the island, I was put in the detention center—
Who knew that even Mexico forbids entrance?

因守家園幾十秋
千思萬想始奔勞
竟至埃崙留候所
誰知墨境禁人遊
₆₇

CHINESE INSCRIPTIONS, 1910–1940

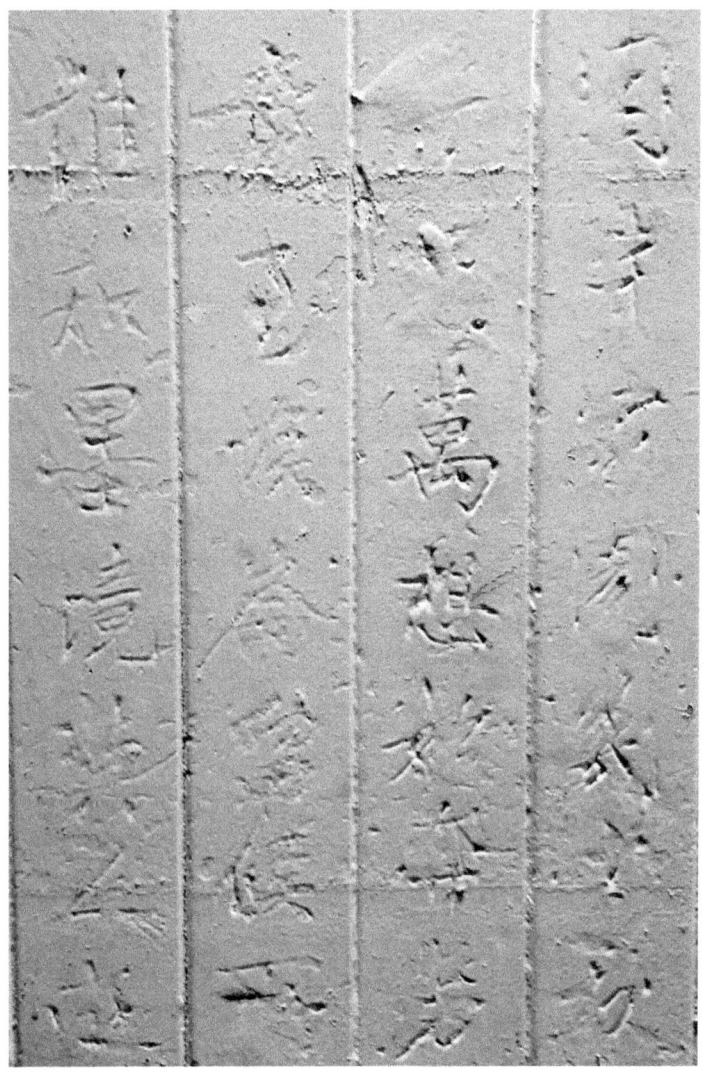

FIGURE 3.9 *"I tended house and home."*

40.

I've been here at Gold Mountain
For twenty-two days.
Know that because I have no money,
I cannot live in Mexico.
Everyone be careful.

此人金山
二十二天
知我無銀
不得住墨
諸君提防
68

41.

Sailors on board ships
Come to the land of the Flowery Flag
Without paying a penny.

行船[的]人
到來花旗
不用分文 [69]

42.

For Everyone:
World Money.

諸君
世界金錢 [70]

The illustration is a good luck symbol, in the shape of an ancient Chinese coin.

FIGURE 3.10 *Good luck money picture.*

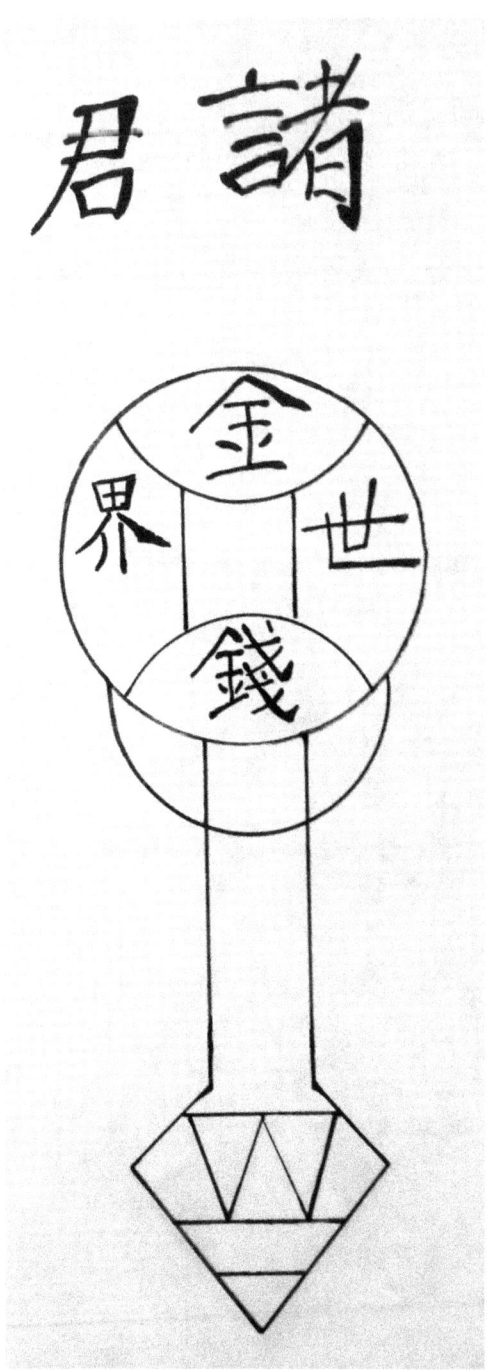

FIGURE 3.11 *Good luck money line drawing.*

43. A Good World

Joyful events come,
 one and then the other;
Daughters leave their chambers,
 and sons ride on dragons.
How to make your honored son
 into a fine son-in-law?
Just take this strict father,
 and make him his father-in-law!
There's no need for the groom to leave home
 to perform the "offering of the geese,"
And why should the bride get all dressed up
 for the "ceremony of return?"
In short, for a lifetime of family happiness,
Don't spread manure in faraway places!

好世界口口
喜事重重復重重
女兒出閣子乘龍
孰得令子為佳婿
且把嚴親作岳翁
奠雁不須甥別〔離〕
歸寧何至髮妝容
總之一生家庭樂
肥水唔流遠處用 71

Unlike the great majority of poems on the walls, which focus on the immediate concerns of detainment, this poem presents a long-term plan for family success—with a twist. A marriage is proposed that will be to the mutual benefit of two families who already have a close connection. The author is apparently the father of a daughter, and he addresses the poem to the father of a son. The poem suggests that the girl and her family are neighbors or even close relatives of the boy's family; traditional Chinese marriage custom would allow cousins to marry, for example, as long as the boy and girl do not share a common surname. The author wishes to bypass the usual pomp, ceremony, and expense of a typical Chinese marriage, and instead use the marriage tie to pool the resources of the two families.

The second line presents two metaphors for coming-of-age. When a daughter "leaves the [women's] chamber," she is preparing to marry and leave home. A son who "rides the dragon" has made a brilliant marriage to a bride whose family has wealth and rank.

"Strict father" is a set term which points to the Confucian role of the father as head of the family; the term appears as early as the works of the philosopher Xunzi (third century BCE). "Father-in-law" here is specifically the father of the bride, and literally means "old man of the [sacred] mountain."

Both "offering of the geese" and "ceremony of return" are ceremonies associated with traditional marriages. Geese mate for life, so in China became symbols of conjugal fidelity. The bridegroom ritually presents a goose or geese to the bride's family to indicate his vows. The "ceremony of return" is for the bride. The traditional Chinese bride left home upon marriage, and moved to the home of her new husband's family. On the third day after the marriage, she was allowed to make a formal visit to her natal home, to give thanks to her parents for raising her. Both of these ceremonies have very early roots, and are mentioned in texts like the *Classic of Poetry* and the *Book of Rites*.

The last line is a version of the Chinese proverb, "don't spread manure on other people's fields" (肥水不流外人田). The phrase implicitly counsels to keep that which benefits the family within the family, whether it be wealth, manure, or—as in this poem—sons and daughters!

44.

Chop the weeds and pull the roots—destroy their glory.

斬草除根絕其光 [72]

"They," presumably, is Americans.

45.

The Flowery Flag:
    the flag waves its three colors, yet only for Americans;
The Wooden Building:
    when the building is left to all, then prisoners will take revenge.

花旗旗其轉三色盡屬美［族］人占據
木樓樓留與一般便將囚［人］償還仇 [73]

This parallel prose inscription appears in *Island* as #76, yet the version there is fragmentary (only 18 characters).

46.

I'm moved by spring flowers in the third month fog;
To the prisoner, the wind is filled with fifth watch cold.

                    Composed by Zhu

感動［春］［花］三月霧
囚人風滿五更寒
　　朱題
74

47.

Today we brothers are imprisoned in a jail—only for the sake of our ancestral land,
Evil poison flows out like a flood.
In future years our armies will become strong at last—then for the ancestral shrines
We will joyfully kill the foreign slaves.

          Composed by Second Brother from Nanyi

今日兄弟困牢籠只為祖國
刻毒流外溢
他年生師正強盛終［以］宗［祠］
由喜殺番奴
　　南邑次［郎］題
75

48.

How can a hero bear to be restrained?
... I should endure the sharp pain.
... Yet my body is engulfed in hot blood,
... And anger fills my chest.
... I listen to others talking in their bunks,
... And am struck deaf and dumb.
... [Thinking of] past days,
I become dazed and confused.

何忍厄英雄
口該耐慘痛
口身淪熱血
口揀憤填胸
口聽他人榻
口囗振瞶聾
口［著］他日事
改口傻昏庸
76

188   VOICES OF ANGEL ISLAND

This remains only a tentative translation, as the first characters of six of the eight lines are not visible, and several others are faint. An illegible signature line follows.

49.

There are worms growing in my liver and lungs.
I'm returning to the mountains of Tang.

有肝肺生虫
回唐山
77

This inscription is carved in poor calligraphy on the exterior of the barracks building. It tells a story equally as affecting as any of the poems inside, though the content is brief and unadorned, and the author probably uneducated. The medical examination was the first major hurdle for those who arrived at Angel Island. Any of a range of parasitic diseases was grounds for deportation. This would-be immigrant's dream is over, and he is returning to China.

50.

Huang Jijuan rebels!

黄季眷作反
78

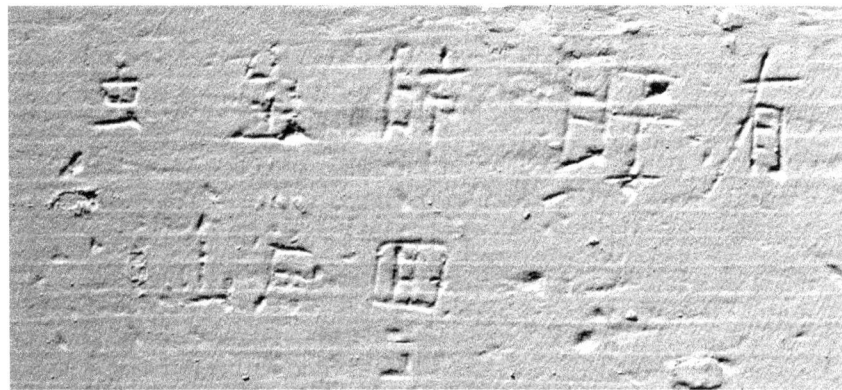

FIGURE 3.12 *"There are worms growing."* Photo: ARG and Daniel Quan.

In 2014, this inscription was discovered by Michael Jasinski, Archeological Specialist for the California Parks and Recreation Department. It is carved on a door that was used as a workbench in the electrical room of the station hospital. The writer has not been identified.

51.

When can I get out of here?　何日出得去[79]

52.

FIGURE 3.13 *Ancestral altar.*

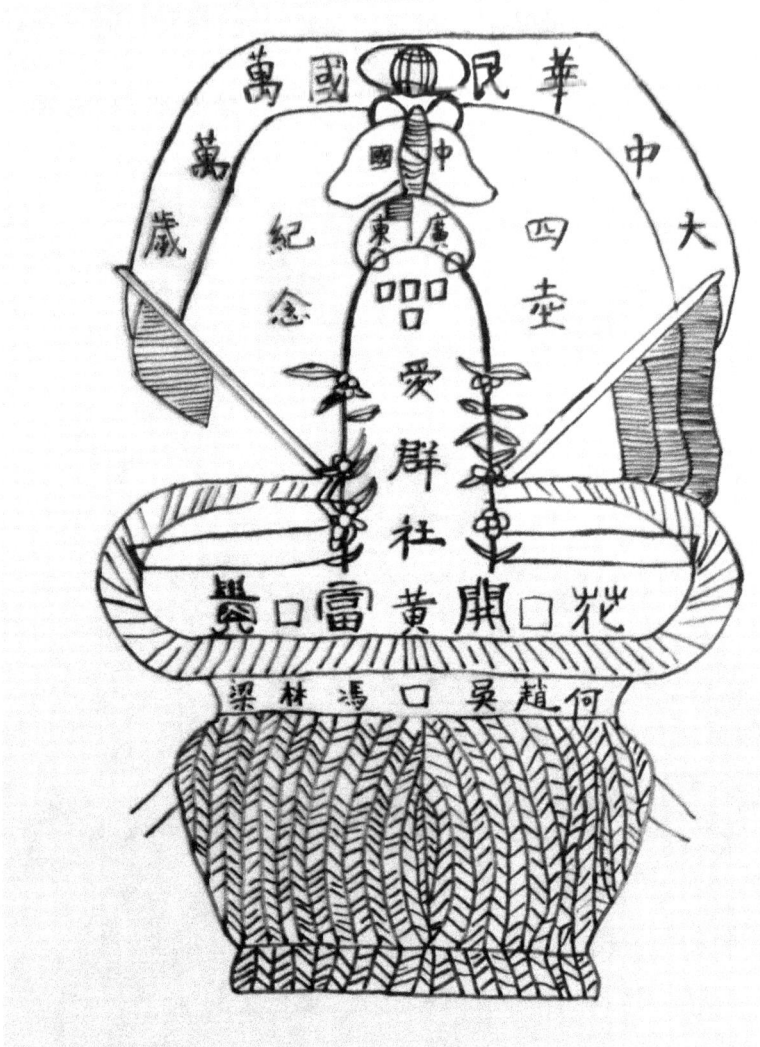

FIGURE 3.14 *Ancestral altar line drawing.*

An ancestral altar is carved on the south wall of Room 205, the Chinese men's dormitory on the second floor. Depicted is a funeral basket, or a memorial basket—a typical offering to the ancestors at the Qingming Festival (also known as the Pure Brightness Festival or Tomb Sweeping Day). A stone or wooden stele with inscription sits in a basket, surrounded by a banner, flags, inscriptions, and flower decorations. The butterfly at top is symbolic of the mystery of human life, based on an allusion to Daoist philosopher Zhuangzi's butterfly dream: Zhuangzi wasn't sure if he was Zhuangzi who dreamed he was a butterfly, or a butterfly who dreamed he was Zhuangzi. Above the butterfly, though it is very faint, is a globe. The altar is nearly four feet high, and its importance to the detainees is evident in the fact that the area around it is mostly free of other inscriptions. While this is not the only such altar in the building (there is another on the first floor), it is the largest, most complex, and most visible.

The banner at the top contains the text:

Long live the great Republic of China!   大中華民國萬萬歲

Two characters are inscribed on the butterfly's wings:

China
中國

A small flag is depicted in the round plaque above the stele, which appears to be the original five-striped flag of the Republic of China. Characters in the plaque read:

Guangdong   廣東

In the space between the banner and the stele are four characters which refer to the Qingming (Tomb Sweeping) Festival. While most traditional Chinese holidays follow the lunar calendar, Qingming was set on the first day of the fifth solar term (in the Chinese series of 24 terms), corresponding to exactly fifteen days after the spring equinox. As the time of the equinox varies slightly from year to year, the date of Qingming also varies. When transposed to the Gregorian calendar, it can fall on April 4, 5, or 6. The wall text places the commemoration on April 6. Qingming fell on that date ten times during the years of the Immigration Station's operation. The first after the founding of the Republic of China was 1915. The four characters read:

Remembering April 6
四陸紀念

At the top of the stele itself are several mostly illegible characters, which may be a date. Below is the main stele text—a vertical line of characters that present a name typical of Chinese benevolent associations. Yet this "association" appears to be unique to Angel Island, and its name was coined to embrace all of the detainees. Thus all will benefit from the ritual commemoration the altar represents.

    Love for the Multitudes Society   愛群社

Where the stele meets the basket, there is a horizontal line of characters in ancient seal-style calligraphy. The phrase signifies good luck and success:

    Blooming flowers, wealth, and nobility   花開富貴

The remainder of the characters are Chinese surnames. Three are interspersed among the seal-style characters—as if they had been added after the initial carving—and the rest are in a horizontal line below.

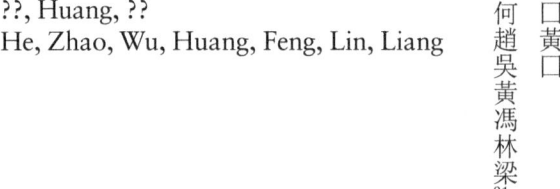

    ??, Huang, ??
    He, Zhao, Wu, Huang, Feng, Lin, Liang

AN ANGEL ISLAND MEMOIR

The following memoir (in Chinese) of Angel Island detention was found among the Him Mark Lai Papers at the Ethnic Studies Library at the University of California, Berkeley, but has not been translated and published before this. The handwritten document was stapled to an envelope bearing the return address of Felicia Lowe's film production company (see text), and so it appears the author mailed it to Lowe, who forwarded it to Him Mark Lai.

Seventy Years Ago in the Wooden Building at the Angel Island Immigration Detention Center: A Brief Record of Events

by Chung Hing Lou 盧萬和

When I was just twenty years old, on the 14th day of the 3rd lunar month (April 30), 1912 I boarded the *Manchuria* in Hong Kong to come to America as the son of a Chinese merchant. On the 12th day of the 4th lunar month (May 28) we arrived in San Francisco. When the ship was just about to reach port, an official dispatched by the Immigration Service came on board and ushered all the new, first-time travelers and some returning travelers onto a smaller ship that went straight to the Angel Island Immigration Detention Center, popularly called the Wooden Building. At the direction of a doctor, an attendant gave all the new travelers cups of Epsom salts in water, and ordered us to drink. Then we were each given a metal foil basin and told to defecate in it. Each person wrote his name and number on his basin. Then the attendant collected the basins of excrement and took them to the doctor, who tested for hookworm. After the examination, those who had hookworm were detained for medical treatment. Hookworm was just a pretext to detain many people and cause trouble for them.

The detention center comprised several wooden buildings, and travelers perched in bunk beds, like in a prison. A Chinese cook was hired, and every day three meals were Chinese food. Immigration officials handled the cases and interrogations of all of the Chinese passengers in the detention center very callously. Cases were delayed. Every time a ship arrived, Japanese people were processed first and they were released. Only then were we Chinese processed. And among us, students were examined first, and sojourners like me afterwards. The Immigration Service employed Chinese translators. Each time a new traveler was interviewed, the interrogator was always accompanied by a translator. The translators all wore expressions of brutal arrogance. They ganged up with the interrogators and used threatening language in coercive examinations. They inquired into every detail, root and branch. Even a small mistake and one risked the disaster of deportation. When a case was appealed, often the process could take months or even years. From my arrival on the 12th of the 4th lunar month (May 28), I was imprisoned in the wooden building at the detention center until the 27th of the 5th lunar month (July 11). I was interrogated three times. Fortunately I was not subjected to bullying and intimidation. Yet upon their return from interrogations many of the new travelers said they had been subjected to such treatment. When I was granted release on the 27th of the 5th lunar month (July 11), I had been imprisoned in the wooden building at the detention center for a month and a half.

I met many there who told me of their grievances. There was a Mr. Li who brought his two sons from the Philippines. He had studied English and could speak it. He had been in the wooden building more than a month and was interrogated twice, but still had not been released. He remained in detention while a multi-faceted investigation was ongoing. There was also an old immigrant who had fallen and injured his foot, and was detained for medical attention. His heart was lacking in goodness, and he hated and envied the students. Every day he played many nasty tricks, like inciting uneducated youths to put filth and lice in the students' clothes and beds. He did all sorts of tricks like that. He was from Heshan, and was an educated man. He had previously written poems on the walls of the wooden building. He said he was in transit to Cuba, but was detained here to cure his foot. He harbored intense hatred for the doctor, and said that sometime he'd like to scratch his eyes out. There was also Reverend Li Yisu from Taishan. He had come with his two sons, and been interrogated many times. Only after a month was he released. The rest were young people like me, sons of merchants. All had to undergo interrogation many times over a long period—one or two months, and occasionally one or two years. They had their fill of the bullying by the workers in the wooden building. Very rarely were relatives allowed to visit, and everyone wore sad expressions.

I have recently received copies of films by Arthur Dong and Felicia Lowe that document experiences at the Angel Island Immigration Station, and their request that those with relevant information to please provide it. Although I was only at the Angel Island Immigration Station for more than a month, my experience there was so bitter that even after the passage of seventy years I can remember even small details. I am thus sending this memoir now. You can use or discard it as you see fit.

Among the old and new immigrants in the wooden building at the Angel Island Immigration Station there were many who recited and composed poetry, but I didn't copy the poems down and have difficulty remembering them. I've composed two *dayou* (doggerel) poems, and record them below for a laugh.

When I came to America, I was not allowed to land;
First I was imprisoned in a cage of a wooden
    building.
Cut off from friends and family coming to visit,
My natural lofty aspirations were never depressed.

前來美國未登臨
先以囚籠木屋禁
隔絕親朋來訪問
天然壯志未消沉

From afar I crossed the oceans on a ten-thousand mile journey,
On a search for achievements that would benefit my life.
We all admired the wealth of Gold Mountain,
And were certain we would find prosperity there!

遠涉重洋萬里行
為求創作利謀生
金山富裕人同慕
料到其中道達享

Mr. Chung Hing Lou was born on August 23, 1892 in China, and died on July 29, 1982 in San Francisco.[82] He presumably immigrated to the United States as a "paper son," as the manifest of the *Manchuria* for the voyage he describes does not include his name. His name appears in several residential directories for the City of San Francisco in the 1960s, and he is on the manifest of the *President Cleveland* on a voyage from Hong Kong to Honolulu, arriving there October 25, 1954, but other public records have not been located.

The *Manchuria* reached San Francisco on May 27, 1912, not May 28 as in the text.

When consumed, Epsom salts (magnesium sulfate) has a laxative effect.

E. Yim Lee, a teacher, was born December 31, 1871 in Sing Ning, Sun Ning (Taishan). He brought his two sons, E. Chung Lee and E. Yuen Lee, to San Francisco from the Philippines, and applied for admission as Section 6—members of classes exempt from the Chinese Exclusion Act. They arrived on the *Manchuria* on May 27, 1912, and listed their final destination as Oakland. Lee was landed on July 13, but only temporarily after he posted a bond. Both sons were deported on July 26 aboard the *Korea*. After a long legal process, Lee's appeal for permanent entry was denied. He was returned to Angel Island on October 16, and deported aboard the *Siberia* on October 26.

Neither the unnamed trickster nor Reverend Li has been identified.

Arthur Dong (曾奕田) and Felicia Lowe (劉詠嫦) are both award-winning documentary filmmakers whose works have focused on the Chinese American experience. In 1982, when Mr. Lou put pen to paper for this memoir, Dong had just recently produced his first film, *Sewing Woman* (1982), which tells the story of his mother's journey to America. Lowe's first film was *China, Land of My Father* (1979), and she was then at work on *Carved in Silence* (1988), which documented the experience of Chinese at the Angel Island Immigration Station.

4

Other Inscriptions, 1910–1940

We sit behind bars and watch with anguish

Laws and regulations limiting specific races and ethnicities are central topics of many histories of immigration, but there were other justifications used to exclude "unwanted" or "unwelcome" immigrants. As Jennifer Gee points out, chief among these was class background. The Immigration Act of 1882 (which is distinct from the Chinese Exclusion Act adopted in the same year) included language that for the first time allowed inspectors to deny entry to those "likely to become a public charge." This was a particularly powerful tool, as it was so subjective and could be stretched to include judgments about mental or physical health.[1] Provisions in immigration law in 1885 banned the entry of contract laborers and penalized all those who assisted their migration.[2] Prior to 1924, when the Chinese Exclusion Act was expanded to cover all Asians, these class laws—as well as diagnosis of "contagious diseases" that were thought endemic to non-white races—were the *de facto* means to enforce at least partial exclusion of Asians other than Chinese. Yet the effect was even more general, for class could be, and was, also used to turn away immigrants and visitors from any point of origin—be it Europe, South America, or Australia.[3] A third limitation rooted in class background was added in the Immigration Act of 1917: aliens sixteen years of age or older who were illiterate in English or their own language were to be denied entry.[4] Other laws were solely directed at women: sexual morality was incorporated in the immigration process by the Page Law of 1875, mentioned in the previous chapter, and the 1910 White-Slave Traffic Act (the Mann Act), which in the immigration context barred entry of women suspected of coming for the purpose "of prostitution or debauchery, or for any other immoral purpose," and anyone who arranged their transportation. In practice, these became a means for class selection as well, as poor women were more likely to be targeted than those of better financial backgrounds.[5]

More generally, it is a sad fact that the proponents of the American eugenics movement had a major impact on setting US immigration policy in the late-nineteenth and early-twentieth centuries.[6] Targets included not only the non-white races, but any person whose procreation was perceived to threaten the dominant groups in the population, i.e., white Northern European and Germanic Protestants. The text of the 1907 Immigration Act is a pertinent example. It reads in part:

> That the following classes of aliens shall be excluded from admission into the United States: All idiots, imbeciles, feeble-minded persons, epileptics, insane persons, and persons who have been insane within five years previous; persons who have had two or more attacks of insanity at any time previously; paupers; persons likely to become a public charge; professional beggars; persons afflicted with tuberculosis or with a loathsome or dangerous contagious disease; persons not comprehended within any of the foregoing excluded classes who are found to be and are certified by the examining surgeon as being mentally or physically defective, such mental or physical defect being of a nature which may affect the ability of such alien to earn a living; persons who have been convicted of or admit having committed a felony or other crime or misdemeanor involving moral turpitude; polygamists, or persons who admit their belief in the practice of polygamy; anarchists, or persons who believe in or advocate the overthrow by force or violence of the Government of the United States, or of all government, or of all forms of law, or the assassination of public officials; prostitutes, or women or girls coming into the United States for the purpose of prostitution or for any other immoral purpose; persons who procure or attempt to bring in prostitutes or women or girls for the purpose of prostitution or for any other immoral purpose . . .[7]

The subheading in the margin of the law reads simply, "Defective persons." The list of banned persons grew larger in the ensuing years. The addition of illiteracy in 1917 as a reason to ban entry has already been mentioned. It was a coded suggestion that even poverty (and by extension, illiteracy) was considered a marker of "genetically inferior stock." The 1917 Immigration Act also added those of "constitutional psychopathic inferiority" to the list. This charge, in tandem with "mentally defective," was in practice the justification to deny entry to those who disclosed or were suspected of homosexual identity.[8] Eugenics also lay behind domestic anti-miscegenation laws and compulsory sterilization programs. California eugenicists were at the forefront of the movement, and were active in promoting their ideas abroad, particularly Germany. Prior to 1964, a total of 20,108 people were sterilized in California, by far the most of any state, and accounting for one-third of all sterilizations nationwide.[9]

The Immigration Act of 1917 is also known as the Asiatic Barred Zone Act, as in addition to its many other restrictions it greatly expanded the Chinese Exclusion laws to cover multiple countries "adjacent to the Continent of Asia." Rather than list them, the law used latitude and longitude to demarcate a huge region, which included South and Southeast Asia, Pacific islands, parts of Siberia, Afghanistan, and Arabia. Japan was not part of the Zone. Eugenics underlay the expansion, but so did popular anti-immigrant and racist sentiments. President Woodrow Wilson vetoed the bill, but members of Congress followed the will of their constituents, and easily garnered the two-thirds vote to override him. A particular influence on popular opinion was the arrival in San Francisco of significant numbers of Sikhs from the Punjab in the 1910s. Anti-immigrant newspapers like the San Francisco *Call* whipped up a firestorm of opposition to the entry of the unassimilable "Hindu Horde" (despite the fact that Sikhs are not Hindus).[10]

Ensuing immigration laws only added new restrictions and barred groups. The Emergency Quota Act of 1921 initiated a system by which the number of immigrants from any one country in a given year was limited to 3 percent of the US resident population from that same country in the 1910 Census. The Immigration Act of 1924 made the quota system permanent, and much, much more restrictive. It set a maximum limit on immigrants from any one nation to 2 percent of the total number of that nationality living in the US, and used 1890 Census numbers for the calculation. The intended effect was to powerfully curtail immigration of Southern Europeans (Italian Catholics, Greek Orthodox), and Russians and Eastern Europeans—particularly Jews—whose US resident populations in 1890 were very, very small. The quota system did not loosen any of the bans of Chinese Exclusion and the Asiatic Barred Zone. The 1924 law added Japan to the Zone, without mentioning it by name. The text instead stipulates, "No alien ineligible to citizenship shall be admitted to the United States." As Asians could not apply for naturalization, Japanese became a *de facto* barred group.[11] In 1934, another group came under restrictions: Filipinos. Up until then, Filipinos had been considered US nationals, and could come and go relatively freely. By the terms of the Tydings-McDuffie Act, adopted to start a ten-year process toward Philippine independence, they were reclassified as aliens for the purposes of US immigration. Filipinos were henceforth allotted the remarkably low quota of 50 immigration visas per year.[12]

It is estimated that people from eighty-two different countries were detained at Angel Island.[13] Yet the number of nationalities represented in decipherable wall inscriptions is far fewer. Besides the East Asian inscriptions presented in previous chapters, inscriptions from the immigration period can be roughly divided into three groups: Russian inscriptions, South Asian inscriptions, and a more miscellaneous group made up mostly of merchant seamen from various countries.

Angel Island was not a major stop for European immigrants, but a significant number were detained there. The Trans-Siberian Railway was in operation by 1904, and so for the first time there was a practicable route for travelers to North and South America via the Pacific. When the Immigration Station opened in 1910, Russians were already arriving at the Port of San Francisco in substantial numbers. The number of arrivals escalated with the beginning of the First World War in 1914, and jumped again in the period of the Revolution of 1917 and the subsequent civil war. In mid-1923, a last large group of 800 refugees was detained at Angel Island. The Immigration Station barracks was not capable of housing so many, so nearby Fort McDowell was also employed.[14] These refugees were survivors of the Siberian Ice March of the last Russian White Army, which was under the command of General M.K. Dieterichs, and were transported from Vladivostok to safety by Admiral Oskar Stark in a fleet of ramshackle ships. The fleet's first stop was Korea, where many refugees and ships were left behind, and then approximately 3,000 people were landed in Shanghai, where they formed the nucleus of the White Russian community that thrived there until the Chinese Communist Revolution. The remnants of Stark's fleet were sold at auction in Manila Bay, where the Russian imperial flag was lowered for the last time.[15]

Russian detainees at Angel Island included some who were very well known. The composer Sergei Prokofiev (1891–1953) was held for three days in 1918. Immigration inspectors asked if he had ever been in jail. He answered that he had.

"That's bad," they said. "Where?"
"On your island!"[16]

In February 1919, Nikolai Avksentyev, former President of the Provisional All-Russian government, was detained at the Immigration Station along with several members of his Cabinet: Vladimir Zenzinov, Andrei Argunov, and E.F. Rogovsky. The short-lived All-Russian government had been founded in Omsk, Siberia in September 1918, as a last-ditch attempt by the White Russians to stem the tide of Bolshevism. It was overthrown in a coup on November 17.[17] A later detainee was Countess Alexandra Tolstoy (1884–1979), youngest daughter of the great writer, who was held for a short while in 1931. She settled in New York, and in 1939 founded the Tolstoy Foundation, and as its president for forty years worked tirelessly to build public support for international refugee relief and human rights.[18]

Only a few hundred South Asians were in the United States before 1906. A much larger number worked in the lumber mills and railroad camps of western Canada. The immigrants to Canada and the US were mostly Sikhs from the Punjab, and many had been veterans of the British India Army. Yet economic conditions in the Punjab, combined with disease and unrest, motivated thousands to look for better prospects abroad. Thousands of laborers arrived in the United States in the next decade, some traveling by ship to San Francisco and others coming overland from Canada. Lumber millwork was to be found in the northwest, but a particular draw was the construction of the Western Pacific Railway line, crossing the Sierra Nevada along the Feather River. By 1907, as many as two thousand South Asians were at work there. After the completion of the railway in 1909, many Punjabis in California turned to agriculture, first as migrant laborers, and then as conditions allowed, as independent farmers. As with other Asian immigrant groups, they challenged—with little success—the increasingly exclusionary policies enacted through 1924. Meanwhile, a smaller but very important South Asian immigrant group comprised students and political refugees, mostly in the San Francisco Bay Area. In 1913, they founded the Ghadar [Revolt] Party, which advocated the violent overthrow of the British in India. The Ghadars quickly gained the support of the Sikh laborers in the countryside, through stirring editorials and revolutionary poems in their party newspaper, also called *Ghadar*. The outbreak of the First World War in 1914 seemed to the community to be a signal to try to liberate India. Many did return there, but their revolution was stillborn: typically they were arrested as soon as they disembarked.[19]

In the interest of promoting international trade, merchant seamen who arrived in the United States from foreign ports were not typically subject to regular immigration procedures, except in certain circumstances. As per Rule 10 of *Immigration Laws: Rules of November 15, 1911*, alien seamen were permitted to land either for shore leave or for any purpose related to their calling, as long as they remained employed on a vessel temporarily in port.[20] A considerable amount of discretion was given to ship masters to ensure their crews' compliance and to report any infractions. Seamen could run afoul of the immigration authorities if they were deserters or stowaways, engaged in business other than that of the vessel, became public charges, or were discharged from employment while in the United States. Those who were detained at Angel Island tended to be there only a short time, until they could prove to the inspectors' satisfaction that they would soon reship on an outgoing vessel.

RUSSIAN WALL INSCRIPTIONS

1.

J. Zeitlin
Gomel

Я. ЦЕЙТЛИНЪ
ГОМЕЛЬ[21]

FIGURE 4.1 *The Zeitlin (Allen) brothers as children. Jacob is at the center. Courtesy Marilyn Mendoza.*

FIGURE 4.2 *The Zeitlin/Hoppenstein family in Gomel, before 1906. From left to right in the front row: Leib (Louis), father Velvel, Jacob, grandmother Malky Hoppenstein, mother Peshe, and Abram (Joe). Courtesy Evan Allen.*

FIGURE 4.3 *Jacob and Anna Allen in the 1950s. Courtesy Marilyn Mendoza.*

Jacob Zeitlin, twenty-one years old and unmarried, arrived in San Francisco aboard the *Manchuria* from Kobe on October 6, 1915. On the passenger list, "Allen" was crossed out and Zeitlin added—probably by an immigration inspector. His occupation was listed as "teacher" ("student" was crossed out), his ethnicity as "Hebrew," and his last permanent residence as "Homel, Mogilev, Russia." He was held on Angel Island for less than a week, awaiting a medical release, and was admitted on October 11.[22]

Homel is an alternate spelling for Gomel, the second-largest city in Belarus, and the administrative center for what is now Gomel Province, to the southeast of the country near the border with Ukraine. Mogilev (also Mahilyow, Mogilyov) is a city and province of eastern Belarus that adjoins the Gomel region. Before the 1917 Revolution, Mogilev was Russian imperial territory, and was the administrative seat for the region that included Gomel. Gomel was a thriving center for Jewish life and culture in the late-nineteenth century and early-twentieth century—it was a typical Eastern European *shtetl*. Yet as in other such centers, the Jews of Gomel became targets: violent pogroms there in 1903 and 1906 resulted in more than two dozen Jewish deaths and the destruction of hundreds of Jewish homes and businesses.[23] During the Second World War, the Jewish community there was completely destroyed in the Holocaust. More recently, Gomel suffered massive contamination by radioactive debris from the Chernobyl nuclear disaster in 1986.

A search through government documents and other sources of information led to contact with Jacob's descendants, who kindly communicated what they know of the family history.[24] The Zeitlins were very well-to-do. Jacob's father Velvel (literally "Wolf," this Yiddish name is often Anglicized as William) was a lawyer. Yet real wealth came from his mother Peshe Hoppenstein Zeitlin's side. The Hoppensteins were in the import/export business. Family lore has it that they even had a special warrant to supply the czar. Peshe could speak seven languages, and fondly recalled taking family riverboat vacations to Germany. Velvel and Peshe had four children: sons Leib (born 1889), Abram (born 1891), and Jacob (born 1894), and a daughter who died in infancy (Figs. 4.1, 4.2). During the violence of the 1903 pogrom, Peshe recalled years later, they buried the family silver in the backyard and were offered shelter with a local Christian family. In the "celebrity sightings department," she also recalled going down the street to see Trotsky. (This would have been on May 10, 1920, when the Bolshevik leader's armored train stopped in Gomel during the Polish-Soviet War. He gave an impassioned speech about the threat of espionage and alleged atrocities by the Polish forces.)[25]

Jacob was not the first of the family to emigrate from Gomel. When the *Columbia* arrived in New York from Glasgow on July 8, 1906, among the passengers were seventeen-year-old "Leib Zutlin" and fifteen-year-old "Abram Zutlin." They were bound for the home of their aunt and uncle in

Lower Manhattan. It is probably not a coincidence that their journey to America occurred only six months after the 1906 pogrom—the second of their young lives. Leib and Abram did not stay in New York for long. They both relocated to Georgia. Though Abram's naturalization documents in 1911 and 1920 were under the name of "Abraham Zeitlin,"[26] by 1910 he was already using the name by which he would be known in America, Joe Allen.[27] Joe was then in Ocilla, in the central part of the state, working as a clerk in dry goods. The family story is that Joe adopted the surname because he had a friend named Allen whom he admired. His brother Leib does not appear to have used the Allen surname at first, yet he did change his given name to Louis; his Declaration of Intention to naturalize in 1910, and his Petition for Naturalization in 1912, both are under the name Louis Zeitlin.[28] Louis was then in Covington, Georgia, working as a clerk. Soon, however, both brothers became Allens. They served in the United States Army during the First World War as Louis Allen and Joe Allen. Louis was posted stateside; he served at Camp Wheeler near Macon, Georgia, and mustered out as a quartermaster sergeant in February 1919.[29] Joe Allen saw one year of overseas service, and mustered out as a corporal.[30]

Meanwhile, as war was brewing in Europe, Velvel and Peshe enrolled Jacob in a music conservatory in hopes of keeping him out of the army. He became a fine violinist. Russia declared war on Germany on August 1, 1914. Hostilities in Europe were certainly the reason why Jacob traveled east when he emigrated in 1915. The Trans-Siberian Railway connected to the Chinese Eastern Railway (a.k.a. Manchurian Railway). The latter had also been constructed by Russia, and the rail hub of Harbin in China's Heilongjiang Province was largely populated by Russian immigrants. From Harbin there was easy access to Chinese ports, travel to Japan, and to the passenger liners that crossed the Pacific.

On the *Manchuria* passenger manifest, Jacob had written that he was on his way to join Louis in Covington, Georgia, but he did not go to Georgia at first. On the eve of American participation in the First World War I, according to his draft card, Jacob Allen was living in Philadelphia, single, and his occupation was "electric welder." Three years later he was living with his wife Sarah Solomon Allen and infant son in Philadelphia, and working as a welder in the automobile industry.[31] They named their son Wolf, after his grandfather; he was called William throughout his life.[32] William had scarlet fever as a child, which caused him to lose his hearing in later life.

In 1918, Velvel died of cancer in Gomel.[33] Three years later, Peshe took ship for America to join her sons—according to family lore she brought with her little but her clothes and "a handful of diamonds."[34] She settled with Jacob and family in Philadelphia. Accustomed to her wealthy lifestyle in Gomel, Peshe was not prepared for the hardships of immigrant working-class life. To spare her feelings, each morning Jacob would dress in a three-piece suit and set off for work. At the factory he would change into his real work clothes and do his job as a welder. Then at day's end he would change back into his suit before returning to Peshe and the family.

In 1923, the couple had a second child, Israel, called Irvin. Yet, tragically, Sarah died in childbirth.[35] Peshe stepped in to help raise the boys. The family stayed in Philadelphia a few more years—they were still there in 1927 when Jacob submitted his Petition for Naturalization (which also requested an official name change from Zeitlin to Allen).[36] Yet by 1930 they had moved to Georgia to join Louis and Joe. They settled in the Sugar Hill District of Buford, about forty miles northeast of Atlanta.[37] Like his brothers, Jacob worked in retail dry goods. Jacob, the boys, and Peshe (now with an American name, Paulina) were still in Buford in 1940; with them was Jacob's new wife Anna (née Siegel), a thirty-two-year-old native of Brooklyn, New York (Fig. 4.3). They had married in Atlanta in 1936. Jacob and Anna had two more children in the 1940s, Evan and Marilyn. They moved again, this time to Elberton, Georgia. William and Irvin were already living on their own by then. In Elberton, the couple opened their own store, Jacob's Shoes, which remained a fixture in the town for decades.

Family remember Jacob as a quiet, kind man who liked sports and small town life. He had hoped to further his education in America, perhaps to become a civil engineer, but the responsibility of supporting his family did not allow it. Daughter Marilyn describes her mother Anna as a *baleboste*, a dynamo, a lively, smart woman who could do it all—a good housewife as well as a fine businesswoman. Yiddish was spoken in the home, Russian when the parents didn't want the children to understand. Religion was important to Jacob and Anna, yet there were only two or three Jewish families in Elberton. So every Sunday Jacob drove the children thirty-five miles to Anderson, South Carolina, where there was a Conservative Synagogue. While Evan and Marilyn joined with children from other towns all around northeast Georgia and western South Carolina to study their Jewish heritage, Jacob would sit and chat with the other fathers from their far-flung community.

By all accounts, Jacob—and Anna—worked very hard, perhaps too hard. They never took vacations, so it is fortunate that in those days in the South shops closed on Sundays and on Wednesday afternoons. Marilyn fondly recalls those Wednesdays, when her parents would close up the shop and leisurely walk home for a family lunch. Jacob Allen died in 1961, after suffering a heart attack.[38] Anna chose to stay in Elberton, and ran Jacob's Shoes until 1984, when she retired at age eighty. She then moved in with Marilyn and her family in New Orleans, and lived there until her passing in 2000.[39]

Peshe Zeitlin Allen naturalized as an American citizen in 1953, at the age of eighty-five. She died in 1966. Louis, who spent much of his career in Toccoa, Georgia, married Eva in 1922. They had no children. Joe married Sanie, another Russian immigrant, but the marriage ended in divorce. He later married Elizabeth Orr, born in Georgia, who was not Jewish. Peshe sat *shiva* for him. Joe and Elizabeth's daughter Beverly Bond still lives in Elberton.

Jacob strongly encouraged his children to pursue education, and all four earned college degrees and undertook postgraduate studies. William received his BA in chemistry from the University of Georgia in 1940, and then began a master's in the field at Georgia Tech. Irvin studied industrial hygiene (what we could call environmental engineering today) at Georgia Tech for his bachelor's degree (1942), and then commenced postgraduate studies there. Yet the Second World War intervened, and neither was able to finish an advanced degree. Evan went to Georgia Tech for his undergraduate studies, and Emory University for a combined MBA and engineering degree. After receiving her BA and MA from the University of Georgia, Marilyn earned a PhD from Loyola University in Chicago, all in psychology.

William married Jeanette (Jerry) Weinstein, a Georgia native, in June 1942. Soon thereafter William was recruited to work on the Manhattan Project, which led to the production of the atomic bomb. He and Jerry moved to Richland Village, Washington, where administrators and scientists working at the nearby Hanford Site were housed. Hanford was where the world's first plutonium production reactor was built. While there he had the opportunity to meet both Einstein and Oppenheimer. During the war, William never told Jerry anything about his work activities. He, too, was in the dark about many aspects of the Manhattan Project, as security concerns required that the work of its 120,000 employees be compartmentalized. Family members remember seeing William cry only twice: when his grandmother died, and when the atomic bomb was dropped on Hiroshima.

After the war, William took a job with American Cyanamid, a major chemical conglomerate, and he, Jerry, and daughter Sandra (Sandy) moved to New Jersey. Daughter Joan was born there. William worked at the company for thirty-five years and never missed a day, rising to become senior chemist and a lead designer on the world's first wastewater treatment facility. Joan describes him as a real Southern gentleman, a wine collector, and art photographer. He was a scuba diving enthusiast, and traveled the world to practice his hobby. On one such trip, to Australia in 1984, he died in a diving accident. His body was never found. He left his wife, two daughters, and two granddaughters.

During the Second World War, Irvin served as engineer on a tugboat at the Norfolk Naval Shipyard in Virginia. After the war, he worked as a chemical engineer, and also taught chemistry at Old Dominion University in Norfolk. Yet he suffered from severe bouts of depression for much of his life. He changed careers, and except for one year testing water resources for the State of Maryland, partnered with relatives operating small businesses—first a tobacconist's shop in Norfolk, and beginning about 1966 a billiard parlor in Baltimore. Irvin married Marcia Brewer (born 1927) and raised three sons: Benjamin, Ira, and Edward. Irvin was a lover of classical music and a fine singer—late in life he joined with his sons in barbershop quartet performances and competition. Marcia died in 1993, and Irvin later married Marjorie Goldstein. Irvin Allen died in 2004. He is survived by Marjorie, his sons and a daughter-in-law, and three grandchildren.

Evan came of age in the 1960s. He began a career in transportation systems, working for Lockheed, the Southern Railway (later the Norfolk Southern Railway), and the United States Railway Association (USRA)—the public-private corporation that created Conrail in the 1970s when the country was faced with a wave of private railway bankruptcies. He developed a unique expertise, and so founded a consulting company which specialized in regulatory economics for utilities. He sold the company in 2000. Evan and his wife Jo Ann have been married for forty-eight years, and live in Falls Church, Virginia. They have two children, Karen and Jeff, and three grandchildren. Evan's religious upbringing in Georgia had a great impact on him. Since his retirement, he has been actively involved in the Reform Judaism Movement, and has served as president of his synagogue.

After earning her doctorate, Marilyn relocated to New Orleans. She has an active clinical psychology practice, and also has taught in the Department of Psychiatry and Neurology at Tulane University Medical School. Married for forty-six years, she and her husband John E. Mendoza, a neuropsychologist, have two children, Jessica and Matthew.

2.

December 25, 1915
The Brothers Faingolid

25 – XII 1915 БР ФАЙНГАЛЬДЪ[40]

In Russian Cyrillic characters, and Arabic and Roman numerals. БР is short for БРАТЬЯ—"brothers."

The Faingolid brothers did not arrive together, but on ships three weeks apart. Irmia Faingolid, a twenty-year-old Jewish tailor from Kiev, Ukraine, arrived in San Francisco on December 25, 1915 aboard the *Persia Maru* from Yokohama. He was ordered deported as LPC—likely to become a public charge—but appealed. The Board of Special Inquiry agreed to land him on bond January 24, 1916, and to revisit his case in six months. Considering the date of the inscription, Irmia was certainly the carver (Fig. 4.4).

Irmia's seventeen-year-old younger brother Isaak Faingolid arrived on January 14, 1916 aboard the *Panama Maru*. Isaak listed his occupation as "auto driver"—in 1916! Isaak was also detained at Angel Island as LPC. During his arrival hearing, inspectors asked him why he had left Russia. Isaak replied, "Because I do not like to be in the army." He told them that his cousin Henry Rubin, a housepainter in Los Angeles, would support him

FIGURE 4.4 *Irmia Faingolid's (Jeremiah Feingold) passport photo. Courtesy Michael Walsh.*

FIGURE 4.5 *George (Isaak) and Amelia Fangold in the 1920s. Courtesy Robert Kolbert.*

while he learned English and found a job. Ever thorough, the immigration authorities interviewed Rubin, who had no idea Isaak was coming. Yet he agreed to take Isaak in, and sent money for the ticket. Isaak was landed after two weeks at Angel Island.[41] Within a year he had relocated to Fresno, and as Isaak Fangold was working as a truck driver for a junk hauling company.[42] By the time of the 1920 Census, he had changed his given name to George, and married Amelia Schwengel (Fig. 4.5). She was the daughter of a German-speaking Mennonite family from Russia, and had immigrated to Fresno with her parents as an infant (her name spelled Amalia) in 1902.[43] George and Amelia's daughter Eda Geraldine was born in 1920. In 1923, George

FIGURE 4.6 *Jerry and Augusta, c. 1965. Courtesy Michael Walsh.*

Fangold became a cattle buyer, a profession he remained in for the rest of his working life. He and Amelia divorced in 1945, yet both remained in the Fresno area. (Amelia remarried to Phillip Fleck.) Eda married Charles M. Kolbert (1905–1960), a career military man fifteen years her senior, and the couple had three children, Carolyn, Charles and Robert. George Fangold died in 1979, and Amelia in 1980.

Irmia (called Ermolai by his family) anglicized his name, and as Jeremiah (Jerry) Feingold settled in San Francisco. When he registered for his draft card at the outset of America's participation in the First World War, he was employed as a busboy at the posh St. Francis Hotel on Powell Street in Union Square. On July 21, 1919, he married Augusta Sukovitzen, who had immigrated with her family in 1906 (Fig. 4.6). The Sukovitzens were members of the Russian Molokan Church, a fundamentalist Christian sect founded in the seventeenth century by peasants who rejected the authority of the Russian Orthodox Church. The Molokans—Russian for "milk-drinkers"—were so-called for their practice of drinking milk on fast days, in defiance of Orthodox authorities. The sect was noted for its strict pacifism and communal organization, and a practice that incorporated a unique style of acapella religious singing. The Molokans faced persecution in Russia, and large numbers were exiled to the Caucasus region during the nineteenth century. In 1878, Russia wrested control of the Kars region from the Ottoman Empire,

FIGURE 4.7 *Jerry's and George's parents and sister Ida in Kiev, c. 1940. Courtesy Michael Walsh.*

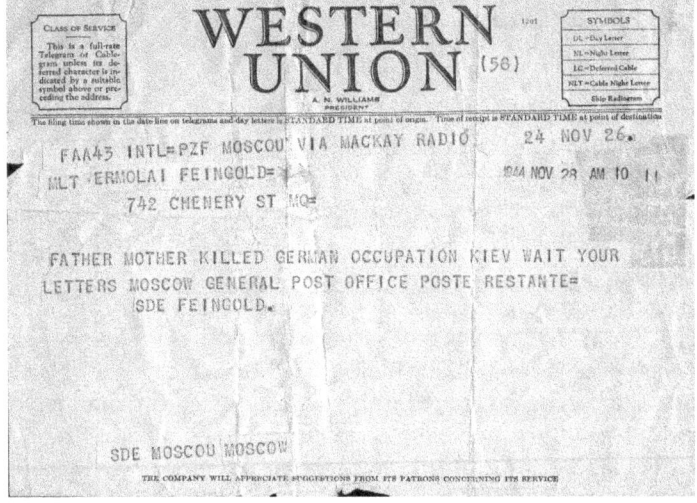

FIGURE 4.8 *Ida's 1944 telegram to Jerry. Courtesy Michael Walsh.*

and a large community of Molokans was exiled there (Kars is presently a province of Turkey). The Sukovitzens were among them. John Sukovitzen (c. 1850–before 1930) and Anastasia M. Kotov Sukovitzen (1862–1949) married before 1883, and had seven known children, all likely born in Kars.[44] Augusta was born around 1895. Before the First World War, several thousand Molokans immigrated to the United States, particularly California. The Sukovitzens and many others settled in the Potrero Hill neighborhood of San Francisco, where the First Russian Christian Molokan Church still stands.

At the time of the 1920 Census, Jeremiah worked as a factory leatherworker, and lived on Howard Street with Augusta and her daughter from a short previous marriage, six-year-old Nellie (Nadia).[45] Ten years later, he was a truck driver for a coal company, while Augusta worked in a laundry. At home on Potrero Hill was their nine-year-old daughter Sophie (Sonia), as well as Augusta's mother Anastasia and sister Frances. By 1940, Jeremiah had changed his occupation again, and worked as a cook's helper in a restaurant. He became a union man, joining the Miscellaneous Culinary Workers Union, Local 110 (AFL) by about 1936 or 1937.

As a blue-collar worker in San Francisco during an age of great labor ferment, Jeremiah was drawn to political activism. He joined the Communist Party as early as 1919, and in the ensuing decades was a spirited participant in the gamut of Party activities.[46] He wrote articles for Party newspapers and newsletters, taught courses like "History of Class Struggles in Czarist Russia" at the California Workers' School (established by the Party), lectured at other similar venues, was a longtime member of the International Workers Order (a mutual benefit and fraternal organization affiliated with the Party), and served on the executive committee of the Russian American Society (identified as a Communist-front organization in the 1955 list of the US Attorney General).[47] He had more than one brush with the law: in January 1930, Jeremiah was arrested after he and a group of other alleged Communists attempted to break up an anti-Soviet meeting at a hall on Sutter Street in San Francisco. During former Kerensky government official Victor M. Chernoff's address to the crowd, at a signal (the waving of a red handkerchief, appropriately) Jeremiah and approximately fifty others jumped up to protest, and a riot ensued. In the melee, a policeman was thrown from the stage and broke his hip. Jeremiah was one of seven arrested.[48] As the Great Depression took hold, the Communist Party established "Unemployed Councils" in multiple cities, to advocate for the poor. Jeremiah was a leader of the San Francisco branch, and on April 1, 1932 was arrested when he and two other activists led fourteen families to the Associated Charities and demanded relief. His case merited a front-page story in the *Western Worker*, under the strident headline, "90-Day Jail Term is Given Feingold: Leader of 'Frisco Jobless is Railroaded."[49] The story notes that a week after his arrest, "Feingold was 'taken for a ride' by plainclothes men and viciously slugged." At his trial he defended himself.

Tho constantly interrupted in a snarling manner by both judge and prosecutor, Feingold spoke for about ten minutes, denounced as lies the prosecution witnesses, explaining the work of the Unemployed Council and the struggle to obtain genuine relief, and concluded by charging his deliberate frame-up was proof that workers have no chance in a capitalist court.

Jeremiah's role in the 1934 San Francisco General Strike is not clear, but as the Communists were closely involved, we can be certain that he participated. By the Second World War period, he was on the FBI's radar. He merited a page on his activities in the "Comintern Apparatus (COMRAP)" files, compiled beginning in 1943 to ascertain the extent of collaborations among Soviet diplomats, the Communist International (Comintern), and the Communist Party of the US. Among several "aliases" for Jeremiah recorded by agents was—amusingly—"Hog Face."[50]

In 1947, Jeremiah opened his own business, called the Russky Kustar (Russian Craftsman), at 1200 Divisadero Street in San Francisco. Initially, he sold Russian wooden toys, but later branched into novelties, phonograph records, and books. His imported book business brought him serious trouble from the authorities during the anti-Communist hysteria of the McCarthy era. The US Post Office considered his shipments dangerous propaganda, and impounded many of them. The Northern California chapter of the American Civil Liberties Union took up Jeremiah's case. From the 36 annual report of the ACLU, for the period July 1, 1955 to June 30, 1956:

> Jeremiah Feingold, a San Francisco book dealer, has had many shipments confiscated, with books destined for such customers as the U.S. Army Language School, the University of California, and the Library of Congress. The P.O. [Post Office] applied a "rotten apple" criterion and held up whole lots which contained some propaganda. Titles by Shakespeare, Chekhov, De Maupassant, and Tolstoy were confiscated. After protests by the Northern California ACLU the department agreed to pass the non-propaganda material and to give the dealer an opportunity to make a case on material held. Latest word is that of a thousand titles held only thirty-eight have been passed.

Jeremiah was even subpoenaed to testify before a subcommittee of the US House of Representatives Un-American Affairs Committee, which held special session in San Francisco on December 10–11, 1956. Jeremiah was a major target of the first day's proceedings, and was verbally raked over the coals. The hearing was chaired by Representative Clyde Doyle of California, and two other House members were present (Harold H. Velde of Illinois and Gordon H. Scherer of Ohio), but most of the questioning came from Staff

Director Richard Arens. Arens was a leading figure in the anti-Communist movement in the later-1950s; his allegations of Communist associations against playwright Arthur Miller were especially widely reported. In 1960, he even questioned the patriotism of President Dwight D. Eisenhower, because the President had introduced his grandchildren to Russian Premier Nikita Khruschev.[51]

Arens began with a long series of tedious questions—over sixty of them—concerning Jeremiah's background, his business, his book suppliers, the dollar amounts of book purchases per year, and so forth. Perhaps Arens was attempting to lull Jeremiah into a false sense of security with softball questions, for then he suddenly launched into his favored subject:

Mr. Arens This gives us a fair idea. Mr. Feingold, are you now, or have you ever been, a member of the Communist Party?

Mr. Feingold Well, I am not now a member of the Communist Party. But so far as the past, my past. I would like to decline on the basis of the Fifth Amendment.

Arens and the Congressmen followed up with more than a dozen almost identical questions:

Were you a member of the Communist Party one year ago? One week ago? At any time since you were served with the subpoena to appear before this committee? At the time of your naturalization in 1945? Have you ever been under the discipline of the Communist Party? Jeremiah pleaded the Fifth to these questions, but when Representative Velde asked him to speculate about the future, his exasperation began to show.

Mr. Velde Mr. Feingold, do you expect to become a Communist Party member again as soon as you leave the jurisdiction of this committee?

[The witness confers with his counsel.]

Mr. Feingold I don't expect to become a Communist Party member. And that is—

Mr. Velde Do you expect at any time later in your life to become a member of the Communist Party?

Mr. Feingold God knows. Maybe I have only two or three days to live.

There was to be no let up. Arens had come very well prepared with documentation, including articles from Communist Party newspapers, and Jeremiah's own attestations of organization memberships on a certificate filed in 1952 for his business, in accordance with the Foreign Agents Registration Act. For example:

Mr. Arens Now I exhibit to you a document which is a reproduction of the *Western Worker*, the western organ of the Communist Party, U. S. A. In this *Western Worker* of January 28, 1935, datelined Fresno, Calif., [Jan. 23] the following appears:
   "Jerry Feingold spoke at the Lenin Memorial meeting held here Sunday night. The meeting was well attended. On Saturday night Comrade Feingold spoke at a meeting of small farmers and agricultural workers held at Kerman near here."
Kindly look at that article, if you please, sir, appearing in the Communist *Western Worker*, which is identified by its masthead as the western organ of the Communist Party, U. S. A., and tell this committee, while you are under oath, whether or not you are he, the Comrade Feingold, alluded to in that article.

   [The witness examines document and confers with his counsel.]

Mr. Feingold I still have the same answer, Mr. Counsel.

Additional questions pertained to Jeremiah's activities with the Russian American Society, and whether that organization had links with the Russian Consulate in San Francisco. Arens even asked whether he had ever carried information or documents to the Consulate, which Jeremiah vehemently denied. Jeremiah was also asked about his associations with other persons under investigation. A rather glaring omission in the day's hearing was mention of any specific books or periodicals sold at Russky Kustar that could be considered propaganda.

Jeremiah's advocacy for the rights of workers carried down the generations. Stepdaughter Nadia was administrative secretary to International Longshore & Warehouse Union President Harry Bridges for thirty-nine years, dating back to when the union was formed in 1937 to her retirement in 1976. Bridges had been born in Australia, and the US government attempted multiple times to use immigration laws to deport him. In 1939, the Angel Island Immigration Station was chosen as the site of the most widely reported of his deportation hearings. We can wonder whether Nadia was present at the hearing, held a dozen yards from where Jeremiah carved his name in 1915.

Nadia married George Walsh, a longshoreman and dedicated ILWU union member and organizer. The membership of Local #10 and later Local #34 elected him to a series of union leadership posts. He dedicated most of his efforts to gaining health care benefits for the workers. In 1950, he mounted an unsuccessful bid for California Secretary of State on the Independent Progressive Party ticket, and received 309,000 votes. The following year he received 30,000 votes in a bid to join the San Francisco Board of Supervisors.[52] Nadia and George's son Bernard (died 2002) was also a longtime Local #34 member. Son Michael is a teacher and sculptor in Ashland, Oregon.

Jeremiah Feingold died in 1974, and Augusta ten years later, both in San Francisco.

Though Jerry and George labored, scrimped, and saved to make their way in the US, at least they were safe on American soil. Their remaining family in Kiev was not so fortunate (Fig. 4.7). Immediately after the capture of the city by the Germans in September 1941, the extermination of its Jews was ordered by Generalmajor Kurt Eberhard, Commander-in-Chief of Kiev, SS Obergruppenführer Friedrich Jeckeln, Police Commander for Army Group South, and SS-Brigadeführer Otto Rasch, Commander of Einsatzgruppe C (one of the paramilitary forces tasked with implementing the Holocaust). The murders were carried out by German units assisted by local police auxiliaries. The Jewish victims—men, women, and children—were forced to strip naked, and then in groups were led into the Babi Yar ravine outside of Kiev and shot. In the two days of September 29th and 30th, 33,771 people were massacred in this way, in what was up to that point the worst single atrocity of the war. Jerry's and George's parents were among the victims. Babi Yar continued to be a killing ground during the rest of the German occupation, not only for Jews, but also for Russian communists, Ukrainian nationalists, Gypsies (Romani), and others. The total number killed is indeterminable; estimates range from 70,000 to 120,000. Sister Ida, happily, had escaped to Moscow. In late 1944, she sent a telegram to Jeremiah, informing him of the murders (Fig. 4.8). The day he received it, Jeremiah wrote a letter, in Russian, in response, though he apparently never sent it. It translates as follows:

San Francisco
November 28, 1944

Dear and beloved Idochka,
I received your telegram today. What a tragedy we are going through. Damned German murderers. It's difficult to write in such a terrible moment. You'll feel some relief my dear sister when you receive this letter. I can imagine how terrible those days were for you and I'll do everything I can to help you and all the Soviet country to survive this terrible time and completely beat the damned Germans, killers of the elderly and children. Dear Idochka, in a couple of days we'll send you a food package and in your response write us what clothes you need (give us the sizes) and we'll try to send them. Idochka please send me your photo, and the last photos of Mom and Dan, killed by the damned Germans.
That's all for now I just cannot write today,
Your loving brother Ermolai
My address is on the other side[53]

3.

M. Slavin

М СЛАВИНЪ[54]

Twenty-one-year-old Moisei Slavin spent one week on Angel Island in 1916. He arrived in San Francisco on March 20 aboard the *Tenyo Maru*, and was landed on March 27. He listed his occupation as "electrical engineer"— what we would call an electrician today. He was a Jew from Odessa, where he left behind his mother, Hana Slavin. He planned to join his brother Samuel Slavin in Buffalo, New York. The 1915 New York State Census places Samuel in Buffalo. He was then thirty years old, single, and working as a machinist. He had been two years in America. First World War draft records show Samuel living on West 115th Street in Manhattan along with his "brother Max Slavin." The 1920 Federal Census shows thirty-four-year-old Samuel and twenty-four-year-old Max living in Manhattan in a West 119th Street lodging house. Samuel was still a machinist, and Max is identified as an electrician. Though Max's arrival year is listed as 1914 instead of 1916, Max and Moisei are almost certainly the same person.

4.

Aleksandr Faitzer

АЛЕКСАНДР ФЕЙЦЕР[55]

Alexander Faitzer, Jr. arrived in San Francisco on May 2, 1920 aboard the *Mount Vernon* from Vladivostok, along with a companion, Samuel Model. The passenger list notes that both "Came to Island 5-8-20 11 AM," and "Left for deportation 6-19-20 6 PM." The cited cause for their detention was that neither had a passport.

The *Mount Vernon* was an enormous four-funnel passenger ship in the US Army Transport Service. It had been a German liner called the *Kronprinzessen Cecilie* until it was seized in Maine when the US entered the First World War. The ship's arrival in San Francisco was part of a clandestine effort on the part of the Allied Command to evacuate soldiers of the 60,000-strong Czechoslovak Legion from Siberia and return them to Europe. At the outset of the Great War, these Czech and Slovak soldiers had fought Austria-Hungary under Russian army command. Yet after the Bolshevik Revolution, when Russia withdrew from participation in the war, the new government decided to send them to Vladivostok to be transported by sea back to Europe. During the long trek the Legion revolted against the Bolsheviks, and began a military campaign against them along the route of the Trans-Siberian Railroad. When the *Mount Vernon* anchored in San

Francisco Bay, over 3,500 Czech and Slovak soldiers and officers were aboard, as well as nearly 700 German and Austrian prisoners-of-war who had been released by Russia to return home. The *Mount Vernon* was not a happy ship—400 of the crew quit in San Francisco, in protest of the poor working conditions. One German prisoner hanged himself on board. Contemporary accounts also note that while in port, there were numerous escapes and attempts to escape the ship. These were not limited to the POWs—one hundred of the Czechs and Slovaks escaped into the city when they had been given bathing privileges ashore, and immigration authorities vowed to track them down and deport them. The *Mount Vernon* left after several days, en route through the Panama Canal to Hamburg and Trieste.[56]

Records of the part of Faitzer and Model in this story, and the details of their detainment at Angel Island, are not available. They were not members of the crew.[57] It is suggestive that the *Mount Vernon* arrived May 2, but the pair was not sent to Angel Island until May 8. Their appeal to remain in the US was denied with the note, "The War Dept. will make arrangements for ret." Both were deported on the *Heffron*, another ship in the Army Transport Service that was used in the evacuation of the Czechoslovak Legion from Vladivostok. The *Heffron* headed back across the Pacific, first to Yokohama and then to Vladivostok to pick up the last elements of the Legion, departing there September 2, 1920. It then traveled to Trieste, Italy, where it disembarked its passengers on November 10, 1920. This ship was later acquired by the Weyerhauser Lumber Company, and sank after hitting mines off the coast of Ireland in 1942.

5.

Fedorov

ФЕДОРОВЪ[58]

Fedorov (also Fedoroff, Federoff, Federov) is a fairly common name. Half a dozen men (and several women) with this surname arrived at the port of San Francisco between 1910 and 1940, but only two appear to have been sent to Angel Island. Fedor Federoff (also Feodor Fedoroff), a native of Nizhny Novgorod in Central Russia, was a seaman who made multiple trips to San Francisco. After the Russian Revolution, ports were put on notice to be on the lookout for Bolshevik agents.[59] Fedor arrived on January 29, 1918 aboard the *Tula* from Vladivostok, was promptly sent to Angel Island on suspicion of being an anarchist, and was held until March 18. During the 1920 Census, he was a patient in the Marine Hospital in the Presidio of San Francisco, and his occupation was listed as "marine fireman." Twenty-two-year-old Alexander Fedoroff's plans were also influenced by events beyond his control. He arrived aboard the *Shinyo Maru* on July 15, 1923, one of a group of twenty-three Russian refugee students from Harbin. Yet the Quota

Act of 1921 was then in force, which set limits on the number of immigrants from other countries, and limited the monthly allowable number to 20 percent of that country's annual allotment. Earlier in July over 500 Russian refugees had arrived at the port of San Francisco, and so the monthly quota was already filled. Alexander and the other Harbin students, as well as another seventy-four Russians from the *Shinyo Maru*, were sent to Angel Island. They languished there for three months as they made appeal after appeal. In the end, all of the students were landed.[60]

6.

L. Ram
---- X [roman numeral 10]
1915

Л. РАМЪ
---- X
1915[61]

Twenty-three-year-old Lazar Ram, from "Ponevezh, Kovno, Russia," arrived in San Francisco on October 27, 1915, aboard the *Mongolia*. His listed destination was New York. He was traveling with Tanchum Joffe, another young man from his hometown. Ponevezh is Panevėžy in present Lithuania; in the late-nineteenth and early twentieth century, it was administered for Russia by the Kovno Governorate, which oversaw an extensive region from its capital in Kovno (Kaunas in Lithuanian). In 1915, the Jews of the western part of the Kovno Governorate, including both Kaunas and Panevėžy, were driven out by the Russian Army and exiled deep into Russia, which may be the reason for Lazar's journey to San Francisco. He and Tanchum were held at Angel Island for two days while awaiting a medical release, and were landed on October 29. This wasn't Lazar's first trip to the United States—he also had landed at New York on September 11, 1910 aboard the ship *Russia* from Libau, Latvia (he spelled his name then as Leiser Ram). New York records give a more specific hometown for Lazar. Ramygala is a small town within the county of Panevėžy, but twenty-four kilometers south of the city on the banks of the Upytė River. When he registered for the draft at America's entry to the First World War in 1917, Lazar was single, living in New York, and working at the Fleischman Distillery as a clerk. On his draft card, his date of birth is listed as November 22, 1892. He then moved south, and by 1919 was working as a clerk at the Capitol Department Store in Fayetteville, North Carolina (Fayetteville City Directory, and 1920 US Census). He was popular in the local Jewish community, and served as secretary of the Young Men's Hebrew Association (YMHA). His departure for Europe in July 1920 was noted in the Social News of the *Fayetteville Observer*:

Compliments to Lazar Ram who left last night for New York, where he will sail in a few days for Europe. The members of the Y.M.H.A. gave a grand ball last evening. The hall was beautifully decorated for the occasion, and delightful dance music was provided. Delicious refreshments were served, and about a hundred guests were present. After $2.45 the dance his friends accompanied Mr. Ram to the railway station. He goes to Lithuania for a stay, and represents several large firms in this country. He was a former secretary of the Y.M.H.A., and last evening he was made an honorary member. His friends presented him with a gold ring in token of their esteem.[62]

At some point, he moved to London (the name and birthday in the records are the same, yet the birth year is listed as 1891). The British National Archives has a listing for a naturalization certificate (BZ174) for Lazar Ram, dated 1932, and notes he had a daughter, Avithal Ram. The same year Lazar was back in Lithuania, working as bookkeeper and general clerk for the British Legation at Kaunas. He lived for many years in London's Bayswater district, and died in 1976.

7.

B. Kabushko
---- 1925

Б. КАБУШКО
---- 1925[63]

Boris Andronicovitch Kabushko arrived in San Francisco from Harbin on January 5, 1925, aboard the *Taiyo Maru*. He was born in Saratov, on the Volga in southern Russia on February 25, 1906. He was coming to join family, including father Andronik (1866–1941), mother Apollinaria (1875–1959), and sister Zoia, who had arrived October 7, 1923 in Seattle and settled in Los Angeles. Andronik initially worked as a laborer there. Another sister, Eugenia, arrived January 15, and lived in San Francisco.[64] At the time of the 1930 Census, Boris was in Corvallis, Oregon, perhaps taking courses at Oregon State University—or he may have been working on a farm, as two years later he earned his degree in agriculture at the University of California, Berkeley. His college yearbook says he was a member of the Blue and Gold Dairy Club and the Forum Club, and a resident of Hollywood.[65] He was married by the mid-1930s, and he and his wife Alexandra—also a native of Saratov—made multiple voyages to China and South America. One of the manifests mentions Boris was in the "dairy manufacturing" business. In 1941, he and Alexandra moved to Sao Paulo, where for over twenty years he served as Technical Director for Kibon, a company which grew to be Brazil's major ice cream producer.[66] Boris died in Florida in 1998.

8.

The Brothers I [and] A Vodniak
БР И А ВОДНАКЪ⁶⁷

БР is short for БРАТЬЯ—"brothers." The "I" (Cyrillic И) and "A" (Cyrillic A) in the inscription are written as a single stylized monogram, with the horizontal stroke in "A" placed within the right portion of the "И." Ionia and Abraham Vodniak arrived on the *Nippon Maru* on December 8, 1917, and were detained at Angel Island as LPC—likely to become public charges. In fact, they were on their way to join their father Ishiker Vodniak, a tailor then living in Vineland, New Jersey, who had immigrated about 1913.[68] The family was originally from Kaniv, a picturesque town on the Dnieper River in central Ukraine. Their mother and three other siblings were also en route, but crossed the Pacific on another ship, and did not reach San Francisco until December 19.[69] It appears that the suspicions of the immigration officials were aroused by the arrival of the two unaccompanied boys, listed on the passenger manifest as seventeen and eleven years old, respectively.

A Board of Special Inquiry was convened.[70] Ionia explained that before making the journey to America, he and Abraham had resided with their mother, elder sister, and two younger brothers in Ekaterinoslav (present Dnipropetrovsk, Ukraine's fourth largest city). Their father sent money every few months for their support, and Ionia, Abraham, and elder sister Ita also worked. Besides their father, two older brothers were also in America, working in Philadelphia. Ionia told the immigration inspectors that since travel funds from his father had not arrived in time, his and his brother's passage from Yokohama had been advanced by the Hebrew Aid Society. Even though Abraham's true age was in fact fifteen, representatives there advised him to claim he was younger to qualify for half-fare! The Board noted the names and addresses of their father and brothers in America, and deferred a decision on the case until further investigation could be made. Meanwhile, upon their arrival in San Francisco, their mother and three siblings were also detained at Angel Island. Once Ishiker Vodniak had been interviewed in Philadelphia, and had wired money to cover transportation for all six family members, they were landed together on December 31.

It was very common for immigrants to take more "American-sounding" names to gain acceptance in US society. The Vodniaks went much further than most. "Vodniak" was changed to "Woodnick," and every member of the family—except Abraham—adopted a new given name as well. Family head Yeshia (Ishiker) Vodniak became Samuel (Sam) Woodnick, and wife Chaya became Clara Woodnick. The two eldest sons already in America, Schmiel Leib (Schmilek) Vodniak and Yankel Vodniak, called themselves Louis (Lou) and Jacob (Jake), respectively.[71] Ionia (Joine) became Joseph

(Joe), Ita became Edith, and the two youngest boys, Israel and Mordche (Max), became Sidney and Martin. However, taking new names did not mean abandoning their cultural and religious heritage: the Woodnicks were strict Orthodox Jews who kept a kosher household.

The Woodnicks were a family of hardworking craftspeople. Sam was a tailor, who in 1917 worked in a sweatshop with ten other garment workers, doing contract work for a firm in New York. He netted about $25 per week. Lou was a barber. Jake was an upholsterer, and around 1921 opened an upholstered furniture factory with a partner in Reading, Pennsylvania.[72] Joseph, Abraham, and Sidney eventually all became upholsterers as well. Before her marriage in 1922, Edith was a factory worker. When he grew old enough to strike out on his own, Martin took a different path. After his marriage, he moved to Wilkes-Barre, Pennsylvania, and worked in his wife's family's grocery business.

Family lore has it that Joseph was initially unhappy in America, and attempted to return home to Europe. But the First World War was still raging, and he was unable to cross through Germany. He rejoined the family, and in the late-1910s had a job selling window shades.[73] He remained restless, and enlisted in the US Army in 1920, and served for three years.[74] He then went to work with his brother Jake in Reading. There he met Bertha Levine. They married in 1925, and in 1928 had a daughter, Claire. Joe worked as foreman, and later manager, of the business through 1933.[75] After 1933 they moved to New York, where the couple ran a combined upholstery and furniture retail business, and lived in the Washington Heights neighborhood of upper Manhattan.[76] Bertha died in 1977 in Florida, and Joe in Houston, Texas in 1986. Claire Woodnick Gherman lives in Houston, where she is a widowed mother of two sons, a grandmother, and a great-grandmother.

Abraham (Abe) found work in a carpenter's shop, according to the 1920 Census. At the time, Sam, Clara, and all their unmarried children lived at 1741 53rd Street in the Parkside neighborhood of West Philadelphia. Lou and his family lived nearby. In the first decades of the last century, residents of Parkside and neighboring Wynnefield were predominately German and Eastern European Jewish immigrants. Abe's bride-to-be, Mary Eadles, lived four blocks away on Paxon Street. They married in 1924 and had a son, Seymour. Abe was having trouble finding and keeping jobs as an upholsterer, and money was tight, so the couple moved in with Mary's parents, Max and Ida Eadles.[77] Max was a sheet metal worker. Seymour remembers 1727 Paxon Street as a happy home, bustling with life and the comings and goings of many relatives. He learned to speak Yiddish before he spoke English.

In the search for work, Abe moved his little family frequently in the ensuing years. In 1928 they moved to Reading, where Abe went to work with Jake and Joe. They stayed five years, before returning to the Eadles' in Philadelphia. Seymour has vivid memories of Philadelphia, and selling papers at the trolley stop for three cents each. They left Philadelphia again in the mid-1930s, this time for New York. There they lived only a few blocks from Joe and his family in Washington Heights. Daughter Doris was born there in 1935. They then moved back to Philadelphia once again, and stayed long enough for Seymour to finish elementary school. In 1937, Abe moved the family once more, to Washington, DC. This time he had a lucky career break. The owner of an upholstery shop where Abe was working retired, and he invited Abe to purchase the business over time. The shop was successful, and provided the family a good living for three decades. However, in 1968 it was burned out in the riots following the assassination of Martin Luther King, Jr. Abraham Woodnick died in Maryland in 1984. Mary Woodnick died in 1996.

Seymour enlisted in the army in 1943, and became an armored car radioman in the 43rd Cavalry Reconnaissance Squadron, part of the 3rd Cavalry Group (Mechanized) under the command of General George S. Patton. He encountered virulent anti-Semitism in the army. Radiomen with the top qualifying grades in training were promised promotion to Technician 4th Grade Sergeant, yet when he joined his unit at Fort Gordon, Georgia, he was the only one denied that rank—he was made Technician 5th Grade Corporal. When he questioned why, the First Sergeant of the company told him, "No Jew boy will ever make sergeant in my outfit." Seymour took the issue to the company commander, who replied that what the First Sergeant said is the way it is. "Corporal, you're dismissed." His barracks mates also subjected him to merciless harassment. Despite the hardships, Seymour always did his duty. The unit landed in Normandy on August 7, 1944, and until VE Day—May 9, 1945—was in almost continuous, harrowing combat as it raced across France and into Germany. The casualty rate was high. In one engagement, the driver sitting right beside Seymour was shot in the head and killed instantly. Except for a period he spent in hospital for burn treatment after an open drum of gasoline exploded in camp (ignited by a fellow soldier burning a "Dear John" letter), Seymour remained with the unit through late 1944. His war ended on December 19, just a few days after the start of the Battle of the Bulge. He was part of a four-man patrol that crossed the Saar River near Oberleuken to carry out reconnaissance. They were discovered by the Germans, and in the ensuing firefight Seymour was wounded in the arm. He received the Purple Heart and was sent home.

After the war, Seymour married Sonia (Sonny) Schoen, and they began a happy life together. He studied interior and furniture design at the Philadelphia Museum School of Art, and began a successful career as a designer and executive in the furniture industry. Sonny died in 1992, and the same year Seymour retired. He turned to a pursuit he had loved since high school—painting. Remarried now, Seymour and his wife Jackie live in Lynchburg, Virginia, where his oils and watercolors are frequently exhibited in local arts centers and galleries.[78] Gatherings with family—two children, four grandchildren, and four great-grandchildren—are a source of happiness.

Doris's earliest memories are of the family's apartment on Kenyon Street in Washington, DC. When she was five, she contracted rheumatic fever, and spent two years in a convalescent home in Maryland. This delayed her start in school. By the time she returned home, Seymour had already left for military service. As a teenager, Doris worked part time alongside her father in the upholstery shop. On a blind date in 1954, she met Saul Abelman. They married, and raised three children together. Unfortunately, Saul died young, at the age of fifty-one. Doris later married Julian Kline, who had two sons of his own. Now retired in Florida, in 2012 they celebrated thirty-two years of marriage. Together they have nine grandchildren.

9.

C. Nizenkoff

К. НИЗЕНКОВ[79]

Four members of the Nizenkoff family arrived in San Francisco together aboard the *Shinyo Maru* from Harbin on September 4, 1930, and all were sent to Angel Island. Family patriarch Constantin Zaharovich Nizenkoff, his wife Nina, and their twenty-one-year-old daughter Anna were not

FIGURE 4.9 *The Nizenkoffs in Russia, c. 1900. Constantine Z. is sitting front left. Courtesy Erik Nizenkoff.*

FIGURE 4.10 *The Nizenkoffs in America, c. 1936. Constantine Z. at back right, Constantine C. at back left, Anna at front right, and Nina holding Ted at front left. Courtesy Erik Nizenkoff.*

detained for long. After they passed their medical examinations, they were landed on September 8. However, his twenty-two-year-old son Constantin Constantinovich had a heart condition, the result of contracting rheumatic fever as a child. Thus he was initially excluded by immigration inspectors as a "person having physical dis. which may affect ability to earn living." He appealed, and was permitted admission once he posted a "Public Charge Bond" of $500; he was not landed until September 22. Constantin C. is thus the more likely writer of this faint inscription.

The Nizenkoffs were from the middle Volga River region in the southeastern part of European Russia. Constantin Z., born in 1881 in the village of Krasnoye Poseleniye, not far from the city of Samara, was an affluent farmer and landowner (Fig. 4.9). He settled in the countryside near the city of Simbirsk (present Ulyanovsk), about 100 miles northwest of Samara. The two children were born there, Constantin C. in the village of Pavlovka, and Anna in nearby Neklyudovka. According to family lore, their mother, Constantin Z.'s first wife, committed suicide. In 1923, Constantin Z. married Nina Alexander. Nina was born in 1890 in Sarapul, a city on the Kama River, a tributary of the Volga. One of fourteen children to a pharmacist and his wife, Nina received an excellent education in St.

Petersburg, and became an agricultural chemist carrying out soybean research. She traveled in lofty circles in the capital; she later said that one of her childhood friends was a Russian princess! The Nizenkoffs' reasons for emigration are not entirely clear, but their considerable wealth and connections with the elite (Constantin Z.'s sister married a colonel in the Imperial Army) would have made them targets of the Bolsheviks. That Simbirsk was Lenin's hometown could not have helped. The family was not able to take much with them when they boarded the Trans-Siberian Railway and began their journey out of the country. Hyperinflation in the first years after the Revolution had made the currency nearly worthless.

Constantin Z. started farming in Cotati, California (in Sonoma County), but the business soon failed. He then moved the family to Washington state, where he purchased twenty acres in Redmond and became a successful egg farmer. (Twenty acres in Redmond, where the Microsoft Corporation now has its headquarters, would be quite an asset today!) The Nizenkoffs welcomed a new addition to the family in 1933, when Nina gave birth to their son Theodor (Ted) (Fig. 4.10). Yet the marriage ended in divorce. Constantin Z. died in Seattle in 1948.

Constantin C. enrolled at the University of Washington, and studied to be a civil engineer. He married Tamara (Tama) Nevolin in 1937, and their son Victor was born the following year. Constantin C. was a lifelong gun hobbyist and an excellent marksman. During the Second World War, he tried to enlist in the army, but was refused due to his heart condition. Instead, he spent the war years working as an engineer at the Mare Island Naval Shipyard. His marriage with Tama ended in divorce.

Tama married engineer John W. Breed, and the couple moved with Victor to the San Francisco Bay Area, and later Texas. She died in Alabama in 1999. Victor took his stepfather's surname—Stanley Victor Breed is a retired firefighter, and now lives in Millbrae, California.

Constantin C. remarried as well, and he and wife Frances lived for many years in Chicago, where he worked for the city as a civil engineer. They retired to Yuma, Arizona, where Constantin C. died in 1990. Frances shared her husband's shooting hobby. On December 3, 1994, while she was performing duties for the Yuma Trap and Skeet Club at a public shooting range, she was shot dead by an unknown assailant. Her body was found a week later. Her murder has never been solved.

Nina moved with Ted to Seattle in the early 1940s. Some of Ted's strongest childhood memories are of their one-room apartment there. Though Nina was a chemist in Russia, with her limited English skills she worked as a seamstress in America. By Ted's own account, he was "acting up" during high school, so Nina sent him to live with Anna. Anna had married Theodor Klemushkin, another Russian immigrant, and settled in San Francisco, where their son William was born in 1941. Nina later joined them there; she died in 1969. Ted stayed in Northern California, and became a successful small businessman. He first operated a dry cleaning supply company, and later shifted over to the concrete business. Once divorced, in 1975 he married Sharon Fernandez, and they settled in Watsonville, in Santa Cruz County. Sharon died in 2013, and Ted the following year. Their two sons both work in the high tech industry.

10.

Bukovsky

БУКОВСКИЙ[80]

When Admiral Oskar Stark sailed the remnants of the White Russian fleet into Manila Bay, nineteen-year-old Michael Boochkovsky was among the Ice March survivors aboard.

The Russians in Manila were offered asylum in the United States. On July 1, 1923, a group of 526 of the refugees, including Michael, arrived in San Francisco aboard the United States Army Transport ship *Merritt*, and were sent for immigration processing at Angel Island.[81] Available records for Michael are few. The passenger manifest shows that he was a native of Kamaniets-Podilskyi, a city in western Ukraine. He moved to Oakland, California, where in 1925 he was a car cleaner, and later worked as a messenger for the public library.[82] A 1928 *Oakland Tribune* article of upcoming events announced that he would play violin solos at the library's annual Christmas party, which was also to feature "a puppet show, old English games, singing, and special dance numbers."[83]

11.

Jacob Neufeld

ЯКОБ НЕЙФЕЛД[84]

There were *three* Jakob Neufelds in detention at Angel Island at the same time in 1930. They came from two different families, but their experiences and reasons for immigrating were similar. All were German Mennonites, whose ancestors had settled in southern Ukraine at the invitation of Catherine the Great beginning in the late-eighteenth century. The two largest farming settlements they established were the Chortitza and Moloschna colonies. The colonies prospered, and the residents lived peacefully and mostly without interference from the Russian government. Yet the First World War and the Russian Revolution brought chaos, depredations, and famine to the region. A wave of Mennonite emigration ensued. With the assistance of overseas Mennonite communities, thousands moved to Canada, the United States, Mexico, and South America. Others moved further west, into Siberia and Central Asia, but gained only a temporary respite as the forced collectivization of farms that began in the late 1920s caused catastrophe in the countryside.

Jakob P. Neufeld, aged seventy-three, his wife Helena, and their nine children arrived in San Francisco aboard the *Asama Maru* on October 9, 1930.[85] Eldest among the children was Jakob J., then twenty years of age. The passenger manifest shows the two-step westward migration of the family. The places of origin for Jakob P. and Helena are noted as Sparrau and Ladekopp, respectively. These were two of the fifty-seven villages of the Moloschna Colony in Ukraine. All of the children, on the other hand, were born in "Selo Raevka, Pawlodar." Pavlodar is a province in northeastern Kazakhstan. A Mennonite settlement had been established there in 1906, and Rayevka was one of its thirteen villages. Jakob P. and his family were held for more than three weeks on Angel Island. Immigration inspectors labeled them LPC, and in addition cast doubt on Jakob P.'s physical health and mental competence. Members of the Mennonite community in Shafter, California, interceded on the family's behalf, and they were finally admitted after posting a bond.

The third Jakob was Jakob Heinrich Neufeld, aged twenty-one, from Tiegerweide. He was traveling with his younger brother Abram and sister Maria, and arrived on the same ship as the larger Neufeld family. Tiegerweide was another of the Moloschna villages. No intermediate stop is noted for the trio. Their stay at Angel Island was relatively brief—they were held as LPC, but released after five days. They were joining their mother Aganetha B. Neufeld and brothers Johann H. and Peter H., who had arrived the previous month on the *Shinyo Maru*. They were then bound for Reedley, California.

While it is unlikely that patriarch Jakob P. roughly scratched his name on the barracks wall with the tip of a knife, either of the two younger Jakobs can be considered candidates.

12.

Y. Binev

Я. БИНЕВЪ[86]

Yankel Bineff, aged twenty-six, arrived in San Francisco on the *Manchuria* on October 6, 1915. Yankel also used the surname Goliman, which was perhaps his first wife's name; on the passenger manifest, Goliman is crossed out and Bineff added. He was held at the Immigration Station for medical observation, and admitted on October 11. Yankel was a native of Tiraspol, a city on the eastern bank of the Dniester River in present-day Moldova. His father Labish

FIGURE 4.11 *Jack and Bella Benoff with son Edward. Courtesy Ethan Benoff.*

was a drayman there.[87] Moldova is a small landlocked country tucked between Romania and Ukraine, and at that time was part of the Russian empire. The family didn't have much and worked hard for what they had. Yankel later frequently joked about how delicious the watermelons were, and they were only one kopek—but no one had a kopek. Yet he considered himself fortunate, as the community in which he lived was free from anti-Semitism and the gentiles there kept the pogroms from reaching their Jewish neighbors. Yankel's second wife Bella was not so fortunate: she came from Kishenev (now known as Chişinău), capital of the Moldovan region, where violent pogroms against the Jews occurred between 1903 and 1905.

Yankel was conscripted into the Russian Army, and was eventually posted to Harbin, China. It was from there that he set out for America, leaving his first wife Perla (Pelia) Goliman and a son and a daughter behind, and giving as his contact in America his brother Shoil Binioff in Kansas City, Missouri.

There is a later notation on the passenger manifest that he naturalized as a US citizen in Philadelphia. The alien registration number in the notation matches the April 26, 1949 naturalization record for Yankel Benoff (born January 1, 1890) filed there. The record also records his formal name change to Jack Benoff (a logical change, as Yankel is a Yiddish diminutive for Jacob). Jack and his second wife Bella settled permanently on Manton Street in Philadelphia, and had two children, Louis (1925–1974) and Edward (born 1933) (Fig. 4.11). Jack worked with his sister Esther's husband William Krimsky as a housepainter, and for a time was a traveling salesman.[88] Jack died in 1961, and Bella in 1970.

Edward Benoff continues to practice law in the Philadelphia region in the firm he founded in 1961, and graciously contributed his reminiscences for this entry. When informed of the existence of the Angel Island inscription by his father, Edward wrote, "It is with a smile that I learned he had left a permanent impression other than with me." The family spoke Yiddish at home, and eventually English. Jack taught himself to read English and read the daily newspaper faithfully. Edward describes his father as short of stature but very strong, and possessed of a spectacular head of silver hair.

> I was told that my dad was a good dancer and particularly liked the Russian and Yiddish folk dancing. When my father danced with my aunt they were truly something to watch ... He was very much involved with daily happenings. Every day we would gather around the radio to hear the news and the commentators. This was particularly true during the war. My brother was in the Second Marine Division serving in the South Pacific. He was a corpsman and was among the first troops to go into Nagasaki. He helped treat the civilian population. He died at age forty-nine of a brain tumor. We always felt that there was some relationship to his service in Nagasaki.

When Jack's two children from his first marriage came of age, they too immigrated to the US to join him. Wolf Binieff (Willie Benoff) married Ida Stoler in 1934 and had two children, and Faiga (Fay) Benoff married Lou Jacobs in 1935 and had one daughter. Louis and wife Lorraine Snyder had two daughters. Edward and his late wife Elaine (née Rosenthal) raised three sons and have seven grandchildren.

RUSSIAN POETRY FROM *RUSSKII GOLOS*

The following two poems were published in the *Russkii Golos* [Russian Voice] newspaper in Harbin, northern Manchuria, in October 1923. Harbin, now the capital of China's Heilongjiang Province, was little more than a fishing village in 1898 when the Russians gained the concession to build the Chinese Eastern Railway, which was then linked with the Trans-Siberian railway. The city grew rapidly, and for a time was home to the largest Russian community in the Far East. After the Russian Revolution in 1917, Harbin was flooded with refugees. While some remained for decades, others moved elsewhere, to Chinese cities like Qingdao, Tianjin, and Shanghai, or to third countries. The Russian texts of the two poems below are not available; the translations by someone identified only as A.Y.G. were included in diplomatic correspondence dated November 1, 1923, from American Consul C.C. Hansen to the Secretary of State in Washington, on the subject of "Russian Student Emigrants to the United States of America." The author of the first was Nicolas Masloff, one of twenty-three Russian students who arrived with other Russian immigrants aboard the *Shinyo Maru* on July 15, 1923. They were detained at Angel Island because their names did not appear on the official immigration quota lists for July. The students were finally admitted in October. The second poem is a satiric look at the quota system and its effects.[89]

13.

In a country free, humane and honorable,
Where all men are brothers and liberty is.
We sit behind bars and watch with anguish
The sea, mountain and the azure ebb-tide.
We sit and grieve for our great steppes,
For the green forests where the nightingale sings.
For the Russian soul, so simple and clear to us,
For the glory and power of former Russia . . .

Oh, the fate of the Russian emigrant is very bitter.
He sees much trouble if he leaves without precautions,
He will come to Angel Island behind the bars to sit.
And be watched, and the guard's eye to watch after him.
He will curse emigration, Angel Island and
Will remember the League, the League of Nations,
And will send it to the devils.[90]

14. Quota

(Little feuilleton)

We did not invent the quota.
This is an American contrivance.

And it is established there, behind the Great Ocean.
But the peace of mind of the residents of Harbin
   depends on that American quota more than on anything else!
Until the quota is filled the Harbiner is in constant agitation.
His head during the day and night feverishly works in the sole direction:
   -"How to get away to America?"-
This fundamental question consists of several other questions:
   -"From who to get the letters of recommendation?"-
This is not an easy question.
Persons, known to the Consulate, before they would give a letter,
   try everything to refuse that favour.
Beginning with "not at home" up to "I beg your pardon, I don't know
      you!"
Then:
How to get the visa out of turn?
If one will wait his visa in the "tails" of turns,
   then he won't get his visa before the "advent of the Messiah"
   when probably the journey to the United States will lose its sense.
Here one needs to recall all his acquaintances and to find out:
   Whether or not the thread of these acquaintances reaches
   the "senior assistant of the junior secretary of the American
      Consulate?"
And finally the most damned question:
   "How to get money for the journey?"
Go around the city with a subscription list?
It's impossible to collect in such a way more than five roubles
   (Thank God even for that!)
Organize a concert or dance?
This surely will bring a deficit.
It's believed that the surest way is: the dark night, a mask, a revolver
      and:
   "Stop, hands up! Will you please lend me some money for
   my journey to America? . . ."
But it's also pretty easy to get by that way not into America,
   but into "not so distant places!"
While the Harbiner worries about all those questions,
   his friends consciously try to impair his nerves.
Every day returning from the office his wife informs him:
   "Have you heard that Nikolay Femistoklovitch is leaving for
      America?"
"Who is that Nikolay Femistoklovitch?"
"I don't know, they talked about him in the office . . ."
The wife's mother at the evening tea, after the sixth cup,
   sighing with difficulty and directing her eyes to

the distant corner of the ceiling, says very meaningfully:
"They received a letter from Mihail Vasilievitch from America.
He writes, that he got a good job . . . He gets six dollars every day
. . ."
". . . Mihail Vasilevitch?"
. . . How? my neighbor told me . . .
. . . [what do] we have to do with Mihail Vasilievitch, we
don't know him and devils with him if he got a job! . . ."
"Why, yes," indifferently says the wife's mother, filling the eighth cup
with tea,
"I said it simply to tell you something . . ."

But how nice and quiet it is in Harbin after the quota is filled!
It's filled now and thank God it's filled up to July next!
For half a year you can forget about references, visa
and about organizing a concert!
Let all these questions bother you in July, but before that awful time
you may sleep quietly, and cheer yourself with suggestions:
My God, July is so far off still, it's impossible that I wouldn't collect
several roubles?
Nonsense, it's impossible!
I won't smoke, won't go to the movies, won't drink.
Sure, I will have some money!
And up to July your wife won't inform you of the names of persons
who left for America,
of those of whom they speak in the office,
and your wife's mother won't talk at the evening tea of those who
left for America
and who got a job where they pay them six dollars per day! . . .
For half a year thoughts of a Harbiner will be released from the press of
the America "question"
and their heads will be able to work in any direction
because the quota is already filled!!!

FINE[91]

SOUTH ASIAN WALL INSCRIPTIONS

15.

Tara Singh, Lahore
... nine months at ...
.... jail.
Tara Singh
19 June 1936[92]

لاہور تر سنگھ
... ਨੌ ਮਹੀਨੇ ਤੇ .... ਜੇਲ
ਤਾਰਾ ਸਿੰਘ
19 ਜੂਨ 1936

The first line is in Urdu script, which is in use primarily in Pakistan today, while the rest is in Gurmukhi script used by the Sikhs of Punjab (Fig. 4.12). The Punjab region straddles the border between Pakistan and India (both countries have states with the name). Tara Singh is a relatively common name among Sikhs. Singh is the surname (or middle name) adopted by all males initiated into the Sikh community, and Tara is a common given name. Multiple people with this name arrived at the port of San Francisco between 1910 and 1940, headed for the US or Canada. The writer of this inscription appears in the Tulare County Sheriff's Office and Jail Records for January 30, 1936, with the notation, "Enroute to Angel Island." He is described as a

FIGURE 4.12 *Tara Singh inscription in Urdu and Gurmukhi.*

forty-five-year-old laborer who had lived in the county for twenty years, and in the United States for twenty-three years. The inscription dates to six months later, which in part explains the partially deciphered portion of the text. He was presumably at Angel Island for immigration investigation or deportation, but the common nature of his name makes it difficult to trace him further. The city of Lahore is now the capital of Pakistan's Punjab Province, but before partition in 1947 was also an administrative division that encompassed areas that are now on the Indian side of the border.

16.

One hundred days
Tara Singh
Sur Singh Village
Lahore Division[93]

ਸੈ ਦਿਨ
ਤਾਰਾ ਸਿੰਘ
ਸੁਰ ਸਿੰਘ
ਲਹੌਰ

In Gurmukhi script. Sur Singh was in the Lahore Division before partition, but is now on the Indian side of the border, in the Tarn Taran District. It is located on Punjab State Highway 21, southwest of Amritsar, and northwest of Patti. The city of Lahore is to the west. The writer of this inscription is likely the same as in the previous one, but that is not certain.

17.

Sayyat – '17

সায়াত – ১৭[94]

In Bengali script. A merchant seaman named Nurdin Sayad arrived in San Francisco on the SS *Matoppo* on October 2, 1917, and this inscription is very likely by him. Nurdin is a variant of Nuruddin, a name of Arabic origin that means "light of religion."[95] Bengal is a Muslim majority region, and most names have Arabic origins. Sayad is described in the crew manifest as a "lascar sailor." This was in inclusive term for crew members from South Asia, Southeast Asia, or the Middle East who were employed on European ships. South Asian lascars just prior to the First World War were mostly Bengali.[96] The *Matoppo* was a freighter owned by the Ellerman & Bucknall Steamship Company, and was in service from 1905 to 1930.

PUNJABI POETRY FROM *GHADAR DE GUNJ*

The revolutionary Ghadar Party, based in San Francisco, was founded in 1913 with the aim of overthrowing the British in India. Its core membership was made up of students and political exiles, while much of its support came from the Sikh laborers and farmworkers in California, the Northwest, and western Canada. The party newspaper, also called *Ghadar* [Revolt], featured vernacular songs and poems that were penned by the revolutionaries to drum up support, but sometimes also incorporated the perspectives of the typical immigrant. The poems and songs were so popular that the party published them separately in several short collections, called *Ghadar de Gunj* [Thunder of Revolt], beginning in 1914. The pamphlets were written in the Gurmukhi script of the Sikhs, but Urdu and even Hindi editions of some were also produced. The authors had their eyes firmly set on India, and most of the poems and songs are political diatribes. Yet some are more general laments about poverty, oppression, and prejudice that speak to the immigrant experience.

18.

The path to the heart is through the heart,
   I come from the heart to you.
The Ghadar workers have strung together choice flowers,
   I am a beautiful, fragrant garland.
From the collected breath of the compassionate ones,
   I have made a river of nationalism flow.
Selecting pearls from the seven seas,
   I have created a precious necklace of verse.[97]

19.

Collecting potatoes from farms we have not earned much,
   our knees bent with hard labour;
Lifting timber our backs are bent,
   and our youth turned to old age;
Labouring wages don't make us rich,
   and for years we have born insults,
Scattered from China to Africa,
   we are hurt and have gone down over the years.

What have we earned in coming to America,
    having left our country for years now?
Everywhere they hate us, calling Coolie! Coolie!
    We are not ashamed enough.[98]

20.

Goras don't like blacks—
    better show what black hands are capable of.
Why work for the Gora bosses?
    let us return to our country!
Let's go back as part of the Ghadar party,
    and dedicate ourselves to liberation from serfdom.
What have we gained from sojourn abroad except frustrations,
    even as years have passed?[99]

Gora (gaura) is a Hindi and Indo-Aryan racial epithet for Europeans or light-skinned persons.

21.

Some push us around, some curse us.
Where is our splendor and prestige today?
The whole world calls us black thieves
The whole world calls us "coolie"
Why doesn't our flag fly anywhere?
Why do we feel low and humiliated?
Why is there no respect for us in the whole world?[100]

22.

My darling sons, come to the battlefield
Carrying the power of knowledge in one hand and a sword in the other.
May a happy heart, contented mind, healthy body like a lion be yours.
Extinguish the fire of selfishness
By pouring over it the water of patriotism.[101]

OTHER INSCRIPTIONS, 1910–1940 239

WALL INSCRIPTIONS IN EUROPEAN LANGUAGES

23.

> 19 – 17/10 – 15
> M. Jensen
> Danmark
> Aarhus[102]

Twenty-two-year-old merchant seaman Martin Jensen arrived in San Francisco aboard the *Henrik* on October 10, 1915. The manifest confirms he was a native of Aarhus, Denmark's second-largest city and its major port. Martin and three other sailors were stowaways who had boarded the ship in Santa Rosalia, Mexico. Immigration Inspector Crawford wrote, "Four <4> Stowaways ordered to Island." All four were held as LPC. Martin had no money at all, and listed no contacts in the US. Yet he and the three others were all admitted on October 23. The way Martin carved the date on the barracks wall is unusual, but it is certainly October 17, 1915.

24.

> Felipe Lerena
> Spain
>
> Felipe Lerena
> España[103]

Twenty-year-old Felipe Mauricio Lerena arrived in San Francisco from Costa Rica on February 17, 1922. A native of Bilbao, Spain, Felipe listed his last permanent residence as Havana, Cuba. He and a fellow merchant seaman were stowaways on the SS *Noorderdijk*, and both were deported on March 23.

25.

> Vivian Vincent
> Tahiti[104]

Vivian Vincent was a merchant seaman, employed as an oiler on the *Beulah* when it arrived in San Francisco from Papeete on April 6, 1927. Then twenty-nine years old, he was a native of Tahiti, and had seven years of experience on ships.

26.

Teao Huri[105]

Teao Huri (born *c.* 1891) was also a merchant seaman from Tahiti. He made at least four trips from Papeete to San Francisco. The first was on the *St. Francois* (arriving December 23, 1917), and the next two on the *Moana* (arriving September 13, 1918 and December 6, 1918). When he arrived again April 14, 1926 aboard the *Beulah*, he had risen to the position of first mate.

27.

Xmas '32!!
J.D. Burgess
Wellington N.Z.
Also in 1923–5[106]

John Douglas Burgess was a professional sailor, and traveled through the port of San Francisco many times, and on many different ships. Born in New Zealand on September 25, 1902, he was employed on merchant ships plying trans-Pacific routes for over five decades (Fig. 4.13). Burgesses were among the first European immigrants to New Zealand, and settled on North Island to grow flax. J.D.'s grandfather was a coastal shipper, and his father William Frederick Burgess was a well-to-do artist and architect. Yet after his father died the family fell on hard times, and his mother took in boarders to make ends meet. They eventually moved to Wellington, New Zealand's major port. J.D.'s sister Grace recalled that he always loved the water, and as a child was always wet. By his own account, after he finished high school in 1916 in Blenheim on South Island, he went to work on the Wellington waterfront, where at age nineteen he was "shanghaied" into service at sea. He recalled, "I was working aboard a ship called the *Maunganui* when she sailed suddenly. With me stuck on board. I ended up months later in San Francisco."[107] (Family members do allow that J.D., a gregarious man and story teller, may have had a tendency to embellish the truth.) This sudden introduction to seafaring was a shock, but led to a long and happy career.

Before the Second World War, his was a frequent name on crew lists for Union Steam Ship Company of New Zealand passenger vessels on the San Francisco route—the *Tahiti, Makura, Maunganui,* and *Aorangi*. He started at the bottom as 2nd Pantryman, and by the early 1930s worked up to 1st Class Steward. He later told his family that in the early days he also often

FIGURE 4.13 *J.D. Burgess at the Panama Canal, 1930. Courtesy Gerri Burgess.*

shipped as John Douglas. As this is a very common name, his claim is not entirely demonstrable. However, there was a John Douglas working as an ordinary seaman on New Zealand/Australia to US western ports routes in the middle to late 1930s, whose age, height, and weight match those of J.D. Moreover, the times of the voyages he took do not overlap with those of J.D. Burgess, nor are the ships the same. "John Douglas" is listed as an American citizen, and one manifest, the April 25, 1934 arrival in San Francisco of the *Golden Cloud* from New Zealand, claims he was born in San Francisco. Yet other public records (Census, military, etc.) show no "John Douglas" of J.D.'s approximate age from the city.

J.D. was fascinated by the US, and became intent on becoming American. He told his family that he had jumped ship three times, and the last time the judge allowed him to stay. Again the claim is not easily demonstrable, yet

FIGURE 4.14 *J.D. Burgess and family,* c. *1950. Courtesy Gerri Burgess.*

the existence of the inscription in the Angel Island barracks noting two detentions is some support. He also told the family that he had spent time in the Midwest driving trucks full of bootleg liquor. They thought it was a tall tale—but when he died they discovered that his Social Security card had been issued in Michigan.

After Pearl Harbor, J.D. said, he joined the US Army Air Corps under the name John Douglas, but when his superiors found he had nautical experience, he was transferred to the merchant marine. No record of the enlistment of "John Douglas" is available, but a record for John Douglas Burgess's enlistment in San Francisco is dated April 7, 1942. On it his place of residence is noted as Uintah, Utah, which is immediately adjacent to the old Hill Field (now Hill Air Force Base), which was a major repair and supply base for the air war effort.

Enlistment and service in the US military made it possible for J.D. to apply for naturalization. It was approved on November 5, 1942 by the District Court in Hawaii. Though J.D.'s active army service was only for one year (he was released March 8, 1943), in fact he served the US military for the duration of the war and for most of his subsequent career. He worked on military transport and supply ships during the Second World War, the Korean War, the Vietnam War, and the periods in between. Many of the vessels were of the Liberty- or Victory-class built in large numbers during the Second World War, like *Virginia City Victory*, *Brigham Victory*, and *Sergeant Jack J Pendleton*. J.D. mostly served as 3rd or even 2nd Mate in charge of navigation. He retired in 1971.

In 1945, J.D. married Bernadine Mae Cook, who was born in Washington state and raised in Oregon, and had moved to San Francisco after high school. She was just nineteen at the time—twenty-four years younger than J.D. The couple had two daughters, Geraldine Grace (Gerri) Burgess in 1947 and Gloria Estella Burgess in 1949 (Fig. 4.14). Gerri Burgess graciously provided information and photographs for this entry. After living for more than a decade in San Francisco, the family moved to a house in Healdsburg, Sonoma County, as the scenery there reminded J.D. of his childhood home in New Zealand. Life was not easy for the family, as J.D. was away more than he was home—though Gerri said that whenever he did come home, it was like Christmas. He was an inveterate letter writer, and sent letters describing the scenery and his experiences from all the far-flung ports he visited. The girls collected the postage stamps, and listened to the sounds of foreign places on the shortwave radios he gave them. Raising the children largely on her own was difficult for Bernadine, for J.D. was only paid off at the end of voyages, and family finances in the periods in between could be sparse. She worked in retail at Woolworths and other places to help make ends meet. In the 1960s, she went back to school to master secretarial skills, and served for most of the latter part of her working life as administrative secretary to academic departments at Santa Rosa Junior College in Sonoma County.

J.D. and Bernadine divorced in 1973, and he married Wilma Beckley Casaurang (1913–2004) in 1975. J.D. Burgess died in 1980, and Bernadine in 2003. Gloria, an artist and court reporter, tragically died in 1985 in a single-vehicle automobile accident on a twisting coastal road in Mendocino County. Gerri Burgess recently retired after forty-two years as an elementary school teacher, mostly near her present home of Cloverdale, California.

28.

W. Keenan
Auck.
N.Z.[108]

Like J.D. Burgess, William Francis Keenan was a professional sailor. Born in New Zealand in 1914, he served most often as an able-bodied seaman on Union Steamship Company of New Zealand ships such as the *Wairuna*, *Monowai*, and *Hauraki*. During the 1930s, he landed at ports on the US Pacific coast multiple times.

29.

Souvenir of Fernando Cardenas 1928
Recuerdo de Fernando Cardenas 1928[109]

Fernando Cardenas was a twenty-one-year-old crew member of the freighter *San Jose* when it landed in San Francisco loaded with fruit on September 9, 1928, after stops in Corinto, Cristobal, Port Limon, and San Jose de Guatemala. He was from Corinto, Nicaragua, and was employed on the ship as a "wiper" in the engine room. He made another trip to San Francisco as a seaman on the *San Jose* in 1928, arriving on October 14. Yet on a third trip to San Francisco in 1928, arriving December 2 on the *San Mateo*, he came as a crew member but applied for and was given immigrant entry. A notation on the manifest shows he applied for naturalization in Puerto Rico in the 1930s, and used the 1928 record to show his lawful entry. The application does not appear to have been successful, for when he arrived in New York aboard the *San Juan* from Puerto Rico on March 19, 1937, he was held for deportation.

30.

Souvenir from
Enrique Piton
June 24, 1932
Recuerdos de
Enrique Piton
6.24.32[110]

Considering the skill of this carving, it should come as no surprise that its writer was a carpenter. Yet Enrique E. Piton (born July 17, 1896) was also a habitual criminal, and spent a large part of his adult life in California prisons. A native of Ciudad Lerdo, Durango, Mexico, he and his brother Ricardo (Richard Frank Piton) crossed the border to the United States in 1914, and settled in Los Angeles.[111] They were still there in 1917, when the US joined the Allies in the First World War.[112] The following year Enrique was arrested and convicted of grand larceny. His sentence was one to ten years confinement in the California State Prison at San Quentin, in Marin County, which he began on March 7, 1918 (Fig. 4.15).[113] He was still in San Quentin at the time of the 1920 Census, but was paroled soon afterwards after serving three years.[114] Little more than one year later he was convicted again of the same crime, and sent back to San Quentin.[115] Authorities there transferred him to Folsom State Prison, in Sacramento County, and he served another three years.[116] Enrique's brother Ricardo,

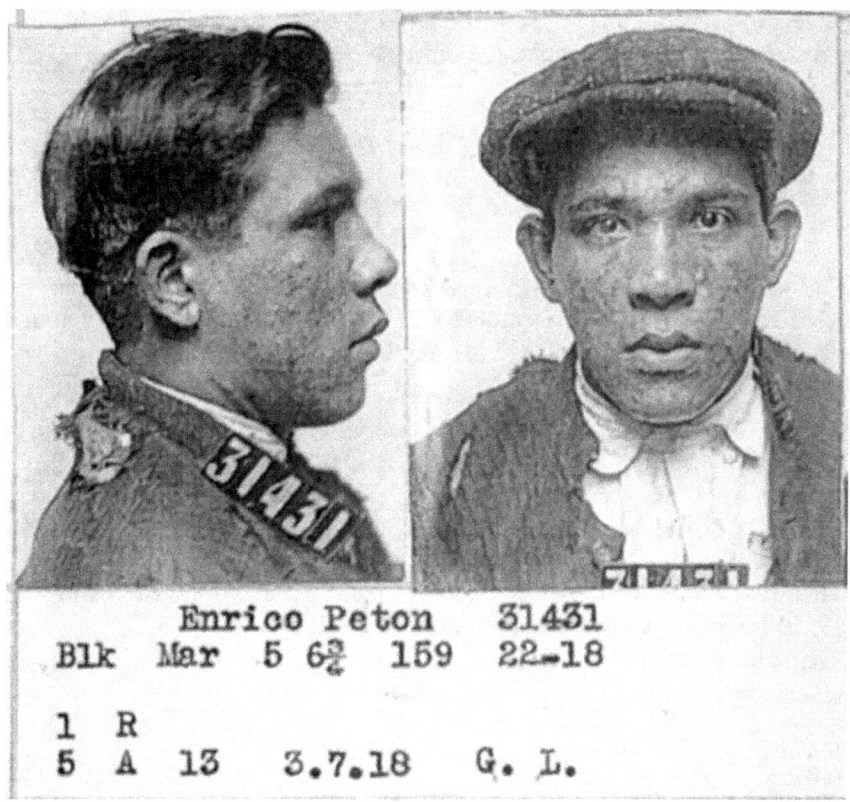

FIGURE 4.15 *Booking photographs of Enrique Pito.*

a longshoreman, became a naturalized US citizen. No naturalization records have yet been found for Enrique. An article appearing in the *Reno Evening Gazette* in early 1924 records a plan to release him from Folsom and immediately deport him to Mexico, yet the authorities were unable to carry through because the Mexican Revolution had disrupted shipping.[117] He was paroled in February, but the records are not clear as to whether he was in fact deported. The San Quentin register also shows a second degree burglary arrest in San Francisco in 1926. He disappears from public records for a decade, until in 1935 he was charged and convicted again, this time for burglary in the second degree. Since he had two prior convictions, this time he was "adjudged an habitual criminal" and sentenced to life, though all his offenses were nonviolent.[118] He was still in Folsom Prison at the time of the 1940 Census, and also when he filed his Second World War draft registration. He was released eventually, as an article in *The Fresno Bee Republican* in 1948 reports he was picked up for serial shoplifting and narcotics possession in Porterville, Tulare County.[119]

The inscription notes the date of June 24, 1932. Records do not explain why he was at Angel Island at the time.

31.

>Ali Hasson [F]iam
>Detroit, Mich!![120]

The 1930 Census shows thirty-seven-year-old Ali Hasson living in Detroit. A native of India, he was employed in the automobile industry. Though married, he was then living in a lodging house.

32.

>Long live Italy! Down with Austria!
>Viva Italy. Abbasso L'Austria.[121]

This inscription, in Italian, is likely from the First World War period. In 1919, Italy finally annexed the German-speaking alpine region of South Tyrol and the nearby Italian-speaking region of Trento, after a decades-long dispute with Austria-Hungary.

33.

>Long Live France!
>Vive la France[122]

34.

>Long Live Mexico!
>Viva Mexico[123]

5

Second World War Wall Inscriptions, 1942–1945

The expectation that one day will bring escape—cold, bleak

The Second World War story of the Immigration Station began well before Pearl Harbor. In December of 1939, the crew of the German liner *Columbus* scuttled the ship off the coast of Virginia to escape attack by a British naval vessel. The crew was picked up by the US Navy heavy cruiser *Tuscaloosa*, and taken to New York. Most of the 512 crew members were transported by train to San Francisco, and confined at Angel Island to await the outcome of diplomatic negotiations concerning the case. Initially, the men had high hopes they would quickly be repatriated, as the United States was still officially neutral in the European conflict. Yet most were of military age, and so Britain refused to give them safe conduct on the seas. They were held at the Immigration Station for fourteen months, though their treatment was lenient. One result of the long wait was a marriage: an interned seaman met and married a local stenographer, and was allowed a three-hour honeymoon tour of San Francisco, under the watchful eyes of two immigration inspectors. Eventually, some of the men were released to return to Germany. In residence when the Administration Building burned down in August of 1940, the remaining crew members helped fight the flames. They were then moved from the Immigration Station to the Quarantine Station on the other side of the island. About the same time, the Justice Department determined that they were neither to be repatriated nor allowed entry into the United States, but instead would be interned at a camp in the interior. In March of 1941, over 400 of them were transported to Fort Stanton in New Mexico, to be detained until the end of the war.[1]

The burning of the Administration Building effectively put an end to the station's usefulness as an immigration processing center. It was closed, and on November 5 the remaining 200 immigration detainees (approximately 150 Chinese and fifty others) were transferred to temporary Immigration and Naturalization Service quarters at 801 Silver Avenue in San Francisco. Due to overcrowding there, work was soon begun on a new immigration detention center behind the Sharp Park Golf Course in Pacifica, California, just south of San Francisco. The entire Angel Island Immigration Station site was turned over to the US Army in 1941, and it became the North Garrison of nearby Fort McDowell. After the bombing of Pearl Harbor, the detention barracks were quickly brought back into use by the new management. A new mess hall, recreation area, and guard towers were built, and the hospital was converted to guards' barracks as the site was prepared for military prisoners. Yet not all were prisoners-of-war.

The forced internment of Japanese Americans from the West Coast is a well-known and tragic story. On February 19, 1942, President Franklin Roosevelt issued Executive Order 9066, which authorized the army to declare areas of the United States as military areas "from which any or all persons may be excluded." Those to be excluded could include persons whose ancestry was in any enemy country, so some Italian Americans and German Americans were relocated and interned, but the vast majority of those affected were of Japanese ancestry. Approximately 120,000 people in California, Oregon, and Washington were forced to leave their homes and relocate to camps operated in remote parts of the western states by the newly established War Relocation Authority (WRA). Those interned by the WRA did not transit the old Angel Island Immigration Station, but the station *was* a stop for hundreds of Japanese internees from Hawaii.

The relocation and internment of Japanese from Hawaii is not well known outside of the islands. A mass relocation of people of Japanese ancestry from the Hawaiian Islands was never implemented, as it was deemed infeasible to move 35 percent of the population, and the territory was in any case already under martial law. Yet immediately after the Pearl Harbor attack on December 7, 1941, local authorities and the FBI arrested over a thousand Issei (first-generation) community leaders; the number eventually rose to more than 2,000. The arrests were not random—in light of the possibility of hostilities with Japan, the FBI and military had begun preparing "custodial detention" name lists several years before. Included were business people, Japanese language school teachers and principals, journalists, Buddhist and Shinto priests, members of martial arts societies, "consular agents" (generally longtime Hawaii residents on islands other than Oahu who, on an unpaid basis, assisted other Japanese to fill out birth, marriage, and death records, and then forwarded them to the Japanese Consulate in Honolulu), and "others of no particular affiliation but who by reason of their extreme nationalistic sentiments would be a danger to our security as well as others who have seen Japanese military service."[2] These people spent the rest of the war as "enemy alien" prisoners. Two major US

Army camps were established in Hawaii: Sand Island in Honolulu Harbor, and Honouliuli about twenty miles to the west. Yet ten large groups of prisoners, comprising 699 people, were transported to the mainland between February 20, 1942 and December 2, 1943. The first mainland stop for seven of these groups, a total of 594 people, was Angel Island. The last three groups transited the new Immigration Service detention camp at Sharp Park. The following itinerary is typical:

Group No. 2 Itinerary
(166 Persons)
Leave: Honolulu   March 19, 1942
Arrive: Angel Island (California)   March 30, 1942
Arrive: Fort Sill (Oklahoma)   Mid April, 1942
Arrive: Camp Livingston (Louisiana)   Early June, 1942

This group was then split into two groups which were sent to the following:

Fort Missoula (Montana)   June, 1943
Santa Fe (New Mexico)   June, 1944

The destinations were all US Army or Justice Department facilities. Prisoners also went to Camp McCoy (Wisconsin), Camp Forrest (Tennessee), Crystal City (Texas), and Lordsburg (New Mexico).[3] Those who transited Angel Island left multiple inscriptions on the barracks walls.

Some Japanese Americans from California and other western states, like their Hawaiian counterparts, were arrested as "enemy aliens" early in the war, and temporarily held at Angel Island. They were then transferred to US Army and Department of Justice camps. A research project led by Grant Din when he was Community Resources Director of the Angel Island Immigration Station Foundation (AIISF) has identified ninety-three such prisoners so far. The AIISF also has names of eighty-one German and Italian "enemy aliens" held there during the war years.[4]

Prisoners-of-war held in the old barracks included the first captured in the war: the commander of a midget submarine at Pearl Harbor, Ensign Kazuo Sakamaki, who then joined the Japanese Hawaiians at Camp McCoy. Yet no other Japanese military prisoners arrived until the summer of 1942, after the battles of Coral Sea and Midway. Mirroring the progress of the war, initially most prisoners-of-war held at Angel Island were Germans from the North Africa campaign. These included a group of high rank: Lieutenant General Karl Bülowius, three other German generals, a colonel, and a major were among those detained at Angel Island.[5] As of June 1943, 36,688 war prisoners were held in twenty-one camps, including the transit camp at Angel Island (the only such camp on the West Coast). Of this number,

22,100 were Germans, 14,516 were Italians, and only sixty-two were Japanese. All of these Japanese prisoners were sent to Camp McCoy, Wisconsin.[6] (In the spring of 1943, the Army decided to dedicate Camp McCoy solely to military prisoners-of-war, primarily Japanese but also including some Germans, and so the Hawaiians and other "enemy aliens" who were there were shipped elsewhere.[7]) Yet even at the end of the war, the total number of Japanese POWs held in the US was only 5,434, a fraction of that of Germans and Italians.[8] Of this number, not all were even military—also detained in the US were a considerable number of conscript laborers from Korea, Okinawa, and other Japanese territories who served the Japanese Imperial Army. There are two clear reasons for the low number. First, Japanese soldiers and sailors were trained to believe that capture by the enemy was shameful and dishonorable, and that death in battle—or suicide if need be—was preferable. The proportion of those captured to those killed was far lower than in Europe and North Africa. Second, most of the Japanese captured in the Pacific Theater were turned over to the allies, and were detained in Australia or New Zealand. Those who were transported to the US mainland were either closer to the US when captured (as those from the Aleutian campaign), or were deemed to have military intelligence value.[9]

A top secret interrogation center to gather intelligence from Japanese POWs was built at the old Byron Hot Springs resort, near Tracy west of San Francisco. The resort had thrived in the late-nineteenth and early-twentieth centuries, and became a playground for the rich and famous who came for the healthful mineral waters and recreation opportunities. In its heyday, Clark Gable, Mae West, Jack London, and Charlie Chaplin visited. Yet in 1938 it went bankrupt, a victim of the Depression. The US government leased it in 1941. After processing at Angel Island, prisoners were sent to Byron Hot Springs for interrogation, and when that was completed, were sent on to permanent camps.[10] As the number of Japanese POWs remained small in the first years of the war, Germans were also interrogated there in significant numbers.

Bryon Hot Springs was officially called Camp Tracy, but in general correspondence was referred to only as PO Box 541 to maintain secrecy. It was one of only two military interrogation centers in the country; the other was Fort Hunt in Virginia, near Washington, DC. Ulrich Straus has written a comprehensive book about the Japanese POW experience, *The Anguish of Surrender*. He writes,

> Great care was taken to ensure that knowledge of the facilities was strictly limited to those with a need to know. In internal documents they were not classified as POW camps but as "temporary detention centers." This ensured the International Committee of the Red Cross and third-party diplomatic protecting powers did not get wind of their existence. Angel

Island near Tiburon in San Francisco Bay was the holding station and "cover" for the intelligence operations at Camp Tracy. All POWs destined for Tracy and their records were routed through Angel Island.[11]

In light of the great public controversy over "enhanced interrogation techniques" used on terror suspects in the first two decades of the twenty-first century, it is illuminating to see how Japanese prisoners were treated in the Second World War. US intelligence at the time responded with the "soft" approach. Japanese POWs were provided good food, good treatment, and medical care, and were even given privileges to purchase amenities at the canteen and permission to use the resort's spas and mud baths. Interrogations were calm and generally polite affairs; two- or three-hour-long sessions were scheduled each day, conducted by interrogators well versed in Japanese language and culture (about half were Nisei).[12] Straus writes,

> ... it was the "soft" approach that paid the best dividends. Japanese POWs hardly knew what to make of the "nice" way they were treated. "Weren't the interrogators still the enemy?" The enemy's unwillingness to assume the proper "enemy role" made it difficult for the prisoner to adopt the correct role prescribed by the Bushido code.[13]

Augmenting interrogations were hidden microphones in the prisoners' cells and on the grounds, and at times Nisei linguists went undercover and joined them in detention. In their turn, Japanese prisoners at Byron Hot Springs provided a great deal of valuable intelligence: information about Japanese biological weapons capabilities, including the existence of the secret Biological Experimental Station in Harbin, Manchuria; detailed descriptions of the Yokosuka and Sasebo naval bases; information about naval training and ships in the fleet; specifications of the weapons systems on Japan's two super-battleships; radar capabilities; code names for some army units; as well as a complete description of the Japanese mega-submarine, the I-1.[14]

Camp McCoy remained the largest camp for Japanese military prisoners, and another at Clarinda, Iowa also held substantial numbers. About 600 were sent to Kenedy, Texas, and small groups were distributed in other places, including Pine Grove Furnace, Pennsylvania, and Hearne, Texas. Angel Island was initially only a transit center, but it then became permanent quarters for about 400 Japanese prisoners, who remained until the end of the war.[15]

There is a description of life for German prisoners in the Angel Island camp as of mid-1943, in an unusual newspaper feature story in the *Los Angeles Times*. Clearly, the fair treatment accorded the prisoners is used here to confirm to the public America's moral superiority in the conflict. The entire article is worth quoting here,

NAZI PRISONERS LIKE WAR CAMP IN UNITED STATES
The following article was written by the first newspaperman to visit the prisoner of war camp at Angel Island, San Francisco Bay

By Roger A. Johnson

ANGEL ISLAND WAR PRISONERS' CAMP, June 9. (U.P.)—

German soldiers captured in North Africa have found a temporary "home" here in San Francisco Bay halfway around the world from Bizerte and El Alamein, and they like it—the environment, the food and the fair treatment.

This is a clearing station where they are "processed" for a time before being transferred to permanent camps scattered throughout the country.

Amidst towering eucalyptus trees that grow in abundance on the three-mile-long island the Internment receives and initiates Axis prisoners into the American fair play. Commander of the camp is Maj. Albert E. Wilfong, Ogden, Utah.

Arrive in shorts

During the early spring months some of the prisoners arrived at foggy San Francisco Bay wearing desert short pants direct from the sands of Egypt. They had one denominator, common to soldiers the world over—pin-up girls.

Their barrack walls were plastered with leggy pictures of Rita Hayworth, Paulette Goddard, Greer Garson, Janet Blair, Ann Miller, Diana Barrymore. They even had a demure shot of Brenda Frazier and a "Petty" girl from Esquire who was making the "V" sign with her fingers.

When they arrived the Germans didn't expect mistreatment because the British and Australians had told them the Americans would give them a square deal. And now they have found reason to know it is true.

They keep a strict discipline. The Nazis were gathered in one room playing German whist and pinochle when we entered.

A blond, good-looking young master sergeant snapped to attention when Maj. Wilfong appeared.

"Achtung," he shouted.

Men Obey Command

The other men—corporals and privates jumped from their seats and stood at rigid attention.

The camp's daily schedule is fixed. Reveille is at 6 a.m., breakfast at 6:30. From 7:30 to 9 a.m. they clean their own quarters. From 9 to 11 a.m. they take their exercise—walk around the island under escort, mow the lawn, or rake leaves. They are paid for their work.

Lunch is from noon to 1 p.m. They rest from 1 to 2 p.m., exercise again from 2 to 4, and eat supper at 5 p.m.

They work in a Victory garden which is handed on from one batch of prisoners to the next. The one arriving in July and August will reap the harvest of Japanese and Germans who did the planting in March and April.[16]

A feature story on Japanese prisoners-of-war at Angel Island published in *The S.F. News* on August 9, 1945 (four days after the atomic bomb was dropped at Hiroshima, and the day after the second bomb at Nagasaki)[17] was rather less charitable, and reflects the casual racism typical of the times.

NO CODDLING FOR JAP PWs ON ANGEL ISLAND
(*Through Angel Island processing station in San Francisco Bay pass the Japanese prisoners of war sent to the United States. The News sent a reporter and cameraman to Angel Island this week, the first detailed story and photographs are the result.—The Editor.*)
—

By George Dusheck
On the eastern slope of Angel Island in San Francisco Bay lies a triangular stockade a city block in area. It is five minutes march from the North Garrison dock. Its high barbed-wire fences, commanded by gun towers, contain a few old wooden buildings, once the detention barracks of the U.S. Immigration Service.

Today the Japanese prisoners of war brought to the United States move in and out of this stockade. This is the Japanese Prisoner Processing Center, commanded by Major John A Whitlock of Spartanburg, S.C.

Before the war Major Whitlock operated a music store in his home city. Now he "processes"—cares for without coddling—the hundreds of Jap prisoners that each month are shipped back to this country. They are delivered to him by the Port of Embarkation. In turn he delivers them to prisoner-of-war camps in the interior of America—in chair cars, not Pullmans.

In between Major Whitlock and his staff teach these small, brown men without a country—they are officially dead in Japan—the rules of life in an American P.W. camp.

They learn the meaning of "military courtesy"—through half a dozen Nisei interpreters. In practice this means that when an American officer approaches a group or enters a room, the first Jap to sight him bawls:

"Kiytsuki!" This word brings every Jap within earshot to immediate attention.

They remain at attention until told to relax. During a recent visit to the processing center one group of Japs, lounging in their own quarters, came to instantaneous attention at the command of their own leader four times in five minutes as the inspecting party passed in and out of the room.

Says Major Whitlock:

"These men are obedient, willing workers, cheerful—and completely unpredictable. I have never had trouble with any one of them, and I will never cease being ready for it."

The Japs are clean. Told to keep their quarters, mess, and recreation areas in good order, they never stop working at it. Their persons and clothes—Class X Army castoffs—are spic and span.

In the short time they are on Angel Island while awaiting transportation to a regular prisoner-of-war camp they are organized into self-disciplining groups. They not only police their own quarters, but also prepare their own meals, and wash the dishes afterwards.

Most of the men are young, in their early twenties. Major Whitlock is convinced some are as young as 12 years. They were farmers or factory workers before the war. There are only a handful of officers, who live in separate quarters.

The group leaders are non-commissioned officers from the Japanese Army or Navy. They enforce a rigid discipline. American guards are under instructions never to use force on these Japs.

"Our relations with the men are consequently right," said Lieutenant M.B. Horn. They obey, and grumble very little. Mostly they want more tobacco, of which they are issued two ounces a week, which painstakingly and awkwardly, by cow-hand standards, they roll into cigarets.

They receive an "adequate diet of unrationed foods." A typical day's menu, served at 6 o'clock in the morning, at noon, and at 5 o'clock in the evening, is:

For breakfast: fruit, rolled oats, dried milk, bread, and coffee. For dinner: fish, rice, vegetable, salad, bread, and water. For supper: soup dried peas, potatoes, vegetable, bread, and tea.

Some time during their stay on Angel Island the prisoners are fingerprinted, photographed. They are given thorough physical examinations. They suffer from the same ailments as Americans who have fought in the same areas—malaria, intestinal parasites, wounds. Major Whitlock estimates that 20 per cent are syphilitic. These are started at once on the long course of alternating arsenic and bismuth shots. They are not treated with valuable penicillin.

These men have no future to look forward to. Some express hope they will be permitted to stay here. A few have offered to join the United States armed services.

They do not ask what will become of them—unwanted by their own country, and despised enemies here. They smoke, gamble with cards, mahjong, and the ancient game of "Go," tend to their persons, feed themselves.

Said Lieutenant Horn:

We don't encourage them to ask such questions. It would just make them start thinking. And anyway—we don't know the answers."

From time to time, groups of 150 to 250 are loaded into archaic day-coaches in Oakland and started for the vast interior of the continent-nation they failed to conquer. Stocky Major Whitlock was asked if he had any final comment to add to the inspection tour.

"Yes," said the South Carolinian, who describes himself as "chief Jap-handler." "Say we don't coddle 'em and that they don't ride in Pullman cars. And thanks!"[18]

Several inscriptions in the barracks are by German prisoners-of-war, but many more are by Japanese. Those by Japanese are often stridently partisan. They apparently did not "like war camp in the United States."

Some of the last prisoners from the Pacific War housed at Angel Island were only boys—Major Whitlock was correct when he estimated some as young as twelve years. The horrific Battle of Okinawa, fought on sea and land from April to June 1945, killed over a quarter million people, up to 150,000 of them civilians. Japanese military leaders deployed every resource available to stop the American advance on the Japanese home islands. More than 1,500 local middle and high school boys were organized into Tekketsu Kinnotai (Iron and Blood Imperial Corps) to aid the army; schoolgirls were also mobilized to serve in medical units. Boys in the Iron and Blood units performed a variety of support functions, but also engaged in front-line combat. More than half died in suicide hand grenade attacks on American tanks and vehicles or in other guerilla actions. Many of the survivors were captured and interned at Honouliuli and Angel Island. Peter Ota of Tustin, California was a young Private First Class when he served as a POW interpreter at Angel Island. In a 2007 article in *Pacific Citizen*, Ota recalled the Okinawan boy soldiers' arrival: "We were shocked. They were kids. They looked like kids who were lost." Ota and the other guards came to know the boys well, listened to their stories, and allowed them to help out around the compound doing office work. "We'd ask them, aren't you homesick? And they would respond: 'No. We don't have any family to go back to.'" After the war the boys were ordered deported to Japan.

Ota recalled, "Some of them came running back crying. They did not want to go. They were forcibly taken on the boat."[19]

The report of an International Red Cross and Department of State inspection visit to Angel Island in July 1945 also mentioned boy soldiers:

> Among the prisoners there was a young boy who claimed to be fifteen years old but who appeared to be certainly not more than eleven. He had been nick-named "peanuts" and is a great favorite. He was especially helpful around the kitchen.[20]

A moving account by one of the boy soldiers himself is Mitsugu Sakihara's "Sparrows of Angel Island," published in 1996. He explained that after being wounded and captured, he was imprisoned at Honouliuli. He was then one of a select group of fifty-three Iron and Blood veterans sent to the mainland. The boys were told that they were to be trained in English and democracy so that after the war they could help in building the new Japan. However, the plan was abandoned as the war ended sooner than expected, and so their journey ended at Angel Island. After spending the autumn there, in December they were put aboard ship for return to Japan, filled with apprehension of what they might find at home.[21]

On August 6, 1945, the US Army Air Force B-29 Enola Gay dropped an atomic bomb on Hiroshima, and three days later the USAAF B-29 Bockscar dropped another on the city of Nagasaki. The twin nuclear catastrophes, combined with conventional and incendiary bombing of eight other cities and a Soviet assault that defeated Japanese forces in Manchuria, prompted the Japanese government to accept the strict Allied terms for surrender on August 15—V-J Day. The formal Instrument of Surrender was signed on the USS *Missouri* in Tokyo Bay on September 2. The end of the war began what was to be the final official task performed at the old immigration station—the repatriation of Japanese POWs, both military and civilian.

Repatriation happened quite quickly. A flurry of telephone conversations and letters among representatives at the Office of the Provost Marshal General (OPMG) and the regional Service Commands in authority over the various prisoner-of-war camps produced written orders on September 7 to transport 241 POWs back to Angel Island, where they would be placed in the custody of the Ninth Service Command. This prisoner group, eight from Pine Grove Furnace, eighty-three from McCoy, forty-six from Clarinda, and 104 from Kenedy and Hearne, was by specific order all of Okinawan origin.[22] On September 25 and 26, orders were issued to transport all 2,697 remaining Japanese POWs at Camp McCoy and another 987 from Clarinda to California, where they were to arrive no later than October 5.[23] Some of these, including approximately 178 prisoners from McCoy who were wounded, ill, or otherwise disabled were sent directly to Angel Island. The rest, including both military and civilian prisoners (mostly Koreans) were sent first to Camp Lamont, in Kern County near Bakersfield, and the nearby branch camps of Lakeland (at Corcoran) and Boswell Ranch (near Corcoran).[24] There they were put to work on the cotton harvest.[25] By late December, these prisoners were sent on to await ships for their repatriation, some from the Port of Embarkation at Los Angeles, and some from Angel Island and the Port of Embarkation at San Francisco.[26]

The *Los Angeles Times* reported,

> San Francisco, Nov. 7. (U.P.)
> Seven hundred Japanese war prisoners and civilian internees left for their homes in Japan today aboard the Sea Flasher. The Angel Island Japanese processing center said the group was the third to be shipped home.[27]

More than a dozen inscriptions by Japanese repatriates are found on the barracks walls, and the November 7 departure as well as an earlier one on September 25, are specifically mentioned. The texts pertain mostly to their travel plans, with an occasional expression of anticipation or anxiety about going home, and are fairly repetitive. It is clear that prisoners were leaving messages for others who were to come later, in multiple places to make sure of notice. The number of full names, surnames, and nicknames included is notable. The war's end had also brought an end to any need for confidentiality. The last group of prisoners departed Angel Island on January 8, 1946. The US Army left Angel Island in September of that year, and the Immigration Station/North Garrison site was abandoned.[28]

BY JAPANESE HAWAIIANS[29]

1.

June 4
As a prisoner.
Hilo City
Shindō

六月四日
監禁者として
ヒロ市
進藤
[30]

Takuji Shindō was from Hilo, Hawaii, where he was proprietor of the Shindo Drug Store. (The land at 350 Kamehameha Avenue where the store once stood is now part of the Hilo Farmers' Market). He was also a co-owner of the Hilo Nippon Club. Born in Kawakami Village, Kamo District, Hiroshima Prefecture in 1889, he immigrated to Hawaii in 1907. Initially, he raised sugar cane near Kurtistown, but his farm business failed and so he moved to Hilo. He was in Group #3 of the ten groups of internees from Hawaii.

The warrant for his arrest on suspicion of being an enemy alien was issued the same day as the Pearl Harbor attack. The February 2, 1942 transcript of the investigative hearing on the case shows that he was a respected businessman who was a leader in community organizations. At various times he served as auditor and secretary of the Hilo Japanese Chamber of Commerce, secretary of the Hilo Japanese Society, and vice president of the United Business Association. He also was a member of the Hilo Hongwanji Fraternity, which supported the Jōdo Shinshū Buddhist temple in the city.

Accused enemy aliens were not permitted to hear the testimony of government witnesses in these special board hearings, so Shindō was not present when Dale R. Curtis, Special Agent of the Federal Bureau of Investigation, took the stand. Curtis claimed that Shindō was present—though admitted he did not participate—when a group of Japanese Hawaiians engaged in a political discussion at the Japanese Chamber of Commerce meeting of January 7, 1941. Topics included the coming world dominance of Japan, and the problem for Japanese Hawaiians of appearing too patriotic to Japan. Shindō was not accused of holding such views, except by association. When questioning of Shindō resumed, he denied that he had heard anything of the sort, and said that he probably had made only a short appearance at the meeting, as he was busy preparing for the subsequent party at the Nippon Club. In response to questions he swore his allegiance to the United States.

Q Being a subject of Japan, I presume you are a loyal subject?
A I cannot say that I am a loyal subject of Japan because I arrived here when I was 17 or 18 years old and I have not done anything for the Japanese government. On the other hand, I have made this my permanent residence and I have enjoyed all the freedom and liberty offered me and I am a loyal American that does not have the citizenship status.
Q Well, why then through the course of many years in the United States, have you adhered so strictly to Japanese customs and practices?
A Whatever I have done, I have done for the community at large and not particularly for the Japanese. I am always willing to give a helping hand to any person of any nationality. It is true that I am a Japanese subject and I am accustomed to the Japanese ways of living and habits, but on the other hand, I have also worked for the

benefit of other nationalities. When the Hawaiian church or Portuguese church come around for donations, I have given it to them. I have also spent my time and expense and worked for the community welfare drive and the promotion of defense stamps and particularly celebration of the 4th of July and so forth, and many other community work. Being a business man, I am always glad to help the whole community and not just for the Japanese alone.

Q   Yes, but don't you see throughout the years, most of your connections have been with exclusively Japanese organizations and societies and with alien Japanese, and you have made, in addition, no effort to throw off Japanese customs and practices and act like an American, although you do not have the privilege of being a citizen?

A   I would feel out of place if I joined any other organization. First, because I cannot speak English and second, I would not be welcome in any other organization of other nationalities. That is particularly true to all nationalities, all racial extraction. The Filipinos have their own society, the Hawaiians have their own societies and the Portuguese have their own societies. Not only the Japanese.

The board agreed on the following findings: that the internee is a subject of Japan; that the internee owes technical allegiance to Japan; and that the internee's activities have been pro-Japanese although not necessarily anti-American. Yet they disagreed on what to do. The president (a federal judge) and the military participant recommended that Shindō be interned for the duration of the war, while the other two members held he should be paroled. The case then went to representatives of military intelligence and the FBI, who recommended internment. Lieutenant General Delos C. Emmons, Military Governor of the Territory of Hawaii, concurred and it was so ordered.[31]

The 109 people in Group #3 arrived at Angel Island on June 1, 1942, and soon thereafter were transported to the camp at Lordsburg, New Mexico, where they arrived on June 18. While at Lordsburg, two sketches of Takuji Shindō were done by a fellow internee, George Hoshida, who was also from Hilo. Hoshida's notebooks containing 260 drawings and watercolors of life in the internment camps are now in the collections of the Japanese American National Museum in Los Angeles. A portrait of Takuji Shindō shows the subject dressed in an undershirt, staring directly at the viewer, with crewcut and lined face (Fig. 5.2). The second sketch is simpler, and depicts only his head and face.

After the war, Takuji Shindō returned to Hilo, where wife Yoshino (1897–1993) and son Richard T. were waiting. He died in 1958. Richard Shindō became a well-known dentist in Hilo, and his wife Bessie K. Shindō taught school.

FIGURE 5.1 *George Hoshida portrait of Takuji Shindo, left. From the collections of the Japanese American National Museum.*

2.

Of 110 people from the Group #3 ship,
Eight are from Waialua.
A safe passage.
June 4, 1942

第三回船百十名中
八名ワイアルア出身
無事通過
六月四日千九百四二年
32

Waialua is on the North Shore of Oahu. It was a major center for Hawaiian sugar production starting in the late-nineteenth century, and so was populated largely by immigrant workers and their families.

SECOND WORLD WAR WALL INSCRIPTIONS, 1942–1945

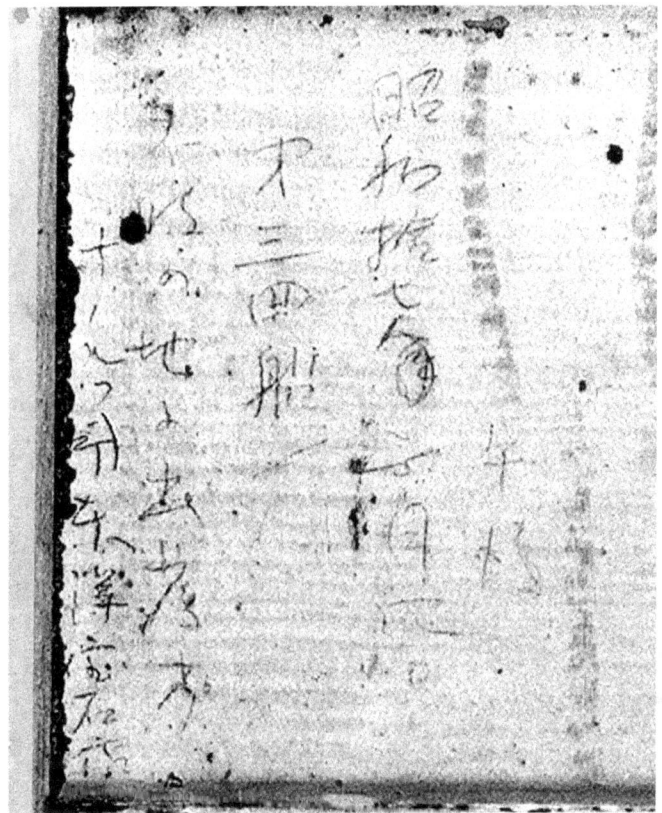

FIGURE 5.2 *Robert Sueoka inscription. Photo: ARG and Daniel Quan.*

3.

After noon on June 4, Seventeenth Year of Shōwa (1942)
Those of us from the Group #3 ship are leaving for an unknown location.
Toyo Jewelry Store, Honolulu City

午後
昭和拾七年六月四日
第三回船
不明の地に出発す
ホノルヽ市東洋宝石店
33

Although unsigned, the store name in the inscription confirms the writer as Robert Iju Sueoka (a.k.a. Robert Yoshinori Sueoka).[34] He was born in 1903 in Atago Village, Yamaguchi Prefecture. His parents, Usaburo and Kinu

Sueoka (also Suyeoka), immigrated to Hawaii in 1906, leaving him in the care of family. Robert joined them in 1918. He had a variety of jobs in the next two decades, including clerking for a brokerage and a tailor shop, and managing a book company.[35] He also clerked for the Honolulu Gold Exchange in 1935. The 1940 Census describes him as a watch salesman with his own business, and the passenger manifest for the October 23, 1941 arrival of the *Tatsuta Maru* from Yokohama gives his occupation as "jeweler."

A warrant for his arrest was issued April 10, 1942, and the investigative hearing for his case was held on April 15. The record confirms his business was Toyo Jewelry at 1234 College Walk, Honolulu. As in Takuji Shindō's hearing, the accused was not permitted to hear the government witness against him. Wayne D. Gregg, Special Agent in the Counter-Intelligence Corps, Military Intelligence Division, focused on Sueoka's recent purchase of Japanese ¥846 for US $141, which he then resold for a profit. Gregg then stated—without providing evidence—that Sueoka was in the market for ¥30,000 to ¥35,000. He also said that Sueoka had in his possession "several snapshots of Japanese navy and army officers and of Japanese troops," and that he had filed an application for Japanese Army deferment through the Japanese Consul.

Buying and selling currencies to profit from favorable exchange rates is not illegal. The suggestion was that Sueoka was a currency speculator betting a Japanese victory would increase the value of the yen. Follow-up questions from the board members to Sueoka in the latter part of the hearing reveal this suspicion—he was even asked about a potential Japanese occupation of the Hawaiian Islands. Yet Sueoka's answers affirmed he had only undertaken the one $141 transaction for profit; he had also changed some dollars to yen in preparation for his trip to Japan in 1941. As for the snapshots—there was only one taken in Hawaii (during the visit of a Japanese training ship) that had been a gift, and the rest he had taken himself in Korea, in 1918! His request for army deferment was a simple printed form required of Japanese nationals; he was, after all, an alien under US law.

A series of questions by the board concerned Sueoka's loyalty to the United States.

Q   How do you feel, which side would you like to see win this war, China and America or Japan and Germany?
A   Well, in my opinion, I like to see freedom. I believe in Democracy so I would like to see freedom and I have been in Japan but there is not as much freedom over there as here.
Q   Which side would you like to see win the war?
A   Well, I like to see the United States win—any side to get freedom.
Q   Would you like to see Japan lose the war?

A Well, not exactly lose, but I never thought of such a thing. The only things I can say is that I just tend to my business. I struggle for my family, to keep it up.
Q Do you think it would be a good thing for freedom and peace if Japan loses this war?
A Yes, sir.
Q Would you like to see Japan lose this war?
A Well, as long as I have freedom here I would like to see the United States win.
Q How about Japan losing the war?
A Yes, sir.
Q You would like to see Japan lose this war?
A Yes.
Q Do you think it would be a good thing if Japan were reduced to an inferior military power?
A Yes, sir.
Q Third-rate military power?
A Yes, sir.
Q So she could not go on a rampage any more, you think that is a good thing?
A Yes, sir.

The board pressed him even further at the end of the hearing, asking whether he would be willing to fight for the United States against Japan. Sueoka answered that he would fight if he was forced to, for example if he was drafted, but that he liked peace and preferred to stay neutral.

Q If the Japanese Army made a landing in Hawaii, on this Island, and nobody asked you to go and fight the Japanese, but you had an opportunity to do a little bit of shooting at them, to prevent them from landing, would you fight the Japanese?
A No, I would run away.

The board recommended that Robert Iju Sueoka be interned for the duration of the war. The decision was unanimous. Military intelligence authorities concurred, and it was so ordered by the Military Governor.[36]

After passing through Angel Island in 1942, Sueoka was imprisoned at Lordsburg, New Mexico with the other Group #3 members. Yet in March 1944, he was allowed a transfer to the Jerome War Relocation Center in Arkansas to join his wife Chiyeko. The couple were then moved to Tule Lake in May. Robert died in Honolulu in 1988, Chiyeko in 1986. An ink sketch of Robert Sueoka is in the George Hoshida Collection in the Japanese American National Museum.

4.

> On June 3, while those of us from the Group #3 ship
> were working at K.P. duty, a problem [came up].
> Our guys did their bests, and their guys apologized.

六月三日吾等三回船は
ケーピーとしては働き一ド問題を
口口吾等は頑張り
彼等は謝罪せり
37

The "problem" appears to have been an altercation in the mess hall with another group of prisoners or with military cooks. See #10 below for another inscription on this incident.

5.

> Evening.
>
> The expectation that one day
> Will bring escape—
> Cold, bleak.
>
>   June 4

時夕
いつの日を
のがる々あてでの
［い］ろさむし
六月四日
38

The central three lines form a *haiku* poem of 5-8-5 syllables (the standard form is 5-7-5). Though no year or group number is mentioned, the date, location, and orientation of the inscription suggest it was also by a Japanese Hawaiian from Group #3.

6.

Everyone is well.
It is almost certain we are leaving for someplace in Texas.
After lunch on June 4, Seventeenth Year of Shōwa (1942).

一同元氣ナリ
テキサストホボ確定ス
某地向出発ス
昭和十七年六月四日中食後

[39]

Group #3 did not in fact go to Texas, but to Lordsburg, New Mexico. The detainees were later transferred to Santa Fe. However, the internment camp for enemy aliens in Crystal City, Texas was the eventual destination for some Japanese Hawaiians from Groups #1, #4, and #7.

7.

Everyone in Group #4 is really trying hard. Japanese boys must raise their morale!
A friend from Waialua

第四回の皆君を大いに頑張れ
日本男児の意気を発揚せよ
ワイアルアの一友人

[40]

Group #4 of the internees from Hawaii comprised forty-five men and women in total, but was split into two groups for transport. The first arrived at Angel Island on June 29, 1942, and then was sent on to Lordsburg, New Mexico. The second group, comprising only women prisoners, transited the new immigration detention center at Sharp Park, in Pacifica south of San Francisco, and then was sent to Crystal City, Texas.

INSCRIPTIONS FROM YASUTARO SOGA

Yasutaro Soga (1873–1957), also known as Keiho Soga, was a leading Issei journalist in Hawaii, and was an influential community leader and activist for over four decades. He was editor and publisher of the daily *Nippu Jiji* newspaper from 1905 until the beginning of the Second World War. The newspaper (later renamed *Hawaii Times*) was a progressive force in that period, advocating for the rights of plantation and mill workers. After the attack on Pearl Harbor, Soga was arrested. He was placed in Group #5 of the Issei leaders sent to mainland concentration camps operated by the Department of Justice. Group #5 was detained at Angel Island from August 15–27, 1942, and then was transported to Lordsburg Internment Camp in New Mexico. Soga remained at Lordsburg until 1943, and then was transferred to Santa Fe Internment Camp for the rest of the war. When the war was over, Soga wrote a memoir about his experience of incarceration he called *Tessaku Seikatsu* (鐵柵生活), which was published serially in *Hawaii Times*, and then in book form in 1948. A translation was published in 2008 with the title *Life Behind Barbed Wire*.[41] Though his description of Angel Island is short, he was intrigued by the writing on the walls and transcribed four Japanese inscriptions he saw on the second floor of the barracks. Two were apparently by Japanese prisoners-of-war, and two were by other Japanese Hawaiians. He also wrote his own inscription on the wall before departure. Although the five inscriptions have not been located and may have been erased or painted over, Soga was a reliable journalist who showed scrupulous attention to factual detail. Thus we can be confident these texts were visible on the walls in 1942. His description of the room in which he and other Group #5 prisoners were held suggests it was Room 205, the large dormitory on the second floor. There are multiple Japanese inscriptions from the Second World War period there, though many are partly or wholly illegible.

8.

Father told me to die bravely in battle.
Mother did not actually *say* for me to become a prisoner, but ... Well, here I am now ...

父は語れり、戦ひには潔よく死せよ。
母は語らざりき、捕虜となれとは、
然るに今の我は…

SECOND WORLD WAR WALL INSCRIPTIONS, 1942–1945   267

The first Japanese POW held at Angel Island was the first captured in the war: Ensign Kazuo Sakamaki. Sakamaki commanded a two-man midget submarine which foundered during the attack on Pearl Harbor. He was brought from Hawaii to Angel Island in March 1942, and then sent to Camp McCoy in Wisconsin. Yasutaro Soga was at Angel Island only five months later, in August. By that time very, very few Japanese POWs had transited there. One group that arrived that same month consisted of eight prisoners from the Battle of Midway. Even as of April 1943, there were only sixty-two Japanese military prisoners on the US mainland.

9.

Wherever I go across the seas,
The whole world is under one roof
Of blue sky.

海を往く八紘一宇空の色。

The inscription is a standard 5-7-5 *haiku* on a patriotic theme. The central phrase, "the whole world under one roof" ("the eight directions are one abode"),[42] frequently appeared in Japanese propaganda before and during the Second World War. While it carried positive implications of universal harmony, it was also used as a justification for Japanese expansionism: the whole world would be placed under the divine authority of the emperor.

10.

Team Leader Kurita showed his Japanese spirit—while doing KP he really shut them up!

栗田隊長日本気質發揮、KP閉口痛快。

See #4 above. Yasuro Kurita (1887–?), a native of Kashiwara in Osaka Prefecture, was a contractor for painting and construction projects in Honolulu.[43] He was in Group #3 of the Issei from Hawaii, and transited Angel Island in June 1942. There is a portrait of him in the George Hoshida Collection at the Japanese American National Museum. He and wife Ryuko Okino Kurita (1901–1999) had three children, James, Harold, and Carol. The family joined him in captivity at Jerome War Relocation Center in Arkansas in 1943. The Kuritas were transferred to Gila River in 1944, and returned to Honolulu in November, 1945.

11.

Arrived San Francisco August 5, and will leave for Honolulu August 7. Takeo Akizaki, Kazuma Araki, Tokumei Atsumi, Kenkichi Fujimoto, Shigeo Fujino, Hiroshi Honda, Tamotsu Iwohara, Masao Ishimoto, Takeo Kagawa, Kazuo Miyamoto, Tokuichi Niimi, Shunichi Ōdō, Seiichi Sugimoto, Masao Sakamoto, Sanji Sakamoto, Shinzaburo Sumida, Manabu Tashiro, Kenjitsu Tsuha, Kouji Kawahara.

八月五日桑港着、八月七日布哇に行く。秋崎武雄を、荒木數馬、厚海德明、藤本憲吉、藤野茂夫を、本田廣司、庵原將、石本正夫、香川武雄を、宮本一男、仁井見得一、王堂俊一、杉本清一、坂本正雄を、坂本三次、住田慎三郎、田代學なぶ、津波憲實、河原廣治

These nineteen men had been in Department of Justice custody as "enemy aliens" like the Hawaiian Issei transported to the mainland, yet in fact all were Hawaiian-born US citizens. So in August 1942 they were returned to Hawaii for status review. Yet this did not end their ordeal. Most remained in detention, and were sent back to the mainland—but this time under the control of the War Relocation Authority. They spent the remainder of the war in Jerome and Tule Lake.

The names are presented as Soga transcribed and published them. Yet he made errors in three of them, two in pronunciation (Japanese allows multiple alternate readings of Kanji characters), and one in Kanji transcription. "Tokumei Atsumi" is Noriaki Atsuumi, who was in Group #1. "Tamotsu Iwohara" is Tamotsu Ihara, who is not on the group lists but was another

Hawaiian-born US citizen. For "Kouji Kawahara," Soga mistook the given name as "Kouji" (廣治) when it is properly "Toraji" (寅治). Toraji Kawahara was in Group #4.

12.

Let us go together
Over seas and mountains.
Our heads held high,
We'll stride boldly—
As we are "the Japs."

海も山も倶に往かなむ眉揚げて足踏みしめてジヤツプス我等

Soga was an accomplished poet in the traditional Japanese *tanka* form. The standard form is structured in five lines of five or seven syllables each: 5-7-5-7-7. This example is only slightly irregular: 6-7-5-7-7.

BY PRISONERS-OF-WAR

13.

Close the door.
There's a draft.

Türe zu wegen Durchzug.[44]

This inscription by a German prisoner is written on the inside of the front exit door. A shorter version is on an interior door:

Close the door!
Türe zu![45]

14.

There were 21 men captured at Attu Island.
Their whereabouts are unknown.

熱田島ノ全部二十一名捕虜
行先不明[46]

FIGURE 5.3   *"Close the door. There's a draft."*

Attu is the westernmost of the Near Islands group of the Aleutian Islands of Alaska. A detachment of 8,500 Japanese forces occupied it and the neighboring islands of Agattu and Kiska in 1942. The Aleutians are American soil, so the Japanese presence there was considered a provocation and a danger because the islands might become a staging point for air attacks on the West Coast. A massive American air, land, and sea force was sent to retake the islands. The battle for Attu that began on May 11, 1943 saw fierce, bloody fighting as the Americans gradually dislodged the Japanese troops from the frozen hills. It culminated on May 29, when a remaining force of approximately 1,000 Japanese mounted a sudden charge on the American positions. When it failed, and defeat was imminent, most of the survivors committed suicide with hand grenades. Only twenty-eight Japanese prisoners were taken. The Americans buried 2,351 Japanese soldiers in mass graves, and it was thought that several hundred more were buried in the hills. Within weeks the remaining Japanese troops in the Aleutians withdrew.[47]

15.

Attu Island
Mukano—
I was in this room for the last two or three days.
Demon Eye
May 2

熱田島

迎野君

小生ハ二三日前此の部屋を立った

鬼の目

五月二日

[48]

16.

We arrived here on September 12.
We did not find our place of death—
We were captured and are detained here.

吾等ハ九月十二日至着セリ

死場処ヲ得ズシテ

捕エラレ此処ニ留置サル

[49]

17.

Long live the Great Japanese Empire!

大日本帝國萬歲
50

18.

Every heart in the Great Japanese Empire thinks of victory. We must win!

必勝
51

大日本帝國心心念勝

19.

Stupid Yankees
Jisei

二清
52

やんきのばか

FIGURE 5.4   *"Long live the Great Japanese Empire!"*

20.

July 12, Nineteenth year of Shōwa (1944).
South Pacific Archipelago

南洋群[53]

昭和十九年七月十二日

21.

On September 10, 1944, came to this island from Hawaii. 42 [?] persons.

四[十][二]名[54]

一九四四九月拾日でハワイから本島に來る

22.

All those at the airbases on Saipan and Tinian islands kept up their spirits until the end!
I am leaving in February of next year.

サイパンテニアン島ノ航空廠ノ皆様ハ元気デ最後マデヤレ
小生ハ出発ス來年二月[55]

FIGURE 5.5 *Saipan and Tinian inscription.*

Saipan and Tinian are the two most important islands in the Marianas, and in 1944 were key battle sites of the Pacific War. The Marianas group was part of the main defense line of the Japanese forces, so both Saipan and Tinian were heavily fortified and garrisoned. The US military was determined to defeat the Japanese there, to follow up on Allied victories in the Solomon, Gilbert, and Marshall Islands and Papua New Guinea. The bloody Battle of Saipan was fought from June 15 to July 9, and the Battle of Tinian followed from July 24 to August 1. On Saipan, the American landing was accomplished with heavy losses on both sides. The Japanese forces regrouped in the hills, and the ensuing days saw vicious hand-to-hand fighting to root them out. On July 7, 3,000 remaining Japanese soldiers mounted a furious suicide charge on the American positions, but were defeated. Hundreds of Japanese civilians also committed suicide rather than be taken prisoner. In total, over 30,000 Japanese troops and 22,000 civilians died, and there were over

14,000 US killed and wounded. The Battle of Tinian followed a similar pattern, with the Japanese troops retreating to the interior and carrying out guerilla attacks. A Japanese suicide charge was also the final act of the battle there. More than 8,000 Japanese soldiers died, and almost 400 Americans. The Americans then controlled both islands, but small groups of Japanese troops held out in the jungles for months. In 1945, the airbase at Tinian was the takeoff point for the missions to drop the atomic bombs on Hiroshima and Nagasaki.

23.

Dangerous person	危險人物
Coming from Saipan.	サイパン□
Ōtsuka [??]	大塚□□
Beware!!	注意せよ

56

One Japanese prisoner who was brought to the US mainland after capture at Saipan had the surname Ōtsuka. Camp Tracy rosters report that Hajime Ōtsuka, an army private, arrived there for interrogation on April 2, 1945. He would have been processed at Angel Island in the preceding days. He had been captured in Saipan on August 21, 1944. While the given name in the inscription is illegible, what can be seen is consistent with Hajime (肇).[57]

Adding to the ominous content of this inscription is the fact that someone later defaced it with a sharp object.

24.

Nakata Tsunemichi	仲田恒道
For the sake of Japanese victory	日本ノ勝利ヲトナエ
Murder by poison	毒殺

58

Nakata has not been identified, which makes it difficult to date this inscription. It could be either from the Second World War or pre-war periods—as Japan was engaged in military actions in Asia throughout much of the early twentieth century. It is carved, which perhaps makes it more likely to be prewar.

25.

Overthrow America and Britain!
The landing on the American mainland is near.

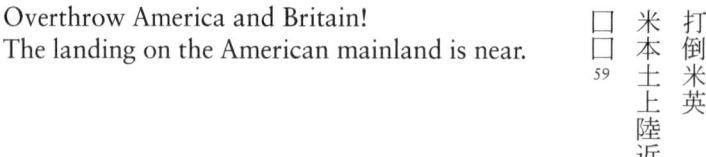

26.

To honor the country
There are not differing ways,
But only one—
Whether one fights on the field of battle
Or toils in the fields at home.

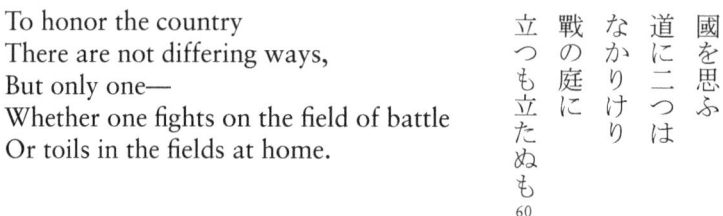

The inscription quotes a famous poem, which is often paired with a story.

During the Sino-Japanese War (1894–1895), an old man and his son were toiling on their farm, pulling a cart along a path between rice paddies. The son was limping and having a difficult time of it. A soldier happened by, and the old man and his son moved aside to make way for him. The soldier said, "Grandfather, it must be a tough job." The old man replied, "Our nation is having a hard time in this war, but my son cannot go to the battlefield as he is lame in his leg. We are very sorry, Sir." The soldier left, and later called an attendant to him. He wrapped some money in a packet and instructed the attendant to give it to the old man and his son. Then he composed this poem. The soldier was Emperor Meiji.

At the time of the Sino-Japanese War, Mutsuhito, Emperor Meiji, was forty-two years old, and had been on the throne for twenty-seven years. To show his concern for the troops, he temporarily relocated the Imperial General Headquarters to Hiroshima, the military staging ground for the conflict.

27.

On July 3, Nineteenth Year of Shōwa (1944), we left New Caledonia.
On the 24th day of the same month, during daytime, we arrived at the port of San Francisco.
On the 25th we disembarked the ship and came to the holding center.
P.W. (prisoners of war), 39 persons.

August 2, Morning: 10 persons left for an unnamed location.
August 5, before noon: 20 persons left for an unnamed location.
August 5, after noon: nine persons left for an unnamed location.

28.

Overthrow America!

29.

Japan must win!

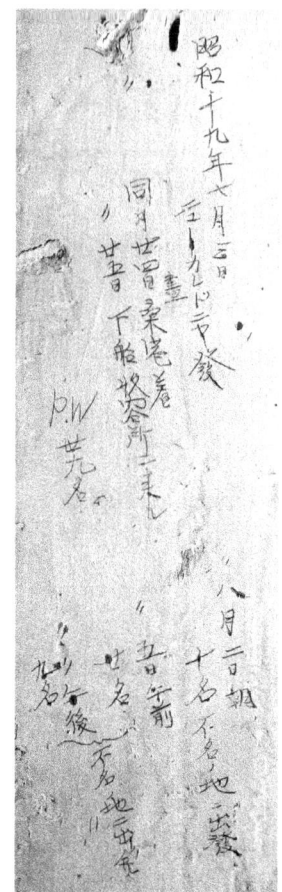

FIGURE 5.6 *Japanese POW diary inscription. Photo: ARG and Daniel Quan.*

30.

January 24, 20th Year of Shōwa (1945)

The love in our hearts for our parents
Cannot match the depth of our parents' love for us.
What will they think
When they learn our fates?

昭和二十年一月二十四日

親思ふ
心にまさる親心
我等の生活
なんと思ふ
64

The inscription is in the form of a *tanka* poem. *Tanka* are usually five segments in a 5-7-5-7-7 syllable pattern. The text here is only slightly irregular: 5-7-5-7-6.

oya omou
kokoro ni masaru
oyagokoro
warera no seikatsu
nan to omou[65]

The first part (5-7-5) is an exact quote from the death poem of Yoshida Shōin (吉田松陰, 1830–1859), an influential intellectual and teacher who was executed as a rebel by the Tokugawa shogunate. Yoshida's poem concludes, "How will they take the news of today?" (けふの音づれ 何と聞くらん). The POW writer gives his own variation of Yoshida's conclusion. That he models his inscription on a death poem suggests that he sees death and capture as equivalent.

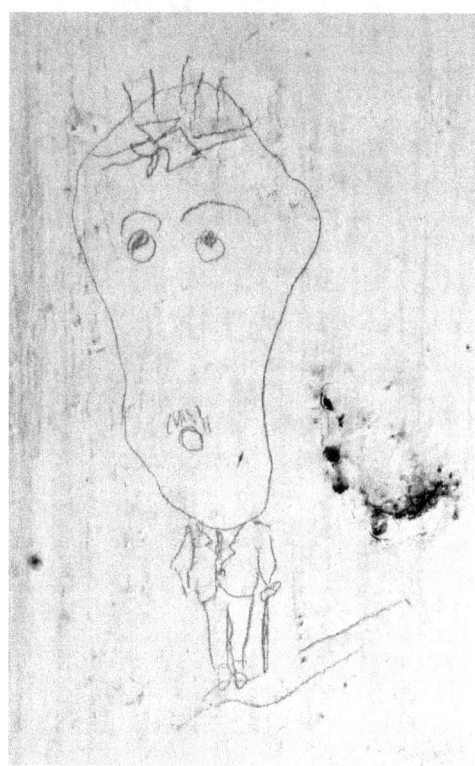

FIGURE 5.7 *Japanese POW cartoon.*

FIGURE 5.8   *Guard station in the barracks.*

FIGURE 5.9   *Guard tower with machine gun swivel mount, seen from the barracks in 1971. Photo: Denis Englander.*

31.

EMERGENCY ONLY
Alarm Instructions
In Case of Emergency Press Both
Buttons for 15 Seconds

For Schedule Signals Press Button
black box for 5 Seconds

For Sgt. of Guard
3 short bells—black box

For Corporal of Guard
2 short bells—black box[66]

BY POST-WAR DEPORTEES

32.

To the Honorable Sergeant Takeda:
On September [?] we will set out.
In high spirits we await our opportunities.
We expect smooth sailing ahead, maybe.
Torikai

武田軍曹殿
九月□□出発ス
大氣で時節を待たう
待てば海路の日和やら
鳥飼
[67]

33.

Fukui, Yoshioka, and Matsuda are going first.
On 9-25 all the rest will set out together.

福井
吉岡よ松田は
先〔へ〕行く
9-25
他一同出発ス
[68]

34.

Mr. Honma:
Eight people are going first.
Twenty people will set out on September 25.
Everyone is well.
Hirata and others

重田氏之中の口多！！
本間さん
平田外一同
八人わ先に行き
二十人わ九月二十五日
出發皆元氣なり
69

35.

To everyone with Mr. Shigeta!!
It seems that the second vanguard group of 600 people will set out on November 7 at 1:00 in the afternoon.
The westward journey direct to Yokohama will take about 15 days.
(Tōshi from Palau)

第二回先発隊（６００名）ハ十一月七日午後一時当地出発セリ
横浜直航ニシテ航程十五日間ナリ
（パラオ遠ヨリ）
70

The Battle of Peleliu was fought in the Palau archipelago from September to November 1944. It was a grueling battle for a small territory with only modest strategic importance. US forces lost almost 2,000 killed and 8,500 wounded in the fight for Peleliu Island and nearby Angaur Island, while more than 10,000 Japanese were killed on Peleliu and another 1,350 on Angaur. Less than 300 prisoners were taken, most of whom were Okinawan and Korean laborers rather than Japanese soldiers.[71]

36.

Regards to Mr. Tanaka Saitō.
November 7, Twentieth year of Shōwa (1945)
About 700 persons will set out for Yokohama.
    Mountain Bandit
    Mr. Kaku
    Tomi
    Ponchū
    Happy
    Shōri
    Saisatsu
We wish you good health.
We may meet again sometime.
Kōhō

昭和二十年十一月七日
約七百名横濱向出發ス
山賊　角サン　富
ポン中　喜生　少リ　才册
請君元氣デ　又会う時
モアリツラン　[項]　方
田中斉[藤]サンニ宜敷ク
72

37.

All of us from McCoy are healthy,
And will leave here on November 7.

マッコイノ皆様元気デ
十一月七日に出発ス
73

McCoy is Camp McCoy, Wisconsin.

38.

To Mr. Sawada Takeo
We are keeping in good health.
Please give our regards to the Hakudo [?] Group and to Mr. Kurokawa.
Kanda ??
Togashi Saburō
Yūkai [??] Masami

沢田武夫君お□
大切に元気でせって□
白堂皆に黒[川]に□って下さい
監田市□
富樫三郎
由[海]正美
74

"Hakudo" has not been identified. It is literally "white hall," and may be a place name.

39.

Please wish good health to . . .
Mr. Kurokawa Teruo should take care of himself.
From Tadao

忠[夫]より

黒川輝夫君お体を大切

口にて元気やって下さい

75

40.

The time has come for me to fulfill my duty.
I think that until it becomes clear whether or not
The separation of life and death will come between us,
I will hold strongly to the proper course.
I pray you will make strong efforts.

More than 600 persons are leaving on November 7.

600名多

11.7 出発ス

御健闘を祈る

我正道に強く口持

想いは一念死生離別の明らかな迄

我使命達成すべき時機来る

76

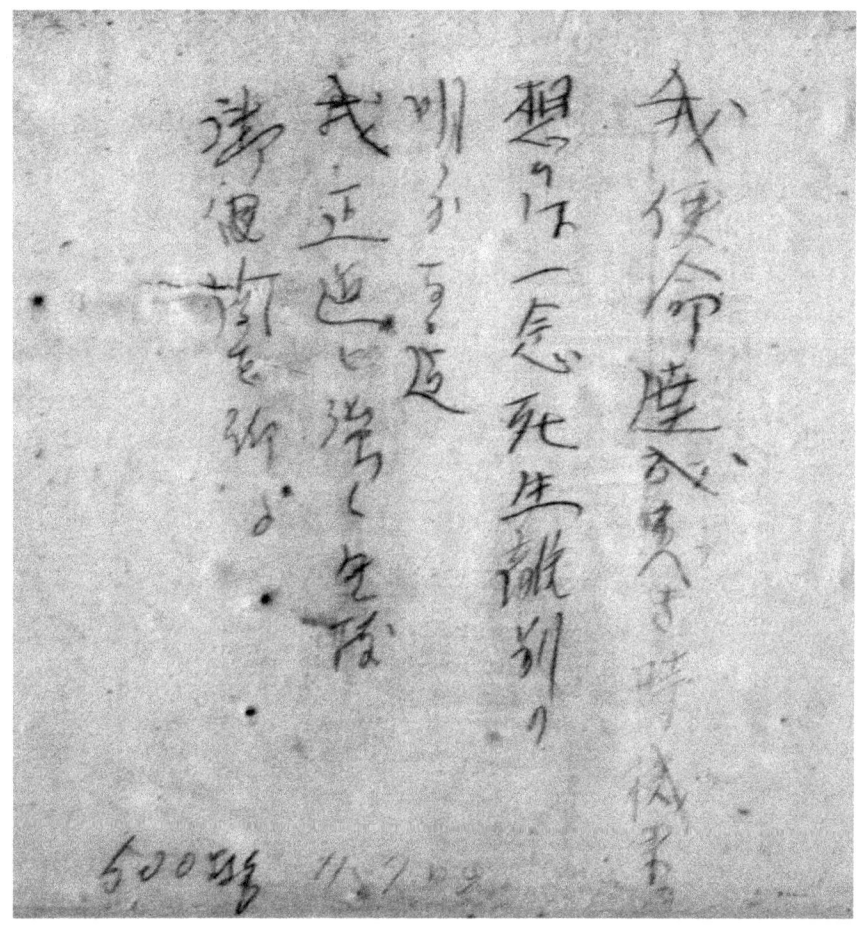

FIGURE 5.10 *"The time has come for me to fulfill my duty."*

Appendices

A. Poem Numbers in *Island*, 1st and 2nd Editions

There are two editions of *Island*, and the numbering systems in them differ. For convenience, the citations in this book follow the 2nd edition (published 2014). The 1st edition divided the poems into two sections, a main section with 69 poems (#1–#69), and an appendix with 66 (#a1–#a66). The 2nd edition combines the two sections into one (#1–#135). Appendix A is provided as a key to relate the two.

1st edition – (2nd edition)

#1 – (#1)	#20 – (#31)	#39 – (#71)
#2 – (#2)	#21 – (#32)	#40 – (#72)
#3 – (#3)	#22 – (#33)	#41 – (#73)
#4 – (#4)	#23 – (#34)	#42 – (#74)
#5 – (#5)	#24 – (#35)	#43 – (#75)
#6 – (#6)	#25 – (#36)	#44 – (#76)
#7 – (#7)	#26 – (#37)	#45 – (#77)
#8 – (#8)	#27 – (#38)	#46 – (#78)
#9 – (#9)	#28 – (#39)	#47 – (#91)
#10 – (#10)	#29 – (#40)	#48 – (#92)
#11 – (#11)	#30 – (#41)	#49 – (#95)
#12 – (#23)	#31 – (#42)	#50 – (#94)
#13 – (#24)	#32 – (#43)	#51 – (#103)
#14 – (#25)	#33 – (#44)	#52 – (#101)
#15 – (#26)	#34 – (#65)	#53 – (#102)
#16 – (#27)	#35 – (#66)	#54 – (#98)
#17 – (#28)	#36 – (#67)	#55 – (#112)
#18 – (#29)	#37 – (#68)	#56 – (#106)
#19 – (#30)	#38 – (#70)	#57 – (#114)

#58 – (#128)	#a15 – (#49)	#a41 – (#87)
#59 – (#123)	#a16 – (#50)	#a42 – (#69)
#60 – (#124)	#a17 – (#51)	#a43 – (#89)
#61 – (#115)	#a18 – (#52)	#a44 – (#118)
#62 – (#130)	#a19 – (#53)	#a45 – (#110)
#63 – (#117)	#a20 – (#19)	#a46 – (#99)
#64 – (#119)	#a21 – (#20)	#a47 – (#104)
#65 – (#125)	#a22 – (#21)	#a48 – (#108)
#66 – (#120)	#a23 – (#54)	#a49 – (#96)
#67 – (#131)	#a24 – (#55)	#a50 – (#97)
#68 – (#132)	#a25 – (#22)	#a51 – (#93)
#69 – (#135)	#a26 – (#56)	#a52 – (#105)
#a1 – (#12)	#a27 – (#57)	#a53 – (#100)
#a2 – (#13)	#a28 – (#58)	#a54 – (#111)
#a3 – (#14)	#a29 – (#59)	#a55 – (#107)
#a4 – (#109)	#a30 – (#82)	#a56 – (#127)
#a5 – (#15)	#a31 – (#60)	#a57 – (#126)
#a6 – (#16)	#a32 – (#61)	#a58 – (#121)
#a7 – (#80)	#a33 – (#83)	#a59 – (#122)
#a8 – (#81)	#a34 – (#79)	#a60 – (#90)
#a9 – (#17)	#a35 – (#84)	#a61 – (#133)
#a10 – (#18)	#a36 – (#85)	#a62 – (#134)
#a11 – (#45)	#a37 – (#86)	#a63 – (#129)
#a12 – (#46)	#a38 – (#116)	#a64 – (#62)
#a13 – (#47)	#a39 – (#113)	#a65 – (#63)
#a14 – (#48)	#a40 – (#88)	#a66 – (#64)

2nd edition – (1st edition)

#1 – (#1)	#16 – (#a6)	#31 – (#20)
#2 – (#2)	#17 – (#a9)	#32 – (#21)
#3 – (#3)	#18 – (#a10)	#33 – (#22)
#4 – (#4)	#19 – (#a20)	#34 – (#23)
#5 – (#5)	#20 – (#a21)	#35 – (#24)
#6 – (#6)	#21 – (#a22)	#36 – (#25)
#7 – (#7)	#22 – (#a25)	#37 – (#26)
#8 – (#8)	#23 – (#12)	#38 – (#27)
#9 – (#9)	#24 – (#13)	#39 – (#28)
#10 – (#10)	#25 – (#14)	#40 – (#29)
#11 – (#11)	#26 – (#15)	#41 – (#30)
#12 – (#a1)	#27 – (#16)	#42 – (#31)
#13 – (#a2)	#28 – (#17)	#43 – (#32)
#14 – (#a3)	#29 – (#18)	#44 – (#33)
#15 – (#a5)	#30 – (#19)	#45 – (#a11)

#46 – (#a12)	#76 – (#44)	#106 – (#56)
#47 – (#a13)	#77 – (#45)	#107 – (#a55)
#48 – (#a14)	#78 – (#46)	#108 – (#a48)
#49 – (#a15)	#79 – (#a34)	#109 – (#a4)
#50 – (#a16)	#80 – (#a7)	#110 – (#a45)
#51 – (#a17)	#81 – (#a8)	#111 – (#a54)
#52 – (#a18)	#82 – (#a30)	#112 – (#a55)
#53 – (#a19)	#83 – (#a33)	#113 – (#a39)
#54 – (#a23)	#84 – (#a35)	#114 – (#57)
#55 – (#a24)	#85 – (#a36)	#115 – (#61)
#56 – (#a26)	#86 – (#a37)	#116 – (#a38)
#57 – (#a27)	#87 – (#a41)	#117 – (#63)
#58 – (#a28)	#88 – (#a40)	#118 – (#a44)
#59 – (#a29)	#89 – (#a43)	#119 – (#64)
#60 – (#a31)	#90 – (#a60)	#120 – (#66)
#61 – (#a32)	#91 – (#47)	#121 – (#a58)
#62 – (#a64)	#92 – (#48)	#122 – (#a59)
#63 – (#a65)	#93 – (#a51)	#123 – (#59)
#64 – (#a66)	#94 – (#50)	#124 – (#60)
#65 – (#34)	#95 – (#49)	#125 – (#65)
#66 – (#35)	#96 – (#a49)	#126 – (#a57)
#67 – (#36)	#97 – (#a50)	#127 – (#a56)
#68 – (#37)	#98 – (#54)	#128 – (#58)
#69 – (#a42)	#99 – (#a46)	#129 – (#a63)
#70 – (#38)	#100 – (#a53)	#130 – (#62)
#71 – (#39)	#101 – (#52)	#131 – (#67)
#72 – (#40)	#102 – (#53)	#132 – (#68)
#73 – (#41)	#103 – (#51)	#133 – (#a61)
#74 – (#42)	#104 – (#a47)	#134 – (#a62)
#75 – (#43)	#105 – (#a52)	#135 – (#69)

B. Wall Locations of *Island* Poems (*Island* 2nd Edition Order)

The notations following → indicate the barracks locations. See the maps and the explanation of the location codes in the Introduction.

#1→205-E-6/7	#7→Not found	#13→105-S-5
#2→109-N-1	#8→205-N-6	#14→105-S-5
#3→105-N-4	#9→205-N-6	#15→205-S-5
#4→105-E-4	#10→Not found	#16→205-S-1
#5→Not found	#11→105-N-2	#17→Not found
#6→105-N-6	#12→206-E-2	#18→Not found

#19→Not found	#58→Not found	#97→Not found
#20→Not found	#59→Not found	#98→205-W-5
#21→205-N-3	#60→205-W-5	#99→Not found
#22→205-S-5	#61→205-N-6	#100→105-N-6
#23→205-W-4	#62→Not found	#101→105-N-5
#24→105-N-4	#63→Not found	#102→105-N-5
#25→105-N-3	#64→Not found	#103→105-N-4
#26→205-N-6	#65→Not found	#104→Not found
#27→Not found	#66→205-E-3	#105→Not found
#28→205-N-3	#67→115-W-5	#106→213-E-1/2
#29→Not found	#68→105-N-2	#107→205-W-1
#30→Not found	#69→105-N-2	#108→205-N-2
#31→105-S-5	#70→205-W-5	#109→205-E-8
#32→105-N-6	#71→205-N-5	#110→205-S-1
#33→205-E-1	#72→205-N-6	#111→205-N-3 *and* 4
#34→105-S-6	#73→205-N-2	#112→205-N-3 *and* 4
#35→105-N-4	#74→205-E-3	#113→205-S-5
#36→105-S-1	#75→207-N-1	#114→205-N-5
#37→205-S-2	#76→105-S-1	#115→205-S-1
#38→Not found	#77→105-N-5	#116→105-S-4
#39→205-N-5	#78→105-E-2	#117→105-S-4
#40→205-S-3	#79→105-E-2	#118→Not found
#41→205-E-5	#80→105-N-2	#119→105-E-5
#42→105-W-1	#81→205-S-6 (partial)	#120→105-E-1
#43→205-S-3	#82→105-S-1	#121→205-N-5
#44→205-N-5	#83→205-N-4	#122→Not found
#45→205-N-3	#84→105-E-5	#123→Not found
#46→205-S-1	#85→205-E-1	#124→205-W-5
#47→205-S-2	#86→Not found	#125→105-E-4
#48→Not found	#87→205-E-6/7	#126→Not found
#49→205-S-1	#88→205-S-1	#127→205-S-3
#50→105-N-5	#89→105-N-3	#128→Not found
#51→Not found	#90→105-N-3	#129→105-S-6
#52→Not found	#91→205-S-2	#130→105-S-6
#53→205-S-3	#92→205-N-2	#131→105-S-2
#54→Not found	#93→205-N-3	#132→105-E-2 *and* E-3
#55→Not found	#94→205-E-1	#133→105-N-1
#56→Not found	#95→105-N-6	#134→105-S-5
#57→Not found	#96→205-S-1	#135→111-N-1

APPENDICES 291

REMARKS: 101 of the 135 *Island* texts have been located on the walls, while thirty-four have not been found. As #18 was by Smiley Jann, and was never written on the wall, and #118 from the two manuscripts is a version of #117 at 105-S-4, they can be dropped from the statistics, leaving thirty-two texts not yet located. Of these, nineteen are in the Tet Yee and Smiley Jann manuscripts, and so were presumably visible on the walls in the 1930s.

A popular early-twentieth century literary miscellany was the *Island* authors' source for two of the thirty-two unlocated poems, and various Chinese newspapers/journals of the 1970s were sources for another ten, as follows:

- The authorship and composition date of the *Yuehai Chunqiu* [Spring and Autumn Annals of the Guangdong Seas] is uncertain; among multiple editions, one was published in San Francisco in 1923 (see Bibliography). One of the entries is "Commentary on Travel to America and Imprisonment in the Wooden Building," and five poems are appended in a separate entry. Yet the prose text makes no mention of Angel Island or detainment of any sort. The appended poems do describe the ordeal of detainment, but do not mention or describe the island. Three of the five poems have been found on the barracks walls (#50 and #130 were noted in *Island*, and #106 was found during recent researches), yet the *Island* authors allow the possibility that they were quoted from this work. Thus we cannot assume the other two *Yuehai Chunqiu* poems (#17 and #54) were ever on the walls.
- In 1974, *Jiujinshan zhoubao* [San Francisco Weekly] published fourteen poems transcribed from the walls. Thirteen have been located, which gives confidence that the missing poem (#65) is—or was in 1974—on the walls.
- Thirteen poems were published by "Pangu Huang" in *Tiansheng zhoubao* [Tiansheng Weekly] in 1979. Pangu Huang is literally "Emperor Pangu"—a pseudonym based on the myth of Pangu, first living being and creator of the world. The article begins with a brief statement that the poems were copied from the walls of the second floor of the barracks more than forty years earlier, and are presented exactly as transcribed. Such vagueness does not inspire confidence, yet nine of the poems have indeed been located on the second floor, all in Room 205. This suggests that the missing poems (#56, #57, #58, and #105) were likely also on the walls of Room 205 in the 1930s, though we cannot say with certainty.
- Readers provided six poems to writers at *Taipingyang zhoubao* [The Chinese Pacific Weekly] in 1978. Three of the poems were submitted by Mr. Allen T. Fong (方引提); two of these were published in the magazine (#10 and #38) in an article by Man Hei Fong (方民希),

and one (#48) was not published, but was forwarded by Man Hei Fong to Him Mark Lai upon receipt. The article notes that Mr. Fong copied the poems more than fifty years earlier—in the 1920s—when he was detained at Angel Island. None of the three has been found on the walls. An article by the magazine's lead writer Jingnan Hu (signed Jingnan) included two couplets and one complete poem (#62, #63, and #64) sent in by a reader identified only as Mr. Chen from Fire Island, New York. Mr. Chen said that he had been at Angel Island in 1924, when he was eleven. He said he did not copy the poems then, but remembered reading them on the walls. None have been found. One of the couplets is #63, translated in *Island* as "Having not yet crossed the Yellow River, my heart is not at peace / After crossing the Yellow River, a double stream of tears flow": 未過黃河心不息/過了黃河雙淚流. This is not an original text, but is rather a variation of a common folk aphorism, often rendered as "Before reaching the Yellow River, one's heart will never cease; / Upon reaching the Yellow River, one's heart then will die": 不到黃河不死心/到了黃河心就死. The gist of the phrase is that one should strive until the end. The source story has the Wu River rather than the Yellow River. After his battle with Liu Bang of Han (*c.* 256–195 BCE) for control of the empire was lost, Xiang Yu of Chu (232–202 BCE) escaped to the banks of the Wu River. Rather than crossing the river into exile, Xiang Yu chose to accept his loss of Heaven's mandate, and thereupon slit his own throat. As for the second couplet (#64), Mr. Chen said that while he was there, a despondent detainee hanged himself, and the lines were written on the wall the next day. Although there are stories about detainee suicides (see Lee and Yung, *Angel Island*, pp. 101–102), the only confirmed Chinese suicide in the barracks was Fong Fook in October 1919. None has so far been documented in the 1920s. The complete (quatrain) poem, #62, is definitely not from the walls of Angel Island. Except for the third line and part of the fourth line, the *Island* text is identical with a famous poem by Yun Daiying, 惲代英 (1895–1931). Yun was an early Communist Party leader and propagandist who was executed by the Nationalists in 1931. His poem, "Written in Prison" (獄中詩), dates to that year, so Mr. Chen could not have seen it at Angel Island in 1924.

Taking into consideration the possibility that at least some of the texts from the miscellany and newspapers/journals were never on the walls, recent efforts have identified the locations of between 77 and 84 percent of the *Island* inscriptions.

C. Wall Locations of *Island* 2nd ed. Poems (Wall Order)

105-N-1: #133
105-N-2: #11, #68, #69, #80
105-N-3: #25, #89, #90
105-N-4: #24, #35, #103
105-N-5: #50, #77, #101, #102
105-N-6: #6, #32, #95, #100
105-S-1: #36, #76, #82
105-S-2: #131
105-S-4: #116, #117
105-S-5: #13, #14, #31, #134
105-S-6: #34, #129, #130
105-E-1: #120
105-E-2: #78, #79, #132
105-E-3: #132
105-E-4: #4, #125
105-E-5: #84. #119
105-W-1: #42
109-N-1: #2
111-N-1: #135
115-W-5: #67
205-N-2: #73, #92, #108
205-N-3: #21, #28, #45, #93, #111, #112
205-N-4: #83, #111, #112,
205-N-5: #39, #44, #71, #114, #121
205-N-6: #8, #9, #26, #61, #72
205-S-1: #16, #46, #49, #88, #96, #110, #115
205-S-2: #37, #47, #91
205-S-3: #40, #43, #53, #127
205-S-5: #15, #22, #113
205-S-6: #81 (partial)
205-E-1: #33, #85, #94
205-E-3: #66, #74
205-E-5: #41
205-E-6/7: #1, #87
205-E-8: #109
205-W-1: #107
205-W-5: #60, #70, #98, #124
206-E-2: #12
207-N-1: #75
213-E-1/2: #106

D. Tet Yee Manuscript Poems and Locations

In this and the following table, manuscript order is indicated first. The Tet Yee manuscript records ninety-six texts (one was copied twice). Fifteen of those with corresponding versions in *Island* have not yet been located on the walls. Listing the poems in the order in which Yee recorded them and noting the known locations helps us to track his movements through the building, and may give an indication of where the missing poems may have been. Comparison with the walls shows Yee was a generally faithful scribe, though three of his texts are incomplete (corresponding to *Island* #24, #32, and #116), and there are minor differences in others (e.g., #14, #31, #82). Two manuscript texts have no versions in *Island* (one twelve-line poem and a couplet fragment), and are marked "NEW." One quatrain text corresponds to *Island* #68 in the first couplet, but has a different conclusion, and so is also marked "NEW."

1. #34→105-S-6ª
2. #55→Not found
3. #44→205-N-5
4. #87→205-E-6/7
5. #53→205-S-3
6. #43→205-S-3
7. #40→205-S-3
8. #37→205-S-2
9. #91→205-S-2
10. #115→205-S-1
11. #1→205-E-6/7
12. #46→205-S-1
13. #88→205-S-1
14. #27→Not found
15. #25→105-N-3
16. #124→205-W-5
17. #85→205-E-1
18. #98→205-W-5
19. #28→205-N-3
20. #21→205-N-3
21. #93→205-N-3
22. #45→205-N-3ᵇ
23. #45→205-N-3
24. #107→205-W-1
25. #22→205-S-5
26. #110→205-S-1
27. #49→205-S-1
28. #47→205-S-2
29. #125→105-E-4
30. #4→105-E-4
31. #94→205-E-1
32. #74→205-E-3
33. #92→205-N-2
34. #73→205-N-2
35. #61→205-N-6
36. #39→205-N-6
37. #26→205-N-6
38. #130→105-S-6ᶜ
39. #130→105-S-6
40. #121→205-N-5
41. #59→Not found
42. #128→Not found
43. #34→105-S-6
44. #118→Not found; related to #117→105-S-4ᵈ
45. #30→Not found
46. #82→105-S-1
47. #97→Not found
48. #7→Not found
49. #123→Not found
50. #20→Not found
51. #5→Not foundᵉ
52. #5→Not found
53. NEW→Not found
54. #116→105-S-4
55. #36→105-S-1
56. #77→105-N-5
57. #108→205-N-2
58. #112→205-N-3 and 4ᶠ
59. #111→205-N-3 and 4
60. #8→205-N-6
61. #96→205-S-1
62. #41→205-E-5
63. #72→205-N-6
64. #114→205-N-5
65. #71→205-N-5
66. #50→105-N-5
67. #70→205-W-5
68. #102→105-N-5
69. #3→105-N-4
70. #103→105-N-4
71. #66→205-E-3
72. #60→205-W-5
73. #100→105-N-6
74. #95→105-N-6
75. #120→105-E-1
76. NEW→105-E-1
77. #6→105-N-6
78. #9→205-N-6
79. #33→205-E-1
80. #35→105-N-4
81. #24→105-N-4
82. #11→105-N-2
83. #32→105-N-6
84. #119→105-E-5
85. #19→Not found
86. #84→105-E-5
87. #78→105-E-2
88. #79→105-E-2
89. #83→205-N-4
90. #42→105-W-1
91. #113→205-S-5
92. #51→Not found
93. #122→Not found
94. #99→Not found
95. NEW→Not found; related to #68→105-N-2ᵍ
96. #14→105-S-5
97. #31→105-S-5

ᵃ Yee also records this poem as his text 43, so the ninety-seven texts in his manuscript are actually ninety-six. ᵇ *Island* uses a single poem number for the quatrains in Yee's texts 22–23. ᶜ *Island* uses a single poem number for the quatrains in Yee's texts 38–39. ᵈ Yee records a pentasyllabic version of #118 (unlocated) corresponding to the tetrasyllabic #117 still visible at 105-S-4. ᵉ Although published as a single eight-line poem in *Island*, Yee marks two quatrains, texts 51–52. ᶠ *Island* #111 and #112 are each carved twice on the walls. ᵍ The first couplet closely matches that of #68 at 105-N-2, but the second couplet differs; Yee's text corresponds closely with the transcription by Smiley Jann.

REMARKS: There are several points of interest here. All of the located poems in the table are in Rooms 105 and 205, the large Chinese men's dormitories. This means that Tet Yee probably did not have access to the other rooms, where a great many Chinese inscriptions are also found. Ten of the missing poems are clustered together, and the located poems that bracket them suggest the south wall of Room 105 might be one place to look for them, if they are ever to be found. It is notable that there is evidence of an alteration to the building at 105-S-6: a door there half covers a row of characters. Inscriptions may have been lost. Bracketing poems also suggest that *Island* #19 may be at or near 105-E-5. When bracketing poems differ, two possible locations are suggested; for example, #27 is preceded in the manuscript by #88 at 205-S-1, and followed by #25 at 105-N-3.

E. Smiley Jann Manuscript Poems and Locations

The Smiley Jann manuscript originally included ninety-nine numbered texts (the number 48 was erroneously used twice), but as pages are missing, ninety-two texts remain. Eighteen texts with corresponding versions in *Island* have not been located on the walls. The order of the entries is of somewhat limited usefulness in locating the missing poems, as Jann groups texts by form, not location. Yet some geographic patterns remain within the categories. Comparison of Jann's texts with the wall carvings reveals numerous differences, which suggests Jann was more likely than Yee to edit or revise. The new twelve-line poem in the Yee manuscript is also recorded by Jann. In addition, two quatrain examples combine first couplets corresponding to published poems with new endings. The first is related to *Island* #68, and was also transcribed by Tet Yee; the second is related to *Island* #34. Thus altogether four new or partially new poems are found in the Yee and Jann manuscripts; all are published in this collection.

1. #118→Not found; related to #117→105-S-4[a]
2. #36→105-S-1
3. #119→105-E-5
4. #5→Not found *and* #14→105-S-5[b]
5. #39→205-N-5
6. #5→Not found (1 half); NEW→Not found (2 half)[c]
7. #23→205-W-4
8. #26→205-N-6
9. #86→Not found
10. #46→205-S-1
11. #8→205-N-6
12. #27→Not found
13. #115→205-S-1
14. #50→105-N-5
15. #101→105-N-5
16. #102→105-N-5
17. #100→105-N-6
18. #71→205-N-5
19. #103→105-N-4[d]

20. #120→105-E-4
21. #95→105-N-6
22. #6→105-N-6
23. #33→205-E-1
24. #19→Not found
25. #35→105-N-4
26. #84→105-E-5
27. #124→205-W-5
28. #107→205-W-1
29. #85→205-E-1
30. #28→205-N-3
31. #22→205-S-5
32. #49→205-S-1
33. #21→205-N-3
34. #93→205-N-3
35. #125→105-E-4
36. #4→105-E-4
37. #51→Not found
38. #79→105-E-2
39. #78→105-E-2
40. #122→Not found
41. #20→Not found
42. NEW→Not found related to #68→105-N-2[e]
43. #116→105-S-4[f]
44. #94→205-E-1
45. #74→205-E-3
46. #61→205-N-6
47. #121→205-N-5
48a. #59→Not found
48b. NEW→Not found; related to #34→105-S-6[g]
49. #29→Not found
50. #30→Not found
51. #127→205-S-3
52. #126→Not found
53. #131→105-S-2
54. #37→205-S-2
55. #91→205-S-2
56. #43→205-S-3
57. #40→205-S-3
58. #41→205-E-5
59. #72→205-N-6
60. #114→205-N-5
61. #70→205-W-5
62. #60→205-W-5
63. #9→205-N-6
64. #32→105-N-6
65. #98→205-W-5
66. #83→205-N-4
67. #42→105-W-1
68. #113→205-S-5
69. #77→105-N-5
70. #104→Not found
71. #123→Not found
72. #108→205-N-2
73. Missing ms. pages
74. Missing ms. pages
75. Missing ms. pages
76. Missing ms. pages
77. Missing ms. pages
78. Missing ms. pages
79. Missing ms. pages
80. #112→205-N-3 and 4[h]
81. #111→205-N-3 and 4
82. #130→105-S-6
83. #128→Not found
84. #55→Not found
85. #99→Not found
86. #96→205-S-1 and #99→Not found[i]
87. #7→Not found
88. #90→105-N-3
89. #52→Not found
90. #18→Not found
91. #24→105-N-4[j]
92. #24→105-N-4; #25→105-N-3
93. #25→105-N-3
94. #80→105-N-2
95. #16→205-S-1
96. #81→205-S-6
97. #15→205-S-5
98. #44→205-N-5

[a] Like Yee, Jann records a pentasyllabic version of #118 (unlocated) corresponding to the tetrasyllabic #117 still visible at 105-S-4. [b] The manuscript quatrain corresponds to both published poems, one couplet from each. [c] Jann records twenty lines, of which the *first* eight are #5, but the *last* twelve comprise a new pentasyllabic poem also recorded by Tet Yee, and published in this volume. [d] The manuscript version is recognizable as #103, but uses a different rhyme and wording. [e] The first couplet is similar to that of #68 at 105-N-2, but the second couplet differs; Jann's version closely matches the transcription by Tet Yee. [f] Jann records four lines, of which three correspond to the ten-line #116. [g] The first couplet corresponds to #34 at 105-S-6, but the second couplet differs. [h] Poems #111 and #112 (Jann's texts 80–81) are each carved twice on the walls. [i] Jann records only eight

lines corresponding to the fourteen-line #96, and the first two are in fact the last couplet of #99 (as yet not located). ⁱ Jann incorrectly divides #24 and #25 into three in his items 91–93.

REMARKS: All of the located poems in the manuscript are in rooms 105 and 205, which suggests that Jann had no access to other rooms. Patterns in the manuscript order indicate several possible locations for unlocated poems. Since Jann combines couplets from #5→*Not found* and #14→105-S-5, #5 should be at or near 105-S-5. Elsewhere he presents as a single poem #5 and the new twelve-line poem also recorded by Tet Yee; this suggests the new poem is also at or near 105-S-5. A similar case is his combination in a single poem of part of #99→*Not found* with #96→205-S-1, which suggests #99 is at or near 205-S-1. Other strong indications: #51→*Not found* is bracketed by #4→105-E-4 and #79→105-E-2; and #52→*Not found* and #18→*Not found* are bracketed by #90→105-N-3 and #24→105-N-4. Bracketing poems provide less specific directions to other unlocated poems, but in some cases do suggest general locations; for example, #27, #29, #30, and #59 are all bracketed by poems in Room 205.

Comparison of the Yee and Jann manuscripts allows further deductions, as twelve of the unlocated poems appear in both: #5, #7, #19, #20, #27, #30, #51, #59, #99, #122, #123, and #128.

- #5: the hypothesis suggested by the Jann manuscript that this poem is at or near 105-S-5 is supported by the Yee manuscript, which has it in the cluster of unlocated poems that it was deduced may be on the south wall of Room 105. Yee also records the new twelve-line poem in that cluster.
- #20: Jann brackets this poem and others by poems found in various locations in Room 105; Yee has it in the cluster of poems it was deduced may be on the south wall of Room 105.
- #27: Jann brackets this poem with poems at locations 205-N-6 and 205-S-1; Yee brackets it with poems at 205-S-1 and 105-N-3. It would appear 205-S-1 is the place to look.
- #59: in both manuscripts, this poem follows #121→205-N-5.
- #99: the hypothesis suggested by the Jann manuscript that this poem is at or near 205-S-1 is generally supported by the evidence of the Yee manuscript, which records it with other unlocated poems (#51 and #122) following #113→205-S-5.
- #128: in Yee's manuscript, this poem precedes #34→105-S-6, and in Jann's manuscript it follows #130→105-S-6.

F. Wall Locations of Carved Pictures

EXTERIOR-N-3:
    "Blue Sky with a White Sun" flag and "Republic of China" in characters

HOSPITAL:
    Rooster carved in plaster (removed from Asian Men's Ward)
    Bird in tree pencil sketch (removed from Asian Men's Ward)
    Cartoon human figure #1 (removed from Asian Men's Ward)
    Cartoon human figure #2 (removed from Asian Men's Ward)

105-N-2:
    Sinking ship

105-N-3:
    Fish

105-N-4:
    Bird in tree
    Pointing hand
    Two birds

105-N-5:
    Horse

105-N-6:
    Two birds
    Small altar—banners and flags surrounding an ancestral tablet in a basket

105-S-4:
    Pair of fish (whales?)
    Fish
    Scaly fish
    Ship

105-S-5:
    Fish

105-E-1:
    Sandpiper and moon

105-E-2:
    Heron

105-W-4:
    Human face doodle
    Chinese flag with five stripes
    Village scenes—five houses, fields, mountains, bird, and fish

115-N-3:
    Revolver

115-E-1:
    New Zealand flag with initials W.H.

115-E-5:	Ship with flag
115-W-2:	"For Everyone: World Money"—good luck coin with inscription
116-S-2:	Ship with rigging and flags
202-N-1:	Winged horse sketch (probably 1970s)
202-N-1:	Horse head (probably 1970s)
202-E-1:	Horse head (probably 1970s) House (probably 1970s)
202-W-1:	Dove (or magpie) with open beak
202-W-2:	Bird (probably 1970s) Head in profile (probably 1970s)
205-N-1:	Ship. Another faint ship to right Rifle and pistol
205-N-3:	Line of three ships with flags
205-N-4:	Ship
205-N-6:	Shark
205-S-1:	Large altar—banners and flags surrounding an ancestral tablet in a basket
205-S-2:	Large fish with open mouth
205-S-5:	Rising fish
205-E-1:	Large heron
205-W-4:	Ship
205-W-4:	Crossed Chinese and American flags
205-W-4:	Flag

205-W-5:
: House
206-N-1:
: Pennant
207-W-1:
: House
209-E-1:
: Cartoon figure by Japanese POW
209-W-1:
: Galloping horse and rider
211-N-3:
: Japanese flag
: Striped flag on stand
211-E-2:
: Swastika inscribed with "Heil Hitler," defaced with an expletive and a peace sign (probably in the 1970s)
213-N-2:
: Two pinwheels
213-N-2:
: Head in profile

NOTES

Introduction

1 *Washington Post*, July 28, 1911, "Revolution in Immigration."
2 Edward L. Haff, District Director for San Francisco District Immigration and Naturalization Service, to Ted Reindollar, May 14, 1936, file 12030/1, RG 85, NAPS.
3 See Lai, Lim, and Yung, *Island* 2nd ed., p. 340.
4 Report by M.W. Glover, November 21, 1910. A copy is in the Him Mark Lai Papers, Ethnic Studies Library, University of California, Berkeley, Carton #1, Folder #36.
5 Lee and Yung, *Angel Island*, p. 23.
6 Ibid., pp. 4, 17–20.
7 Ibid., Appendix Table 2, pp. 328–329.
8 A figure also suggested by Lee and Yung. Ibid., p. 4.
9 Architectural Resources Group and Daniel Quan Design. "Poetry and Inscriptions: Translation and Analysis."
10 Although we identified up to 70 new Chinese texts that had not previously been published, at that time we were able to completely transcribe and translate less than a dozen. The locations of inscriptions in other languages were recorded, but little else was done with them.
11 See Lai, "Island of Immortals," p. 91.
12 Thanks to the University of Washington Press for permission to cite these examples.
13 Translation and transcription from *Island*, pp. 66–67. Wall text is at 105-N-4.
14 Ibid., pp. 66–67. Wall text is at 205-W-4.
15 Ibid., pp. 140–141. The text is carved twice on the walls, at 205-N-3 and 205-N-4.
16 Ibid., pp. 58–59. Wall text is at 205-S-5.
17 On restoration efforts, see Lee and Yung, *Angel Island*, pp. 299–314.

Chapter 1

1 Spickard, *Japanese Americans*, p. 15. Spickard suggests that the reason so many immigrants came from these localities was not because of any particular economic hardship relative to other parts of Japan, but that labor recruiters were especially active there. See also Gee, "Sifting the Arrivals," p. 6.

2 The Gentlemen's Agreement was not a treaty document, but rather an informal understanding based on correspondence between the US and Japanese governments. See Ichihashi, *Japanese in the United States*, pp. 244–246. Ichihashi quotes a summary of the points in the agreement in the *Annual Report of the United States Commissioner-General of Immigration, 1908* (Washington, 1908), pp. 221–222. On the general topic of early Japanese immigration, see Ichioka, *The Issei*.

3 Ichioka, *The Issei*, p. 165.

4 *Los Angeles Times*, April 8, 1911, "Photographic Marriages: San Francisco Judge Suspects an Immoral Purpose Back of Them and Will Thoroughly Investigate." Until 1917, US authorities required that picture brides be remarried under US law before they were granted admission.

5 Lee and Yung, *Angel Island*, pp. 111–143, esp. 117–127. See also Gee, "Sifting the Arrivals."

6 Ichioka, *The Issei*, pp. 1–6, 146–156, 226–243.

7 Japanese agricultural colonies were also founded in Southern California, at Dundee and Santa Ana. See Azuma, *Between Two Empires*, p. 24.

8 See Ichioka, *The Issei*, pp. 146–153; Noda, *Yamato Colony*; and Matsumoto, *Farming the Home Place*.

9 Ichioka, *The Issei*, pp. 1–6, 146–156, 226–243.

10 Suzuki, "Important or Impotent?," p. 131.

11 Ibid., p. 139.

12 See Azuma, *Between Two Empires*, esp. pp. 3–14, 17–31, 61–85. Quote on p. 213.

13 See https://www.nichibei.org/ (accessed April 1, 2020).

14 I presented a selection of materials from this chapter at the 2016 event on the island.

15 Hospital.

16 211-N-4.

17 In Japan, surnames precede given names, yet for uniformity's sake Western order will be followed in this book.

18 Passenger manifests and public records cited in this book can be accessed on https://www.ancestry.com, unless otherwise specified. The manifests are often collected together with "Records of Aliens Held for Special Inquiry." Those in the latter lists who arrived in San Francisco were definitely held at Angel Island. Case files for some Angel Island detainees are held at the National Archives and Records Administration (NARA) center in San Bruno, CA.

19 My grateful thanks to Masaru's daughter Teruko Tamaru, his granddaughter Donna Hokoda Ebata, and all the Miyamoto/Hokoda descendants for providing information and photographs for this entry.

20 The hometown is noted on the passenger manifest for the *Siberia Maru* for San Francisco arrival on May 31, 1924. Chiyokichi and Yoshio were aboard. Both were held at Angel Island for medical observation.

21 1900 US Census.

22 They arrived February 28, 1908, aboard the *Siberia*. An immigration inspector noted on the manifest that Chiyokichi had no passport, only a consul certificate. "Losing" his Hokoda passport was certainly the first step to regaining his Miyamoto surname.

23 His name is recorded as C. Miyamoto.

24 1920 U.S. Census.

25 For examples: On May 23, 1918, twelve-year-old Minoru Miyamoto arrived in San Francisco, on his way to Fresno, after a trip to Japan; he listed his contact in Japan as "cousin" Gunzo Kuramoto in Kawauchi Village. Chiyokichi brought Yoshio to California in 1924, arriving in San Francisco on May 31 aboard the *Siberia Maru*; at the time, Mitsuyo was staying at home in Kawauchi Village.

26 Taichi (age forty-six) and Kinuyo (sixteen) were detained for two days after arriving in San Francisco from Japan aboard the *Tenyo Maru* on February 17, 1918.

27 He arrived in Honolulu on October 22, 1920 on the *Shinyo Maru*, leaving as his contact address "Mr. C. Miyamoto, Road B Box 133, Reedley Cal."

28 When he married, Masaru's brother Minoru also adopted a new surname. His bride Shizuko Masuda had no brothers, so he became Minoru Masuda.

29 Masaru, Kinuyo, and Katsumi arrived in San Francisco aboard the *Tenyo Maru* on February 22, but were not admitted until February 24. San Francisco, California, Chinese Applications for Admission, 1903–1947, for Masaru, Kinuyo, and Katsumi Hokoda, February 22, 1928.

30 The 1930 Census shows the family living at 1011 Cole Avenue in the Hollywood district of Los Angeles.

31 See Burton, Lord, and Lord, "Gila River."

32 See Dalton, "Exile in the U.S.," in "Home Sweet Home Front: Dayton During World War II." Masato is mentioned by name.

33 Seth Mydans, "Aged War Detainees Still Unpaid for Lost Freedom," *New York Times*, August 17, 1989.

34 The monument states that 174 Nukui residents were killed, but the actual number is said to be higher. Mikio Kanda counts 198 killed; see his *Widows of Hiroshima*.

35 Toshio remained in Japan, but Mildred and the children returned to live in California. She later penned a memoir about her experiences. See Shimonishi-Lamb, *And Then a Rainbow*.

36 115-E-1.
37 File 14159/12-29 at NARA concerns Ichitaro's detention; the file consists of seven pages—two contain testimony and the rest describe his hookworm treatment.
38 Records of Border Crossing from Canada to the United States, May 1907. Ichitaro and Hide subsequently boarded the SS *City of Puebla* at Victoria, and arrived in San Francisco May 22.
39 At 608 ½ West 6th Street.
40 First World War draft registration.
41 1920 Census.
42 On the SS *Manchuria*.
43 She arrived in Seattle aboard the *Chicago Maru* on September 7, 1918.
44 First World War draft registration.
45 1920 Census.
46 1930 Census. Their home on Leland Way is near the corner of Sunset and Vine.
47 1940 Census; California Marriage Index; California Birth Index.
48 Ohio Death Record, June 6, 1948.
49 They arrived in San Francisco on February 28, 1934 on the *Chichibu Maru*.
50 Grateful thanks to Catherine Miskow and David Yasumi for their input and perspectives on Yasumi family history.
51 211-S-3.
52 211-W-7. The writer uses *katakana* characters for the district and village: 志摩郡片田村. The village name appears to be followed by a date. The Arabic numerals 5, 1, 3, appear.
53 Seinojo Hamaguchi (born 1889) arrived aboard the *Taiyō Maru* on April 5, 1926; Yoshimatsu Hamaguchi on April 30, 1926; Matsubei Hamaguchi and Konami Hamaguchi on November 25, 1927; Bunpei Hamaguchi (born 1897) and his wife Kise Hamaguchi on March 18, 1929; Genshichi Hamaguchi (born 1903) and Shinobu Hamaguchi (born 1907) on May 24, 1929. Finally, Isaburō Hamaguchi arrived January 2, 1930, and Yashichi Hamaguchi (born 1913) on July 4, 1930.
54 As did two others whose records only indicate a Mie Prefecture origin, Chozo Hamaguchi and Hisaichi Hamaguchi, who arrived in San Francisco on June 19, 1930.
55 C. Robert Ryono grew up on Terminal Island, and wrote a memoir about the Japanese American experience there. See Ryono, *Although Patriotic, We Were Drydocked*.
56 211-W-1.
57 1910 Census.
58 1920 Census.
59 116-S-1. Inscribed in the Latin alphabet.
60 According to Second World War internment records.

61 1930 Census.
62 1910 Census.
63 1920 Census.
64 Social Security Death Index. Second World War internment records have her birth either as October 15 or 18, 1891.
65 The arrival record has Takuyo Irie.
66 Arrived Honolulu aboard the *City of Peking* on February 24, 1903.
67 California Death Index.
68 207-E-1. A simple signature line follows, comprising the word "person" and a geographical name that is illegible.
69 115-N-1.
70 The 1953 Nevada death certificate for Nao Yamashita lists her father as Matsuichi Yamashita, and a 1934 death certificate for Tsurukichi and Nao's baby daughter Roma Yamashita specifies that Yamashita was Nao's maiden name.
71 Vernon Robinson, "A 'Grand Homecoming' for Grand Marshal," *Moapa Valley Progress* (October 21, 2009). Available online at: https://mvprogress.com/2009/10/21/a-grand-homecoming-for-grand-marshal/ (accessed April 1, 2020).
72 "Sgt. Shigeru Yamashita," Japanese American Veterans Association website at: https://www.javadc.org/yamashita%20shigeru.htm (accessed April 1, 2020).
73 See "Junwo 'Jimmy' Yamashita," on the "Discover Nikkei: Japanese Migrants and Their Descendants" webpage at: https://www.discovernikkei.org/en/resources/military/623/ (accessed April 1, 2020).
74 Army Enlistment Record, September 30, 1944.
75 211-W-1.
76 NARA microfilm M1410, manifest 27184, sheet 16, line 30. Grateful thanks to William Greene of NARA for recovering this information.
77 104-E-2.
78 211-CW-1. The inscription is scratched in the paint on a metal column.
79 According to Katsumi Kubota's First World War draft registration card.
80 211-W-9.
81 In the transcriptions, outmoded variant (*hentai*) *kana* symbols (*hiragana/katakana*) have been replaced with modern equivalents, and some old Kanji character forms have been replaced with modern ones as per the official Tōyō Kanji Lists. Otherwise, the transcriptions reflect what was printed in the newspaper, even where irregularities occur—inconsistent use of punctuation and *furigana* phonetic superscript, archaic or unusual spellings of words and *furigana*, and possible typographical errors. Various forms of poetry, each with different meters and rules, were published in *Nichibei*.
82 *Nichibei Shimbun* (hereafter *NCB*), August 22, 23, 25, 27, 30, and September 1, 1915.
83 Record #14517/24-16; Box #952. Arrived July 20, 1915 on the *Manchuria*.

84 Record #14462/16-6; Box #94. Arrived June 29, 1915 on the *Siberia*; deported on the *China* on July 24, 1915.
85 See, for example, Hata and Hata, "George Shima: 'The Potato King of California.'"
86 Record #14371/9-1; Box #913. Arrived May 25, 1915 on the *Manchuria*; deported on August 7, 1915 on the *Tenyo Maru*.
87 *Los Angeles Times*, January 3, 1915.
88 *Shin sekai* [New World], May 31, 1914.
89 Lee and Yung, *Angel Island*, p. 118.
90 "Habeas Corpus Writ Asked for Picture Brides," *San Francisco Chronicle*, February 5, 1920, p. 4.
91 *NCB*, May 9, 1917.
92 *Nichibei* articles list Tamiye's address: No. 1040 in the Nishihiro Neighborhood of Minamihiro Village (now part of Hirogawa Town), Arida District, Wakayama Prefecture.
93 Kisuke Furukawa arrived in Seattle from Kobe on May 31, 1906 aboard the *Kanagawa Maru*.
94 Tomishima Shige had arrived aboard the *Venezuela* on March 30, 1917.
95 Kisuke Furukawa died July 11, 1938.
96 *NCB*, September 16, 1913.
97 *NCB*, January 1, 1913.
98 *NCB*, January 1, 1913.
99 *NCB*, October 16, 1913.
100 *NCB*, May 26, 1917.
101 *NCB*, October 3, 1913.
102 *NCB*, January 1, 1914.
103 *NCB*, January 9, 1914.
104 *NCB*, October 26, 1913.
105 *NCB*, March 22, 1924.
106 *NCB*, September 21, 1913.
107 *NCB*, September 20, 1914.
108 *NCB*, November 12, 1914.
109 The best known depiction of the pair is by Sekien Toriyama (1712–1788) in *Gazu Hyakki Tsurezure Bukuro* [The Illustrated Bag of One Hundred Random Demons], volume 2.
110 *NCB*, January 24, 1915.
111 *NCB*, March 26, 1916.
112 Shinsaku's First World War draft card three years later describes him as a laborer, working for a Mrs. Chandler and residing at 2241 Channing Way in Berkeley.

113 Case ID 250263, Case #14202/017-25, Box #00892.
114 See Shimizu, *Eien to mukyū* [Eternity and Endlessness]; and *Wind of Spring*.
115 *NCB*, August 16, 1914.
116 *NCB*, July 22, 1913.
117 *NCB*, February 21, 1927; March 14, 1927; and March 21, 1927. At some point, Karl Yoneda did English versions of some of the poems, which are included among his papers. Fourteen selections are published in Lee and Yung, *Angel Island*, pp. 112–113; and several appear in his autobiography, *Ganbatte: Sixty-Year Struggle of a Kibei Worker*, pp. 11–12. Yet there are significant discrepancies between these English versions and the original Japanese poems in *Nichibei*. In particular, Yoneda makes short three-line English *haiku* out of what were longer and more complex originals. Moreover, the Japanese versions of the poems in the Japanese translation of Yoneda's autobiography bear little relation to the texts published in the newspaper, and apparently were translated from his English versions. The translations here are new, and closely follow the *Nichibei* texts.
118 *NCB*, January 17, 1915.
119 *NCB*, January 9, 1914.
120 *NCB*, September 2, 1917.
121 *NCB*, October 17, 1912.
122 *NCB*, January 1, 1914.
123 *NCB*, November 5, 1921.
124 *NCB*, October 21, 1917.
125 *NCB*, November 19, 1916.
126 *NCB*, November 26, 1921.
127 *NCB*, October 18, 1912.
128 *NCB*, September 29, 1912.
129 *NCB*, January 1, 1914.
130 *NCB*, October 25, 1913.
131 *NCB*, October 8, 1917.
132 *NCB*, January 1, 1913.
133 *NCB*, October 6, 1912.
134 *NCB*, January 1, 1913.
135 *NCB*, October 13, 1912.
136 *NCB*, October 25, 1913.
137 *NCB*, January 1, 1916.
138 *NCB*, January 1, 1913.
139 *NCB*, January 1, 1913. A poem in the same issue is also by Shōei, and gives his surname as Itō.
140 *NCB*, January 1, 1913.

141 *NCB*, October 24, 1913.
142 *NCB*, January 1, 1913.
143 *NCB*, January 1, 1913.
144 *NCB*, January 1, 1914.
145 *NCB*, January 1, 1914.
146 *NCB*, January 1, 1915.
147 *NCB*, May 16, 1916.
148 *NCB*, September 23, 1913.
149 *NCB*, January 1, 1916.
150 *NCB*, January 1, 1915.
151 *NCB*, August 1, 1921.
152 *NCB*, September 16, 1913.
153 *NCB*, September 16, 1913.
154 *NCB*, October 6, 1912.
155 Note: for 續 read 續.
156 *NCB*, November 17, 1912.
157 *NCB*, October 6, 1912.
158 *NCB*, January 1, 1913.
159 *NCB*, March 31, 1915.
160 *NCB*, December 17, 1916.
161 *NCB*, October 6, 1912.
162 *NCB*, October 6, 1912.
163 *NCB*, July 25, 1921.
164 *NCB*, October 6, 1912.
165 *NCB*, April 30, 1916.
166 *NCB*, August 28, 1922.
167 *NCB*, January 1, 1917.
168 *NCB*, October 6, 1912.
169 *NCB*, October 6, 1912.
170 *NCB*, July 25, 1921.
171 *NCB*, October 6, 1912.
172 *NCB*, January 1, 1913.
173 *NCB*, January 1, 1913.
174 *NCB*, January 1, 1915.
175 *NCB*, January 1, 1915.
176 *NCB*, January 1, 1917.
177 *NCB*, January 1, 1917.
178 *NCB*, January 1, 1913.

179 *NCB*, January 1, 1913.
180 *NCB*, January 17, 1915.
181 *NCB*, April 7, 1913.
182 *NCB*, February 5, 1917.
183 Noda, *Yamato Colony*, pp. 34–36.
184 *NCB*, July 9, 1913.
185 *NCB*, January 1, 1921.
186 *NCB*, January 1, 1916.
187 *NCB*, August 16, 1914.
188 *NCB*, September 15, 1921.
189 *NCB*, January 1, 1921.
190 *NCB*, January 1, 1921.
191 *NCB*, August 5, 1921.
192 *NCB*, August 5, 1921.
193 *NCB*, June 26, 1918.
194 *NCB*, June 16, 1917.

Chapter 2

1 Choy, *Koreans in America*, pp. 23–24.
2 Ibid., pp. 24–27; Richard S. Kim, *The Quest for Statehood*, pp. 15–17.
3 Richard S. Kim, *The Quest for Statehood*, pp. 17–25. See also Lee and Yung, *Angel Island*, pp. 177–209; Warren Y. Kim, *Koreans in America*; Choy, *Koreans in America*, pp. 69–78; and Gee, "Sifting the Arrivals."
4 *Report of the Commisioner General of Immigration, 1908*; see Ichihashi, *Japanese in the United States*, pp. 244–246.
5 Lee and Yung, *Angel Island*, p. 181.
6 Chang and Patterson, *The Koreans in Hawai'i*, pp. 63–66.
7 Richard S. Kim, *The Quest for Statehood*, p. 15. Bong-Youn Choy notes that another group of Koreans numbering fewer than three hundred was issued passports by the Japanese authorities to study in the United States. To obtain such a passport likely required political connections, or the payment of bribes. Most of this group returned to Korea after finishing advanced studies. Choy, *Koreans in America*, p. 78.
8 Lee and Yung, *Angel Island*, pp. 184–185.
9 Schmid, *Korea Between Empires*, pp. 247–248.
10 Richard S. Kim, *The Quest for Statehood*, p. 46.
11 See "Korean American Population By State," available online at: https://asiamattersforamerica.org/korea/data/population (accessed April 1, 2020).

12 211-CE-1. The location is the easternmost column in the middle of the room.
13 INS-SF case file #26104/1-2.
14 See Sohoni and Vafa, "The Fight to be American: Military Naturalization and Asian Citizenship."
15 211-E-1.
16 Lee arrived on the SS *President Taft*. His immigration case file is at the National Archives in San Bruno, #23132/14-21 in /C/25/1/8/9 Box 1890.
17 The second syllable is fairly clearly "In" 인, though "Han" 한 is possible, if three small strokes have been obscured by paint. Yet either way, since Romanization of Korean was not standardized until decades later, "Han" as the transliteration would not be surprising. For the third syllable, the initial and vowel "Si-" are clear. The "k" ㄱ (or "g") final is probably what is below, as a line is visible, though "l" ㄹ is not out of the question, giving the syllable a reading of "Sil."
18 *Honolulu Star-Bulletin*, December 11, 1945. Citations from Palmer, "Koreans in Honolulu Newspapers."
19 Grateful thanks to Young Hoon Jeong for inputting the Korean texts of the poems.
20 *Sinhan Minbo* (hereafter *SHMB*), January 5, 1928.
21 According to the passenger manifest of the *President Pierce*, which arrived at Seattle on May 20, 1929. His name therein is spelled Won Jung Park.
22 *SHMB*, August 8, 1929.
23 *SHMB*, April 30, 1925.
24 Former AIISF Community Relations Director Grant Din located Choi's name on the 1925 passenger manifest, and former Executive Director Eddie Wong reviewed and photographed his immigration file at NARA, San Bruno. The AIISF website includes the translation of "A Night at the Immigration Station" and a short biographical note by Grant Din; see https://www.aiisf.org/stories-by-author/592-choi-kyung-sik. AIISF also provided the materials to the DePauw University Library, which has posted them online as the Kyung Sik Choi Papers; see https://palni.contentdm.oclc.org/digital/search/searchterm/the%20Kyung%20Sik%20Choi%20Papers.
25 The description and photograph appear on page 267 of the yearbook, and can be viewed online at: https://palni.contentdm.oclc.org/cdm/compoundobject/collection/archives/id/34706/rec/12. The individual identified as "P. Choi" matches the Chosen Christian College graduation photograph of Kyung Sik Choi found in his immigration file.
26 Grateful thanks to Assistant University Archivist Janet C. Olson at Northwestern University for finding Choi's student records, as well as providing a link to the Commencement Program that includes his degree information: https://archive.org/details/annualcommenceme1930nort. See p. 28.
27 Grateful thanks to Reference Assistant Oscar Chavez at the University of Chicago Library, Special Collections Research Center, for confirming Phillip Kyungsik Choi's enrollment at the university.

28 State of Illinois death certificate, Cook County, file #6006378, March 1, 1932. Strong evidence that Phillip Choi and Philip Kyungsik Choi are the same person is that both the 1932 death record and the 1925 *Taiyo Maru* passenger manifest list father's name as Hyun Choi.
29 *SHMB*, April 19, 1923.
30 Cha, *Koreans in Central California*, pp. 157–161.
31 *SHMB*, July 5, 1923.
32 *SHMB*, December 22, 1921.
33 *SHMB*, July 26, 1923.
34 Choi, *Gender and Mission Encounters in Korea*, pp. 155–157. Kim arrived in San Francisco aboard the *President Pierce* on July 12, 1923.
35 *SHMB*, February 17, 1927.
36 *SHMB*, November 7, 1913.
37 The original song was written by Jack Judge and Harry Williams in 1912.
38 *SHMB*, February 24, 1917.
39 *SHMB*, April 7, 1921.
40 *SHMB*, July 4, 1929.
41 *SHMB*, December 22, 1927.
42 *SHMB*, October 13, 1927.
43 *SHMB*, September 23, 1928.
44 *SHMB*, November 26, 1924.
45 *SHMB*, December 25, 1924.
46 *SHMB*, April 12, 1925.
47 *SHMB*, July 23, 1925.
48 *SHMB*, July 31, 1924.
49 *SHMB*, November 3, 1930.
50 Charr, *The Golden Mountain*. Biographical note based on editor Patterson's introduction; and on "Easurk Emsen Charr," in Zhao and Park, *Asian Americans*, vol. 1, pp. 198–200.

Chapter 3

1 See Kanazawa, "Immigration, Exclusion, and Taxation."
2 The last major railroad project to link California with rail lines to the east was the Feather River Route, built by the Western Pacific Railroad from 1906–1909.
3 See the "Chinese Railroad Workers in North America Project at Stanford University," available online at: https://web.stanford.edu/group/chineserailroad/cgi-bin/website/ (accessed April 1, 2020). This invaluable resource on Chinese

4   On occupations of Chinese immigrants in the nineteenth century, see Tsai, *The Chinese Experience in America*, pp. 10–32.
5   Lee and Yung, *Angel Island*, p. 6.
6   Ibid., p. 75.
7   Abrams, "Polygamy, Prostitution, and the Federalization of Immigration Law," p. 695.
8   Ibid., p. 698.
9   On the development and initial implementation of the Exclusion Laws, see Lee, *At America's Gates*, chapters 1–3. See also Lee and Yung, *Angel Island*, chapter two (esp. pp. 74–84).
10 Lew-Williams, *The Chinese Must Go*, pp. 48–52, 53–62; a list of the expulsion locations is on pp. 247–251.
11 Ibid., pp. 202–204.
12 Ibid., p. 238.
13 Ibid., p. 237.
14 Hing, *Making and Remaking Asian America*, pp. 22–23.
15 Young, *Alien Nation*, p. 131.
16 Lew-Williams, *The Chinese Must Go*, p. 238.
17 Madeline Hsu cites several examples of firms that fraudulently provided business partnership documentation to would-be immigrants; see Hsu, *Dreaming of Gold, Dreaming of Home*, pp. 73–74.
18 Lee and Yung, *Angel Island*, pp. 84–85; Lee, *At America's Gates*, p. 83.
19 On this topic, see Hsu, *Dreaming of Gold, Dreaming of Home*.
20 Lee, *At America's Gates*, p. 201. See also Wang, "The Soul of Poetry Lives Forever in Hell."
21 On immigrant and community strategies, see Gee, *Sifting the Arrivals*, chapter 4.
22 An estimate of 90 percent is cited in Lee and Yung, *Angel Island*, p. 84.
23 Lee, *At America's Gates*, p. 207.
24 Lai, Lim, and Yung, *Island*, 2nd edition, pp. 339–342.
25 105-S-1.
26 205-S-1. The writer transliterates, rather than translates, the word "China." "Steamship" is rendered as 火船, the word commonly used for 汽船 in Cantonese dialects of the period. The SS *China* was built for the Pacific Mail Steamship Company in 1889, which employed it on trans-Pacific routes until selling it in 1915. It was acquired by the China Mail Steamship Company, and continued in service until laid up in 1923, and scrapped in 1925.
27 205-N-4.
28 Kang Youwei 康有為, "漢族宜憂外分勿內爭論" [The Han Race Should Worry about Division from Without, and Avoid Dissent Within], in *Wanmu caotang*

yigao, **juan** 1. Reprinted in Jiang Yihua et al., eds., *Kang Youwei quanji*, vol. 9 (Beijing: Zhongguo renmin daxue chubanshe, 2007). Available online at: https://cnthinkers.com/thinkerweb/literature/441660 (accessed April 1, 2020).

29 105-N-4.
30 Zhang, *Events in the Empire of 1908*.
31 105-E-1.
32 Ext-N-3/4.
33 205-E-6. A partially legible date precedes.
34 105-N-2.
35 205-S-2.
36 205-S-5. In lines 2 and 8, the wall has 固 for 故.
37 205-N-6.
38 205-N-1.
39 213-N-4.
40 213-S-4/5.
41 205-E-3. 容乜易 jung4 mat1 ji6 is a Cantonese colloquialism.
42 105-S-1. The more common text has the third character of the first line as 明 (bright).
43 105-S-5.
44 Location not found.
45 205-E-8. For 頼 in line 1, the wall uses the alternate form 賴.
46 105-N-1.
47 The quatrain follows an AAxA rhyme (in Cantonese, lau 留, zau 舟, lau 流). The six-line poem follows AAxAxA (in Cantonese, ging 京, nin 年, sing 聲, jing 刑). "Nin" is an acceptable rhyme for the others as southern dialects do not clearly differentiate "n" and "ng" endings.
48 205-W-4. Even though the first character is not visible, the final line is translated as "deported to Tang" (撥返唐) based on other uses of the phrase on the walls.
49 105-S-2.
50 105-W-2.
51 105-S-5.
52 205-N-5. The signature line does not appear after the poem, as is typical, but before it. The poem is prefaced, "[I here] inscribe another heptasyllabic quatrain poem." Thus it is by the same author as the longer poem to the right on the wall, which corresponds to #39 in *Island*. The signature line comes before both poems.
53 Jiang, Yongjing 蔣永敬, *Historical Records of the Revolution Overseas* 華僑開國革命史料 (Taipei: Zhengzhong Books, 1977), pp. 169–171.
54 105-W-4.
55 213-S-1.

56 205-E-3.
57 205-W-3.
58 105-N-6.
59 105-N-4.
60 115-E-1.
61 115-W-5.
62 Location not found. In the last line, 鬼 (devils) is short for the derisive term 白鬼 (white devils). The last character in the line, 蝦 (literally "shrimp"), is a Cantonese colloquial word equivalent to 欺負 (to bully; to take advantage of).
63 Not found on the walls. *Island* #34 is at 105-S-6.
64 105-S-1.
65 202-W-2. A similar statement is found at 206-S-1.
66 115-W-2. The wall has 荳 rather than 痘 in line 5. The rhyme scheme here combines syllables with "n" and "ng" endings. There are several similar examples in *Island*, like #67 and #114.
67 109-E-2.
68 115-W-2.
69 115-W-11.
70 115-W-2.
71 211-E-1.
72 205-S-7.
73 105-S-1.
74 205-W-5.
75 205-S-6. The first eleven characters match part of a parallel couplet in the Smiley Jann manuscript, published in Island as #81. Jann's version has not been located on the walls.
76 116-E-2.
77 EXT-E-6.
78 The door is now in California State Parks storage at Angel Island State Park.
79 Hospital, Room 221-E-9.
80 The wall text has 坴 for 陸.
81 205-S-1.
82 California Death Index

Chapter 4

1 For the text, see https://www.loc.gov/law/help/statutes-at-large/47-congress/session-1/c47s1ch376.pdf (accessed April 1, 2020).

2 For the text of the 1885 Alien Contract Labor Law, see https://www.loc.gov/law/help/statutes-at-large/48-congress/Session%202/c48s2ch164.pdf (accessed April 1, 2020).
3 Gee, "Sifting the Arrivals," pp. 100–138.
4 For the text of the 1917 Immigration Act (a.k.a. the Asiatic Barred Zone Act), see https://www.loc.gov/law/help/statutes-at-large/64-congress/session-2/c64s2ch29.pdf (accessed April 1, 2020).
5 Gee, "Sifting the Arrivals," pp. 245–267. For the text of the Mann Act, see https://www.loc.gov/law/help/statutes-at-large/61-congress/session-2/c61s2ch395.pdf (accessed April 1, 2020).
6 For example, see Baynton, *Defectives in the Land.*
7 For the text, see https://www.loc.gov/law/help/statutes-at-large/59-congress/session-2/c59s2ch1134.pdf (accessed April 1, 2020).
8 See Carro, "From Constitutional Psychopathic Inferiority to AIDS," esp. pp. 206–209.
9 Lutz Kaelber, *Eugenics: Compulsory Sterilization in 50 American States,* available online at; https://www.uvm.edu/%7Elkaelber/eugenics/CA/CA.html (accessed April 1, 2020).
10 Lee and Yung, *Angel Island,* pp. 149–151.
11 For the text of the 1924 law, see https://www.loc.gov/law/help/statutes-at-large/68-congress/session-1/c68s1ch190.pdf (accessed April 1, 2020).
12 For the text, see https://www.loc.gov/law/help/statutes-at-large/73-congress/session-2/c73s2ch84.pdf (accessed April 1, 2020).
13 See https://www.aiisf.org/ (accessed April 1, 2020).
14 *Los Angeles Times,* July 4, 1923, "More Refugees Join Those Held on Angel Island."
15 On Russian and other non-Asian immigration through Angel Island, see Sakovitch, "Angel Island Immigration Station Reconsidered."
16 He arrived in San Francisco on August 21, 1918, aboard the SS *Grotius.* See Nestyev, *Prokofiev,* p. 168; Press, "Prokofiev's Vexing Entry into the USA." See also Lee and Yung, *Angel Island,* pp. 229–230.
17 *San Francisco Chronicle,* February 10, 1919, "Ex-President of Russia is Visitor in S.F.: Kerensky Lieutenant and Party Detained at Angel Island."
18 See Lee and Yung, *Angel Island,* pp. 218–219, 230–231.
19 Jensen, *Passage from India.* A useful resource on early Sikh immigrants to the United States is "Sikh Pioneers," available online at: https://www.sikhpioneers.org/ (accessed April 1, 2020).
20 This compilation is a guide for enforcement based on the Immigration Act of 1907. See https://books.google.com/books?id=V4JCAQAAMAAJ&pg (accessed April 1, 2020), pp. 25–27.
21 211-E-5. The carving employs italic rather than standard Cyrillic letters.
22 The "Record of Aliens Held for Special Inquiry" that details Jacob's Angel Island detention lists the Allen surname and omits Zeitlin.

23 Zoglin, "Gomel."
24 Grateful thanks to Jacob's children Evan Allen and Marilyn Allen Mendoza, and to his grandchildren Joan Allen (William's daughter) and Ira Allen (Irvin's son).
25 Winbury, "Trotsky's War Train," p. 529; Davies, *White Eagle, Red Star*, p. 139.
26 His Declaration of Intention was filed February 2, 1911, and the Petition for Naturalization on June 28, 1920.
27 1910 Census.
28 Dated May 31, 1910 and June 27, 1912, respectively.
29 Louis E. Allen, Georgia, First World War Service Card.
30 Joe Allen, Georgia, First World War Service Card.
31 1920 Census. Sarah Solomon Allen was born in "Polatska, Russia"—Polatsk, in central Belarus. Sarah, three siblings, and mother Rebecca arrived in Philadelphia from Liverpool aboard the *Merion* on March 20, 1913.
32 Born April 30, 1919 in Philadelphia.
33 Year noted in the Petition for Naturalization of Peshe Zeitlin Allen, May 19, 1953.
34 As "Pesse Zeitlin" she arrived in New York aboard the *Polonia* from Libau, Latvia on August 17, 1921.
35 Death certificate for Sarah Allen, Philadelphia, November 16, 1923, File #117637.
36 Dated May 26, 1927.
37 The district was later incorporated as the City of Sugar Hill.
38 Died June 4, 1961, Georgia Certificate #12715.
39 Died June 4, 2000, Social Security Death Index.
40 213-S-3.
41 File #14949/2-17 from box 1013.
42 First World War draft registration card. As on the passenger manifest for his arrival, he listed as next-of-kin his father in Kiev.
43 The Schwengel family arrived in New York on the *Statendam* from Rotterdam on March 10, 1902. Father Johan, twenty-eight, is described as a laborer. Mother Amalia was eighteen. Another family of Schwengels arrived on the same ship, and also listed Fresno as their destination.
44 Their eldest son, Efim John Sukovitzen, was born in 1883. His obituary in the *San Francisco Examiner* on January 3, 1950 specifies his birth in Kars. See https://www.findagrave.com/cgi-bin/fg.cgi?page=gr&GRid=23627222.
45 Nadia's father was William Jonoff (born *c.* 1887).
46 The Communist Party's west coast newspaper, *People's Daily World*, July 14, 1939, included the following notice: "Let's celebrate the 20th wedding anniversary of Jerry and Augusta Feingold and the 20th anniversary of his membership in the Party. Saturday, July 22, 136 Valencia Street, at 8 p.m. Russian food, music and dancing. Admission 19 cents." Cited during Jeremiah Feingold's testimony before the House Un-American Activities Committee; see below.

47 These details were also cited during his testimony.

48 "Riot at Russ Rally Lands Seven in Jail," *Oakland Tribune*, January 6, 1930; "Court Assails Radicals for Riot at Rally," *Oakland Tribune*, January 7, 1930.

49 *Western Worker*, June 1, 1932. Available online at: https://www.marxists.org/history/usa/pubs/westernworker/1932/v1n11-jun-01-1932.pdf (accessed April 1, 2020).

50 Federal Bureau of Investigation, Subject: Comintern Apparatus, File Number #100-203581 Section 63, Part 2, pp. 513–514. Summary Report dated March 6, 1946. Available online at: https://archive.org/details/FBIFileCOMRAP (accessed April 1, 2020).

51 "Richard Arens, 56, Hill Staff Chief, Dies," *Washington Post*, October 27, 1969.

52 "George Walsh: An Unfriendly Witness," *The Dispatcher*, Published by the International Longshore and Warehouse Union, June 2005, p. 11. Available online at: https://www.ilwu.org/wp-content/uploads/2011/08/june05.pdf (accessed April 1, 2020).

53 My thanks to Svetlana Kristal and Roza Trilesskaya for the translation.

54 211-S-2.

55 211-S-3.

56 "Transport Visits San Francisco En Route from Siberia to Europe," *Popular Mechanics*, vol. 34 (1920), p. 217; "400 of Crew Quit Mount Vernon," *San Francisco Chronicle*, May 4, 1920; "U.S. Transport Crew, Soldiers Clash on Ship," *San Francisco Chronicle*, May 11, 1920; "Departure of the Mount Vernon," *The Panama Canal Record*, vol. 13, no. 41 (May 26, 1920).

57 The arrival manifest lists the crew, but not passengers.

58 211-E-1.

59 See Yung and Lee, *Angel Island*, pp. 228–231.

60 Ibid., pp. 233–237.

61 211-S-2.

62 "Social News," *Fayetteville Observer*, July 29, 1920.

63 211-E-1.

64 See passenger manifests for January 15, 1923 San Francisco and October 7, 1923 Seattle.

65 *Blue and Gold Yearbook*, Class of 1932, University of California, Berkeley (Berkeley, California).

66 Kibon was founded as US Harkson do Brasil. The name was later changed to Cia Harkson Industria e Comércio Kibon. The company is now owned by Unilever. Boris's name appears in multiple company reports published in Sao Paulo's Diário Oficial da União (DOU).

67 211-S-2.

68 The arrival records for Ishiker have not been found, but there is a notation on the arrival records for his two eldest sons in 1913 that he had crossed from Canada through Vermont in 1913; see below.

69 *Shinyo Maru*, arrived San Francisco December 19, 1917.
70 See Case File #16742/18-3.
71 The two had immigrated together, arriving in Philadelphia aboard the *Brandenburg* from Bremen on December 25, 1913.
72 Registered as the Enterprise Upholstered Furniture Company.
73 Noted on his First World War draft registration and in the 1920 Census.
74 Joe Woodnick enlisted August 15, 1920, and mustered out on August 9, 1923.
75 As per the 1930 Census, and US city directories for Reading from 1926 through 1933.
76 1940 Census.
77 At the time of his naturalization in 1926, Abe and Mary were living elsewhere in the city, so the move to Paxon Street must date later.
78 Mark Thomas, "Altavista Area YMCA opens new art exhibit," *Altavista Journal*, Wednesday, June 16, 2010.
79 211-E-1.
80 211-E-3.
81 Sakovick and Bailey write that the group was large, and so processing was carried out at Fort McDowell, yet some were held at the immigration station while their cases were examined; see "Anniversary at the Immigration Station." Boochkovsky is the only close match to Bukovsky among immigrants who arrived in San Francisco during the years of the immigration stations' operation.
82 *Oakland City Directory*, 1925, 1933, 1934.
83 *Oakland Tribune*, December 28, 1928.
84 211-E-1.
85 The Neufeld family's story is recounted in Lee and Yung, *Angel Island*, pp. 238–240, 244–245.
86 211-E-1.
87 Yankel's father's first name is noted on Yankel's June 6, 1961 Pennsylvania death certificate. His mother's maiden name is given as Rhoda. When he married Bella Silverman, his parents are identified as Leizer and Rhoda Benoff. Rhoda translates as Rose. Labish is perhaps a nickname.
88 Occupations noted on his Second World War draft registration record and in the 1940 Census.
89 The diplomatic letter (marked "No. 1714"), including both poems, is in the Records of the Immigration and Naturalization Service, Subject Correspondence Files, Asian Immigration and Exclusion 1898–1941, located at the National Archives and Records Administration (NARA), San Bruno, CA. It was provided me by Prof. Judy Yung, who I gratefully acknowledge. Lee and Yung include the first poem printed here in *Angel Island*, along with part of a *Russkii Golos* article describing the Russian students' activities while at the immigration station; see pp. 233–236.

90 *Russkii Golos*, Harbin, October 19, 1923.

91 *Russkii Golos*, Harbin, October 27, 1923.

92 213-W-1.

93 211-CW-1 On a column in the center of the room.

94 211-S-2.

95 The Ancestry.com entry, taken from the crew manifest, erroneously has Nardin as the given name.

96 Ansari, *The Infidel Within*, p. 37.

97 From the 1931 issue of *Ghadar de Gunj*; quoted in Malini Sood, "Expatriate Nationalism," p. 168.

98 Quoted in Tatla, "A Sikh Manifesto?" Text is slightly edited, and punctuation has been added.

99 Quoted in Tatla, "A Sikh Manifesto." Text is slightly edited, and punctuation has been added.

100 *Ghadar*, no. 1, 1. Quoted in Vatuk and Vatuk, "Protest Songs of East Indians on the West Coast, U.S.A.," p. 376. See also Sood, "Expatriate Nationalism," p. 192.

101 *Deshbhakti ke Geet*, 10; quoted in Vatuk and Vatuk, "Protest Songs," p. 379. See also Sood, "Expatriate Nationalism," p. 208.

102 211-N-3.

103 104-E-2.

104 210-S-1.

105 211 N-6.

106 204-N-2.

107 "Really Nothing to Come 6000 Miles for Centenary," *The Marlborough Express*, October 1972. During and after the First World War, the *Maunganui* was in government service. Released in 1919, the ship underwent an extensive refit in Wellington and Port Chalmers, NZ. It sailed for the first time for San Francisco in 1922, arriving July 31. This timeline fits J.D. Burgess's recollection, though his name does not appear on the crew manifest.

108 207-N-3.

109 213-S-4.

110 211-E-7.

111 Ricardo entered at El Paso on or about November 1, 1914, according to his naturalization record. The 1920 Census lists Enrique's arrival year as 1914.

112 First World War draft registration records.

113 San Quentin Inmate Register, Prisoner #31431. His name was listed as Enrico Peton.

114 He appears in the 1920 Census as Enrico Petoni. Parole was granted on March 30, 1920, though it appears he was not discharged until July 7.

115 San Quentin Prison Inmate Register, Prisoner #35644, received November 29, 1921.
116 Folsom Prison Inmate Register, Prisoner #11974, received December 2, 1921.
117 "Convicts Await Deportation," *Reno Evening Gazette*, January 3, 1924.
118 Folsom State Prison Inmate Register, Prisoner #19949, received October 18, 1935.
119 "Shoplifting Suspect is Held on Dope Charge," *Fresno Bee Republican*, June 2, 1948.
120 211-N-3.
121 116-S-1. "Austria" lacks the "r."
122 204-N-1.
123 115-E-1.

Chapter 5

1 The case remained in the headlines for months. See, for examples, *Los Angeles Times*, January 19, 1940, "Scuttled Liner's Crew Awaits Passage for Dash to Homeland"; August 30, 1940, "Scuttled Nazi Ship Crew May Be Taken Inland"; *Washington Post*, August 30, 1940, "U.S. to Transfer 451 Nazi Seamen"; and *New York Times*, March 10, 1941, "Interned German Weds."
2 Kashima, *Judgment Without Trial*, pp. 67–74, quote p. 68.
3 Statistics and itineraries courtesy of the Japanese Cultural Center of Hawai'i.
4 See "Internment of Japanese Americans on Angel Island during World War II," available online at: https://www.aiisf.org/history (accessed April 1, 2020). This project was funded, in part, by a grant from the US Department of the Interior, National Park Service, Japanese American Confinement Sites Grant Program.
5 Soennichsen, *Miwoks to Missiles*, p. 138.
6 *Washington Post*, June 5, 1943, "Captives Held in U.S.: 36,688 Prisoners Here."
7 Caldwell et al., "Archaeological and Documentary Investigation of Fort McCoy's Japanese Prisoner of War Camp, South Post, Fort McCoy."
8 This is the official figure as reported in the *New York Times*, July 8, 1946, "Last Prisoners to Sail." It is slightly higher than the 5,080 figure reported September 13, 1945, "War Captives in the U.S. to be Gone by Spring: Total of Prisoners Here is Put at 417,034." Krammer, "Japanese Prisoners of War in America," counts 5,424; see p. 67.
9 Krammer, "Japanese Prisoners of War in America," pp. 68–70.
10 Ibid., pp. 71–75.
11 Straus, *The Anguish of Surrender: Japanese POWs of World War II*, pp. 135–136. A more recent book on intelligence gathering at Byron Hot Springs is Corbin, *The History of Camp Tracy: Japanese WWII POWs and the Future of Interrogation*.

12 Krammer, "Japanese Prisoners of War in America," pp. 71–75.
13 Straus, *The Anguish of Surrender*, p. 134.
14 Ibid., p. 137.
15 Krammer, "Japanese Prisoners of War in America," p. 76.
16 Robert A. Johnson, "Nazi Prisoners Like War Camp in United States," *Los Angeles Times*, June 10, 1943. *The New York Times* carried a similar story on June 13, 1943, which included photographs.
17 The bombs were dropped on Japan on August 6 and 9 (August 5 and 8 in the United States).
18 George Dusheck, "No Coddling for Jap PWs on Angel Island," *The S.F. News*, August 9, 1945.
19 Lynda Lin, "The Voices of the Past are Written on the Walls," *Pacific Citizen*, October 19, 2007
20 Visit to Japanese Prisoner of War Camp, Angel Island, San Francisco, California, by Mr. Paul Schnyder representing the International Committee of the Red Cross, and Mr. Leonard L. O'Bryon of the Special War Problems Division, Department of State, July 2, 1945. Available online at: Digital Collections, University of Wisconsin-Madison Libraries, https://digicoll.library.wisc.edu/cgi-bin/WI/WI-idx?type=article&did=Research194146.AngelIsland.i0008&id=WI.AngelIsland&isize— (accessed April 1, 2020).
21 Sakihara, "Sparrows of Angel Island." In 1951, Sakihara returned to the United States, and earned his BA and MA from the University of Oregon, and his PhD from the University of Hawaii, where he taught in the Department of History for over thirty years.
22 "Transfer of Japanese Prisoners of War," Letter by Colonel A.M. Tollefson, Director, Prisoner of War Operations Division, Provost Marshal General's Office to Commanding General, Ninth Service Command, Salt Lake City, Utah, September 7, 1945; Box 2482, Reporting Branch, Subject Files 1942–46; Entry 461, Enemy POW Information Bureau; Records Group 389, Office of the Provost Marshal General; National Archives at College Park, College Park, MD. Two other letters by Tollefson, dated September 7, are adjacent; they are to the Commanding General of the Sixth Service Command in Chicago (who oversaw Camp McCoy) and the Commanding General of the Seventh Service Command in Omaha (who oversaw Camp Clarinda), and ordered them to transfer Okinawan prisoners to join the group of 241.
23 "Transfer of Japanese Prisoners of War," Letter by Colonel A.M. Tollefson, Director, Prisoner of War Operations Division, Provost Marshal General's Office to Commanding General, Sixth Service Command, Chicago, Illinois, September 26, 1945; Box 2482, Reporting Branch, Subject Files 1942–46; Entry 461, Enemy POW Information Bureau; Records Group 389, Office of the Provost Marshal General; National Archives at College Park, College Park, MD. "Transfer of Japanese Prisoners of War," Letter by Colonel A.M. Tollefson, Director, Prisoner of War Operations Division, Provost Marshal General's Office to Commanding General, Seventh Service Command, Omaha, Nebraska, September 25, 1945; Box 2482, Reporting Branch, Subject Files 1942–46; Entry

461, Enemy POW Information Bureau; Records Group 389, Office of the Provost Marshal General; National Archives at College Park, College Park, MD.

24 Handwritten notes concerning disposition of Japanese prisoners; Box 2482, Reporting Branch, Subject Files 1942–46; Entry 461, Enemy POW Information Bureau; Records Group 389, Office of the Provost Marshal General; National Archives at College Park, College Park, MD.

25 "Japs to Pick Kern Cotton: Vanguard of Nip War Prisoners Numbering 800 at Lamont Camp," *Los Angeles Times*, October 7, 1945.

26 Krammer, "Japanese Prisoners of War in America," pp. 89–90.

27 *Los Angeles Times*, November 8, 1945, "Ship Taking 700 Japs Back Home."

28 Soennichsen, *Miwoks to Missiles*, p. 139.

29 Grateful thanks to Makiko Asano for assistance in inscriptions decipherment.

30 212-W-3. While this and the following six inscriptions remain on the barracks walls, they are unfortunately not viewable by the public. Room 212 is now part of the elevator shaft added during restoration of the building. Two other short inscriptions there are mostly illegible.

31 "Record of the Hearings of a Board of Officers and Civilians Convened Pursuant to Special Orders No. 33, Headquarters, Hawaiian Department, Dated at Fort Shafter, T.H., 2 February, 1942, in the case of Takuji Shindo," ISN-HJ-1077-CI; Box 2636; Enemy Prisoner of War Information Bureau Subject Files, 1942–46, Entry 461; Records of the Office of the Provost Marshal General, Records Group 389; National Archives at College Park, College Park, MD.

32 212-W-4.

33 212-W-3.

34 Information about the store appears in the records of the investigative hearing for Sueoka's case. See below for citation. A second individual in Group #3 also worked in the jewelry business. Keizaburo (also Keisaburo) Hirano (1885–1965) was the proprietor of the Honolulu Gold Exchange. Thanks to Tatsumi Hayashi at the Japanese Cultural Center of Hawaii for identifying the occupations of both Hirano and Sueoka, which led to the identification of the writer.

35 Information from Honolulu City directories.

36 "Record of the Hearings of a Board of Officers and Civilians Convened Pusuant to Special Orders No. 33, Headquarters, Hawaiian Department, Dated at Fort Shafter, T.H., 19 December 1941, In the Case of Robert Iju Sueoka, alias Robert Yoshinori Sueoka," ISN-HJ-383-CI; Box 2637; Enemy Prisoner of War Information Bureau Subject Files, 1942–1946, Entry 461; Records of the Office of the Provost Marshal General, Records Group 389; National Archives at College Park, College Park, MD.

37 212-W-1.

38 212-W-4.

39 212-W-1.

40 212-W-1.

41 Soga, *Tessaku seikatsu*; the inscriptions are on pp. 90–92. Soga, trans. by Hirai, *Life Behind Barbed Wire*; inscriptions on pp. 69–71. The translations here are new.
42 The character 紘 literally means "cap string." The "eight strings" was a metaphor for the eight directions, i.e., the whole world.
43 1930 Census and 1940 Census.
44 102-N-1. On the inside of the front door.
45 205-W-1.
46 211-N-4.
47 US National Parks Service, "The Battle of Attu: 60 Years Later."
48 109-W-1.
49 109-W-1.
50 115-N-4.
51 210-W-1.
52 102-N-2.
53 209-W-1.
54 209-S-3.
55 109-W-1.
56 209-N-1.
57 See File "PW lists – Tracy, 5 March 1945–11 July 1945"; Box 759; Captured Personnel and Materiel Branch—Country Files, Entry 179D; Records of the War Department General and Special Staffs, Records Group 165; National Archives at College Park, College Park, MD. See also "Advance Information from the Preliminary Interrogation of 16 Ps/W, April 5, 1945," Box 763.
58 115-N-1.
59 206-W-2.
60 210-E-3.
61 212-W-2. This is the only inscription in Room 212—presently the elevator shaft—that can still be viewed. It is on the doorjamb and is visible when the elevator door is open.
62 210-E-3.
63 206-S-2.
64 213-W-1.
65 In the final line, "nan" counts as two, as it comprises two *kana* なん.
66 116-N-3.
67 213-S-2.
68 213-S-2.
69 213-E-7.
70 213-E-3/4.
71 Moran and Rottman, *Peleliu 1944*, p. 89.

72 213-N-2.
73 105-S-2.
74 105-E-5.
75 105-E-5.
76 115-S-7. An additional half dozen similar messages by repatriates are found at 205-N-4, 205-N-6, 205-E-2, 205-PE-1 (on a column at the center of the room), and 213-W-2.

BIBLIOGRAPHY

Abrams, Kerry. "Polygamy, Prostitution, and the Federalization of Immigration Law." *Columbia Law Review*, vol. 105, no. 3 (April 2005): 641–716. Available online at: https://scholarship.law.duke.edu/faculty_scholarship/3826/ (accessed April 1, 2020).

Ansari, Humayun. *The Infidel Within: The History of Muslims in Britain, 1800 to the Present*. London: C. Hurst & Co. Publishers, 2004.

Architectural Resources Group and Daniel Quan Design. "Poetry and Inscriptions: Translation and Analysis." Prepared for the California Department of Parks and Recreation and Angel Island Immigration Station Foundation, 2004.

Azuma, Eiichiro. *Between Two Empires: Race, History, and Transnationalism in Japanese America*. Oxford, UK and New York, NY: Oxford University Press, 2005.

Barde, Robert. "The Scandalous Ship *Mongolia*." *Steamboat Bill (Journal of the Steamship Historical Society of America)*, no. 250 (Spring 2004): 112–118.

Barde, Robert. *Immigration at the Golden Gate: Passenger Ships, Exclusion, and Angel Island*. Westport, CT: Praeger, 2008.

Baynton, Douglas C. *Defectives in the Land: Disability and Immigration in the Age of Eugenics*. Chicago, IL: University of Chicago Press, 2016.

Burton, M. Farrell, F. Lord, and R. Lord. "Gila River," in "Confinement and Ethnicity: An Overview of Japanese American Relocation Sites." *Publications in Anthropology*, no. 74. Western Archeological and Conservation Center, National Park Service: 1999; rev. July 2000. Available online at: https://www.nps.gov/parkhistory/online_books/anthropology74/ (accessed April 1, 2020).

Caldwell, Karyn L., and Wendell P. Greek, principal investigators. Written by Heather L. Spencer. "Archaeological and Documentary Investigation of Fort McCoy's Japanese Prisoner of War Camp, South Post, Fort McCoy." Unites States Army Reserve Command, Fort McCoy. *Archaeological Resource Management Series, Reports of Investigation*, no. 5 (January 1996). Available online at: https://digicoll.library.wisc.edu/cgi-bin/WI/WI-idx?type=turn&entity=WI.InspectionReports.p0058&id=WI.InspectionReports&isize=M&q1=roster (accessed April 1, 2020).

Carro, Jorge L. "From Constitutional Psychopathic Inferiority to AIDS: What is the Future for Homosexual Aliens?" *Yale Law & Policy Review*, vol. 7, no. 1 (1989): 201–228. Available online at: https://digitalcommons.law.yale.edu/ylpr/vol7/iss1/6/ (accessed April 1, 2020).

Cha, Marn. J. *Koreans in Central California (1903–1957): A Study of Settlement and Transnational Politics*. Lanham, MD: University Press of America, 2010.

Chan, Sucheng, ed. *Entry Denied: Exclusion and the Chinese Community in America, 1882–1943*. Philadelphia, PA: Temple University Press, 1991.

Chang, Roberta, and Wayne Patterson. *The Koreans in Hawai'i: A Pictorial History, 1903–2003*. Honolulu, HI: University of Hawai'i Press, 2003.
Charr, Easurk Emsen, edited and with an introduction by Wayne Patterson. *The Golden Mountain: The Autobiography of a Korean Immigrant, 1905–1960*. Urbana, IL: University of Illinois Press, 1996.
Choi, Hyaeweol. *Gender and Mission Encounters in Korea: New Women, Old Ways*. Berkeley, CA: University of California Press, 2009.
Choy, Bong-Youn. *Koreans in America*. Chicago, IL: Nelson Hall, 1979.
Corbin, Alexander D. *The History of Camp Tracy: Japanese WWII POWs and the Future of Interrogation*. Fort Belvoir, VA: Ziedon Press, 2009.
Dalton, Curt. "Exile in the U.S.," in "Home Sweet Home Front: Dayton During World War II." *Dayton History Books Online* at: https://www.daytonhistorybooks.com/page/page/1652450.htm, © 2000 (accessed April 1, 2020).
Davies, Norman. *White Eagle, Red Star: The Polish-Soviet War, 1919–20*. New York: St. Martin's Press.
Gardner, Martha. *The Qualities of a Citizen: Women, Immigration, and Citizenship, 1870–1965*. Princeton, NJ: Princeton University Press, 2009.
Gee, Jennifer. "Sifting the Arrivals: Asian Immigrants and the Angel Island Immigration Station, 1910–1940." PhD dissertation, Stanford University, 1999.
Hata, Don and Nadine Hata. "George Shima: 'The Potato King of California.'" *Journal of the West*, vol. 25, no. 1 (January 1986): 55–63.
Hing, Bill Ong. *Making and Remaking Asian America through Immigration Policy, 1850–1990*. Stanford, CA: Stanford University Press, 1993.
Hsu, Madeline Y. *Dreaming of Gold, Dreaming of Home: Transnationalism and Migration between the United States and South China, 1882–1943*. Stanford, CA: Stanford University Press, 2000.
Ichihashi, Yamato. *Japanese in the United States: A Critical Study of the Problems of the Japanese Immigrants and Their Children*. Stanford, CA: Stanford University Press, 1932. Reissued New York: Arno Press, 1969.
Ichioka, Yuji. *The Issei: The World of the First Generation Immigrants, 1885–1924*. New York, NY: Free Press, 1998.
Jensen, Joan. *Passage from India: Asian Indian Immigrants in North America*. New Haven, CT: Yale University Press, 1988.
Jiang, Yongjing 蔣永敬. *Historical Records of the Revolution Overseas* 華僑開國革命史料. Taipei: Zhengzhong Books, 1977.
Kanazawa, Mark. "Immigration, Exclusion, and Taxation: Anti-Chinese Legislation in Gold Rush California." *Journal of Economic History*, vol. 65, no. 3 (September 2005): 779–805. Available online at: https://www.jstor.org/stable/3875017?seq=1 (accessed April 1, 2020).
Kanda, Mikio. *Widows of Hiroshima: The Life Stories of Nineteen Peasant Wives*. New York, NY: St. Martin's Press, 1989.
Kang, Youwei 康有為. "Hanzu yi you waifen wu neizheng lun" 漢族宜憂外分勿內爭論 [The Han Race Should Worry about Division from Without, and Avoid Dissent Within], in *Wanmu caotang yigao*, juan 1. Reprinted in Jiang Yihua et al., eds. *Kang Youwei quanji* [Complete Works of Kang Youwei], vol. 9. Beijing: Zhongguo renmin daxue chubanshe, 2007. Available online at: https://cnthinkers.com/thinkerweb/literature/441660 (accessed April 1, 2020).

Kashima, Tetsuden. *Judgment Without Trial: Japanese American Imprisonment During World War II*. Seattle, WA: University of Washington Press, 2004.

Kim, Richard S. *The Quest for Statehood: Korean Immigrant Nationalism and U.S. Sovereignty, 1905–1945*. New York, NY: Oxford University Press, 2011.

Kim, Warren Y. *Koreans in America*. Seoul, Republic of Korea: Po Chin Chai Printing Co., 1971.

Krammer, Arnold. "Japanese Prisoners of War in America." *Pacific Historical Review*, vol. 52, no. 1 (February 1983): 67–91. Available online at: https://www.jstor.org/stable/3639455 (accessed April 1, 2020).

Lai, Him Mark. "Island of Immortals: Chinese Immigrants and the Angel Island Immigration Station." *California History*, vol. 57, no. 1 (Spring 1978): 88–103. Available online at: https://www.jstor.org/stable/25157818 (accessed April 1, 2020).

Lai, Him Mark, Genny Lim, and Judy Yung. *Island: Poetry and History of Chinese Immigrants on Angel Island, 1910–1940*. San Francisco, CA: HOC DOI [History of Chinese Detained on Island] Project, 1980. Reprint Seattle, WA, and London, UK: University of Washington Press, 1991; 2nd edition, 2014.

Lee, Erika. *At America's Gates: Chinese Immigration During the Exclusion Era, 1882–1943*. Chapel Hill, NC: University of North Carolina Press, 2003.

Lee, Erika and Judy Yung. *Angel Island: Immigrant Gateway to America*. New York, NY, and Oxford: Oxford University Press, 2010.

Lew-Williams, Beth. *The Chinese Must Go: Violence, Exclusion, and the Making of the Alien in America*. Cambridge, MA: Harvard University Press, 2018.

Matsumoto, Valerie J. *Farming the Home Place: A Japanese American Community in California, 1919–1982*. Ithaca, NY: Cornell University Press, 1993.

Moran, Jim, and Gordon L. Rottman. *Peleliu 1944: The Forgotten Corner of Hell*. Oxford, UK: Osprey Publishing, 2002.

Nestyev, Israel V. *Prokofiev*. Stanford, CA: Stanford University Press, 1961.

Noda, Kesa. *Yamato Colony: 1906–1960*. Livingston, CA: Livingston-Merced JACL Chapter, 1981.

Palmer, Brandon. "Koreans in Honolulu Newspapers, 1903–1945." Available online at: https://scholarspace.manoa.hawaii.edu/bitstream/10125/25505/1/Koreans%20in%20Honolulu%20Newspapers%2c%201903-1945.pdf (accessed April 1, 2020).

Press, Stephen. "Prokofiev's Vexing Entry into the USA." *Three Oranges Journal*, no. 6 (November 2003). Available online at: https://www.sprkfv.net/journal/three06/vexing1.html (accessed April 1, 2020).

Ryono, C. Robert. *Although Patriotic, We Were Drydocked*. Los Angeles, CA: Terminal Islanders, 1994. Available online at: https://ryono.net/terminalisland/terminalisland.html (accessed April 1, 2020).

Sakihara, Mitsugu. "Sparrows of Angel Island: The Experience of a Young Japanese Prisoner of War." *Manoa*, vol. 8, no. 1 (Summer 1996): 108–121.

Sakovich, Maria. "Angel Island Immigration Station Reconsidered: Non-Asian Encounters with the Immigration Laws, 1910–1940." MA thesis, California State University, Sonoma, 2002.

Sakovich, Maria, and Eugenia Bailey. "July 1, 2013 – Anniversary at the Immigration Station on Angel Island." San Francisco, CA: Museum of Russian Culture. Available online at: https://www.mrcsf.org/news/125/ (accessed April 1, 2020).

Salyer, Lucy. *Laws Harsh as Tigers: Chinese Immigrants and the Shaping of Modern Immigration Law*. Chapel Hill, NC: University of North Carolina Press, 1995.
Schmid, Andre. *Korea between Empires, 1895–1919*. New York, NY: Columbia University Press, 2002.
Shimizu, Kashin. *Eien to mukyū: shiikashū* [Eternity and Endlessness: Poems]. N.p., 1921.
Shimizu, Kashin. *Wind of Spring: A Book of Poems*. San Francisco, CA: Beishin Press, 1923.
Shimonishi-Lamb, Mili. *And Then a Rainbow*. Santa Barbara, CA: Fithian Press, 1990.
Soennichsen, John. *Miwoks to Missiles: A History of Angel Island*. San Francisco, CA: Angel Island Association, 2001.
Soga, Keiho (Yasutaro Soga). *Tessaku seikatsu* [Life Behind Barbed Wire]. Honolulu, HI: Hawaii Times, 1948.
Soga, Yasutaro (Keiho), translated by Kihei Hirai, with an introduction by Tetsuden Kashima. *Life Behind Barbed Wire: The World War II Internment Memoirs of a Hawai'i Issei*. Honolulu, HI: University of Hawai'i Press, 2008.
Sohoni, Deenesh, and Amin Vafa. "The Fight to be American: Military Naturalization and Asian Citizenship." *Asian American Law Journal*, vol. 17 (January 2010): 119–151. Available at: https://scholarworks.wm.edu/aspubs/492/ (accessed April 1, 2020).
Sood, Malini. "Expatriate Nationalism and Ethnic Radicalism: The Ghadar Party in North America, 1910–1920." PhD dissertation, State University of New York at Stony Brook, 1995.
Spickard, Paul R. *Japanese Americans: The Formation and Transformations of an Ethnic Group*, revised edition. New Brunswick, NJ: Rutgers University Press, 2009.
Straus, Ulrich. *The Anguish of Surrender: Japanese POWs of World War II*. Seattle, WA: University of Washington Press, 2003.
Suzuki, Masao. "Important or Impotent? Taking Another Look at the 1920 California Alien Land Law." *Journal of Economic History*, vol. 64, no. 1 (March 2004): 125–143. Available online at: https://www.jstor.org/stable/pdf/3874944?seq=1 (accessed April 1, 2020).
Tatla, Darshan S. "A Sikh Manifesto? A Reading of the Ghadar Poetry." *Panjab Past and Present: The Ghadar Movement* (Special Issue), vol. 44, part 1 (April 2013): 61–80. Also available online at: https://www.academia.edu/8144256/A_Sikh_Manifesto_A_Reading_of_the_Ghadar_Poetry (accessed April 1, 2020).
Tsai, Shih-Shan Henry. *The Chinese Experience in America*. Bloomington, IN: Indiana University Press, 1986.
US National Parks Service. "The Battle of Attu: 60 Years Later." Available online at: https://www.nps.gov/articles/battle-of-attu.htm (accessed April 1, 2020).
Vatuk, Ved Prakash, and Sylvia Vatuk. "Protest Songs of East Indians on the West Coast, U.S.A." *Folklore* (Calcutta), vol. 7, no. 10 (October 1966): 370–382.
Wang, Xingchu 王性初. "Shi de linghun zai diyu yongsheng: Meiguo Tianshidao huawen yishi xinkao yu yanjiu qianzhan" 詩的靈魂在地獄中永生—美國天使島華文遺詩新考與研究前瞻 [The Soul of Poetry Lives Forever in Hell – A First Look at New Discoveries and Research on the Extant Poems at Angel Island in

America]. Revised July 2005. Available online at: https://www.fgu.edu.tw/~wclrc/drafts/America/wang-xing-chu/wang-xing-chu_01.htm (accessed April 1, 2020).

Winbury, Rex. "Trotsky's War Train." *History Today*, vol. 25, no. 8 (1975): 523–531.

Yoneda, Karl. *Ganbatte: Sixty-Year Struggle of a Kibei Worker*. Berkeley, CA: University of California Press, 1983.

Young, Elliott. *Alien Nation: Chinese Migration in the Americas from the Coolie Era through World War II*. Chapel Hill, NC: University of North Carolina Press, 2014.

Yu, Connie Young. "Rediscovered Voices: Chinese Immigrants and Angel Island." *Amerasia Journal*, vol. 4, no. 2 (1977): 123–139.

Yung, Judy. *Unbound Voices: A Documentary History of Chinese Women in San Francisco*. Berkeley, CA: University of California Press, 1999.

Zhang Yan 張研. *1908 Diguo wangshi* 1908 帝国往事 [Events in the Empire of 1908]. Chongqing: Chongqing Publishing, 2007.

Zhao, Xiaojian, and Edward J.W. Park, eds. *Asian Americans: An Encylopedia of Social, Cultural, Economic, and Political History*, 3 vols. Santa Barbara, CA: Greenwood, 2013.

Zoglin, Paul. "Gomel." Available online at: https://kehilalinks.jewishgen.org/homyel/gomel_history.html, © 2009 (updated September 2017; accessed April 1, 2020).

INDEX

Page numbers in **bold** refer to figures.

A Good World 185–6
A Night at Angel Island (Itoshima) 61
A Night at the Immigration Station (Choi) 124–5
Aarhus, Denmark 239
Abiko, Kyutaro 21
Akei 60, 89
Ali Hasson 246
Alien Poll Tax 1921, 110
Allen, Anna **203**, 206
Allen, Irvin 207–8
Allen, William 207
American Civil Liberties Union 214
American Communist Party 69
American Legion 147
ancestral altar **189**, 190–2, **190**, 299
Angel Island (Cloud) 123
Angel Island Immigration Station 46–57
　arrival 47, 54, 149, 193
　barracks 2, 3, 4, 4–5
　barracks map, first floor **16**
　barracks map, second floor **17**
　burning of the Administration Building 247
　Chinese rage 51
　closure 247–8
　conservation 14–16
　construction 1
　as a detention facility 3
　dining halls 171
　dormitories 3
　European Sitting Room 164–7, **166**
　fecal samples 48, 64, 193
　guard station **280**
　guard tower **280**

　Korean poems 123–5
　Lou, Chung Hing memoir 192–5
　meals 47–8, 48, 54, 55, 56, 193
　medical examinations 48
　named National Historic Landmark 15
　nationalities represented 199
　opening 21
　pier and baggage shed **15**
　purpose 1
　restoration 6
　site 1
　suicides 58–9
　women 53–9
　Yoneda poems 69–75
Angel Island Immigration Station Foundation 4–5, 15
Angel Island Immigration Station Historical Advisory Committee 15
Angel of Angel Island 61–2
Angell Treaty 1880, 151
Anti-Coolie Act 1862, 150
anti-immigrant sentiment 4, 19
anti-Semitism 224, 230
Araki, Dr. George 15
Architectural Resources Group 4–5
Arens, Richard 215–16
Argunov, Andrei 200
Asei 63
Asiatic Barred Zone 22, 199
Asiatic Exclusion League 19
assimilation 103
Attu Island, 270–1
Autumn Grass (Tokiro) 77
Avksentyev, Nikolai 200

INDEX

Bak, Yang-Rae 135, 136
Barbering Place **158**, 159
Before Sleep (Ha) 140
Berkeley, California 36–7
Bilbao, Spain 239
Bineff, Bella 230, **230**, 231
Bineff, Edward **230**, 231
Bineff, Yankel 229–31, **230**
bird sketch **45**
Blaine, James 150
Board of Special Inquiry 208, 222
Bogyu 81
Boochkovsky, Michael 228
Boroku 78, 79
British National Archives 221
Bukovsky 228
Bülowius, Lieutenant General Karl 249
Burgess, Geraldine Grace (Gerri) 243
Burgess, Gloria Estella 243
Burgess, John Douglas 240–3, **241, 242**
Burlingame-Seward Treaty 1868, 149, 151
Byron Hot Springs 250, 251

California, University of, Ethnic Studies Library 192
California Alien Land Law 1913, 21, 22, 28, 109
California State Legislature 15
California State Parks 4–5
calligraphy 188
 Chinese inscriptions 6, 9–10, **10, 11**, 12, **12**
 Japanese inscriptions 10
Camp (Heki) 93
Camp McCoy 251, 256, 283
Camp Tracy 250
Canada 200, 201, 228
Cardenas, Fernando 244
cartoon **46**, 298
census records 26, 33, 36, 37, 40, 56, 105, 106, 213, 218, 221, 241, 244, 245, 262
Central Pacific Railroad 149–50
ceremony of return 185–6
Cha, Pyeongnim Ui-Seok 145–7
Chahorin 100

Charr, Easurk Emsen 146–7
Chernoff, Victor M. 213
children 100, 102–3
China
 competition with Japan 114
 modernization 113
 Qing overthrown 25
 Tangxi 176
China, Republic of 157, 161, 168, 178, 191
China Mail Steamship Company 177
Chinese Communist Party 44
Chinese Eastern Railway 114, 205
Chinese Exclusion Act 1892, 22, 121, 149, 151, 153, 154, **154**–5, 195, 197
Chinese immigration and immigrants 149–55
 admissions 154
 Angel Island Memoir 192–5
 criminalization 152
 detentions 3, 154
 employment 149–50
 the Five Nationalities 177–8
 interrogations 153–4
 laws governing 4, 150–3, 154–5
 Mexico 180–1
 numbers 149
 origins 149
 rage 51
 wages 150
 women 151
Chinese inscriptions 5–14, **10, 11, 12, 13, 14**, 149–96
 A Good World 185–6
 ancestral altar **189**, 190–2, **190**
 Angel Island Memoir 192–5
 Barbering Place **158**, 159
 calligraphy 6, 9–10, **10, 11**, 12, **12**, 164, 188
 Clouds and hills all around 155, **156**
 extended parallel couplets 8–9
 General Zhao Zilong's Whole Body was Courage 179–80
 Great Blessings to Those Who Enter This House 161
 I tended house and home 180, **181**

INDEX

Island #2, 10, **12**
Island #15, 8–9
Island #23, 7
Island #60, 10, **11**
Island #112, 7–8
It's hard for Chinese 174, **175**
Li Hai poem 159–60, **160**
Meiji and Xuantong dates 24–5, **24**
poetry 5–8, 155–88
Quiet Night Thoughts 168
Random Thoughts 169–70
Random Thoughts Deep at Night 7
sailing ship **160**
shi forms 6–7
There are worms growing 188, **188**
two birds **159**
wall inscriptions 155–92
When you go downstairs for meals 171, **172**
Chinese Revolution 1911, 157
Chiroku 92
Choi, Gyeong-Sik 124–5
Choyu, Matsubara 68, **68**
Chung Hing Lou 195
citizenship 147, 152
  renunciation 34
City of Iron 155
class selection 197
Cleveland, Ohio 34
clonorchiasis 123
Close the door. There's a draft 270, **271**
Cloud 123
Clouds and hills all around 155, **156**
Columbus SS, 247
Coming of Autumn, The (Suzuki) 80
coming-of-age 185
communism 44
Communist Party 213, 215
Congress of Industrial Organizations 69–70
conservation 14–16
Cook, Bernadine Mae 243
counterfeit children 95
Crocker, Charles 149–50
Crossing the Sierra Mountains (Man of Yaksan Mountain) 142
Curtis, Dale R. 258

customs officials 47
Czechoslovak Legion 219

D. W. 139
Dayton, Ohio 29
Declaration of Intention 204
dekasegi ideal 21
Delano, California 125–6
Denmark, Aarhus 239
DePauw University 124–5
deportation 1, 35, 44, 48, 49–50, 52, 53, 63–4, 123, 170, 188
  appeals 49
  picture brides 57
Depression, the 146, 213
detainees, numbers 3
detention, longest 3
Dieterichs, M.K. 200
Din, Grant 249, 310n24
discrimination 107–12
Disembarking at San Francisco Bay (S) 133–4
Dondonbo 82, 87
Dong, Arthur 194, 195
Dusheck, George 253–7

Eighteen Years in the United States (One Who Laments the Times) 143–4
Emergency Quota Act 1921, 199
Emmons, Lieutenant General Delos C. 259
employment histories, Japanese immigrants 32–5
enemy aliens 3, 248–9, 250, 258, 268–9
Englander, Denis 15
Enrique Piton inscription **13**
Ensenada 36
Etsujin 97, 100
eugenics movement 198, 199
Europe, welcome to immigrants from 1
exclusion 50, 108, 119, 152
Exclusion Act 1882, 4
Executive Order 9066, 248

Faingold brothers 208, **209**, 210–11, **210**, **211**, **212**, 213–17
Faitzer, Aleksandr 218–19

false documents 95
Fangold, Amelia 210–11, **210**
Farewell (Lee) 122–3
fecal samples 48, 64, 193
Federoff, Alexander 219–20
Federoff, Fedor 219
Fedorov 219–20
Feingold, Augusta 211, **211**, 213
Filipinos 199
First World War 22, 111–12, 118–19, 146, 179, 200, 205, 211, 218, 223, 228, 319n107
fishermen, Japanese 36
Five Nationalities, the 177–8
Floating Jade Tower, Pyongyang 133, 134
Folsom Prison 244, 245
Fort Logan, Colorado 118
Fort McDowell 200, 248
Fort Stanton 247
Four Poems on Parting: Leaving Stockton (Lee), 135–6
Fourth of July, The 126
France 246
Fuki 69
Fumio 101
Fundora 65
Fundoshi-ikkan 77
Furukawa, Kisuke 58, 59
Furukawa, Tamiye 58–9
Futaba 61–2, 112

Geary Act 1892, 152
Gee, Jennifer 197
General Zhao Zilong's Whole Body was Courage 179–80
Gentlemen's Agreement 1907–1908, 4, 19, 21, 57, 115, 302n2
German Americans 248
Get me out of here fast! 39–42, **39**, **40**
Ghadar [Revolt] Party 201
Ghadar de Gunj 237–8
Gila River War Relocation Center 29
Gojogen 110
Gold Rush, the 149
Gomel 204
good luck money 182, **183**, **184**
grief 7–8

Ha, Wun 129–30, 140, 141
Hamaguchi, Isaburo 36
Hamaguchi, Matsubei 36
Hamaguchi, Yaohichi 36
Han, Back 126
Harbin 231–2
Harei 81
Hatanaka, Choichiro 49, 53
Hatanaka, Chosaburo 53
Hawaii 19, 20, 26, 28, 37, 114, 115, 116, 118, 248
Hawaii Times (newspaper) 266
Haworth, the Reverend B.C. 50, 53
Hearst, William Randolph 108–9
Hebrew Aid Society 222
Heki 93
Hera Village, Hiroshima Prefecture, Japan 33
Herdboy, the 66
Hijitetsubo 83
Hikariso 90
Hikawa 60, 87
Him Mark Lai Papers 192
Hindus 95
Hiroshima 31
Hitoyasu 94
Hokoda, Asaboro and Mitsuyo 26, **28**, 29
Holocaust, the 217
homesickness 168
Hometown Thoughts (Ju) 137–8
Hometown Thoughts (Son) 127–8
hookworm 25, 32, 42, 68, 123, 193
Horn, Lieutenant M.B. 254
Hoshida, George 259, **261**
Hotel Hollywood 33–4
House of Representatives Un-American Affairs Committee 214–16
Huang Zuming 164–7, **166**
Huri, Teao 240

I Miss You, My Brother! (Ha) 129–30
I tended house and home 180, **181**
Ichioka, Yuji 21
Ijiri, Ijuin 79
Ikeda, Masa 105
Il, Hae 125–6
imaging technologies 17

immigrants
  fear of 4
  origins 3
Immigration Act 1892, 197
Immigration Act 1917, 22, 197, 198–9
Immigration Act 1924, 199
immigration controversies 4
immigration hearings 118–19
Immigration Laws: Rules of November 15, 1911, Rule 10, 201
immigration policy 197–9
immigration system 152–3
In-Bal Ryu inscription 117–19, **117**
innkeepers 179–80
inscriptions 5, 5–14
  authors **13**
  pictures 14, **14**
  prose 12
  writers 9
In-Sik Lee inscriptions 120–1, **120**
International Longshoremen's and Warehousemen's Union 69
International Red Cross 256
interrogations 47, 48, 51–2, 153–4, 193–4
Iriye, Tokuzo 37
Is racial bias justifiable? 38
Island: Poetry and History of Chinese Immigrants on Angel Island, 1910–1940 (Lai, Lim and Yung) 6, 154
  #2, 10, **12**
  #13, **13**
  #15, 8–9
  #23, 7
  #27, 178
  #34, 178
  #60, 10, **11**
  #68, 177
  #76, 186
  #109, 170
  #112, 7–8
  #133, 170
  editions 287
  location codes 16–17
  numbering systems 287
  poem numbers 287–9
  wall locations 289–93
Isle of Demons, the 66–7
Italian Americans 248
Italy 246
Itoshima, Chinami 61, 82
It's hard for Chinese (Liu XX) 174, **175**

Jane Couch Memorial Home 55–6
Jangbaek Mountain Recluse 132–3
Japan 40–1, 42–3
  competition with China 114
  declares Korea protectorate 114
  Hera Village, Hiroshima Prefecture 33
  Meiji period 25
  Mine Village, Usui District, Gunma Prefecture 67
  modernization 113
  Nukui, Kawauchi Village, Asa District, Hiroshima Prefecture 26, 31, 303n34
  Takata District 42
  territorial expansion 178–9
Japanese Americans
  internment 21–2, 23, 28–9, 36, 38, 70, 248, 248–9
  reparations 29
  repatriation 31
Japanese and Korean Exclusion League 19
Japanese Association 49, 50, 53, 57, 58
Japanese Communist Party 44
Japanese Hawaiian inscriptions 257–66, **260**, **261**
  Group #3, 260, 264, 265, 268
  Group #4, 265
  Group #5, 266–9
  Yasutaro Soga 266–9
Japanese immigration and immigrants
  agricultural colonies 21–2, 302n7
  Angel Island Immigration Station experiences 46–57
  dekasegi ideal 21
  discrimination 107–12
  employment histories 32–5
  identity 22
  laborers 21

laws governing 4, 19
origins 19
periods 21–2
personal sacrifices 32–5
women 20, 53–9, 107–8
Japanese inscriptions
  1910–1940, 19–112
  bird sketch 45
  calligraphy 12
  Get me out of here fast! 39–42, **39**, **40**
  Ichitaro Yasumi 32–5, **32**
  Is racial bias justifiable? 38
  Isaburo Hamaguchi 36
  Kinzo Tsujitaka 35
  Maichi Sakoi 42
  Masami Miyata 36–7
  Meiji and Xuantong dates 24–5, **24**
  Miyamoto 25–31, **27**, **28**, **30**
  Motoichi Oku 37–8
  Noboru Kubota 43–4
  Overthrow American imperialism! 44
  People of Yamato 42–3
  poems and prose 22–3, 46–112
  rooster carving 45
  Second World War 22
  wall inscriptions 22, 24–44, **24**, **27**, **28**, **30**, **32**, **39**, **40**, **45**
  see also Nichibei Shimbun [The Japanese-American News]
Japanese New Year 67
Japanese-American identity 22
Japan-Korea Treaty 1876, 114
Jasinski, Michael 189
Jensen, Martin 239
Jerome War Relocation Center 263
Jiang Ziya 163
Joffe, Tanchum 220
Johnson, Roger A. 252–3
Joun 107
Ju, Yeo-Sam 137–8
Ju, Yeo-Sop 138

Kabushko, Alexandra 221
Kabushko, Andronik 221
Kabushko, Boris Andronicovitch 221
Kagebenkei 64, 66–7, 108

Kakumaru 86, 96
Kano, Henry Hiroshi 34
Kanzan 63
Kashio 69
Kasho 107
Kawakita, Shigeto 49, 52
Kearney, Denis 150
Keenan, William Francis 243
Keimei 99
Kim, Evelyn Nien-wha 146, 147
Kim, Maria 128
Kimiko, Ruri 104
Kimyoan 85, 102, 103
Kinshu 84
Kinsuishi 109
Kitahira 97
Kodama, Keiko 83
Kojin 76
Kong Din Quong 3
Korea 113–14
Korean American community 116
Korean immigration and immigrants 113–16, 309n7
  numbers 114–15
  political activity 116
Korean inscriptions 113–47
  In-Bal Ryu 117–19, **117**
  In-Sik Lee 120–1, **120**
  nationalist sentiments 145–7
  poetry 122–47
  wall inscriptions 116, 117–21, **117**, **120**
Korean Mutual Cooperation Association 115
Korean National Association 115
Koso 85
Kozuki 107
Kubota, Kame 43
Kubota, Katsumi 43
Kubota, Noboru 43–4
Kuniko 66, 67
Kureizumi 110
Kurita, Yasuro 267–8

Ladies' Agreement 20
Lai, Him Mark 6
Land of the Flowery Flag 162
languages 4

Laugh, The 140
Leaving San Francisco (Ha) 141
Lee, Reverend David Dae Wei 115
Lee, Erika 3, 4
Lee, George Hansik 120–1, **120**
Lee, Jeong-Dae 135–6
Lee, Jeong-Du 122–3, 135–6
Lerena, Felipe Mauricio 239
Let's Go Home (Cha) 145–7
Lew, Philip 117–19, **117**
Lew-Williams, Beth 151
Li Bo 168
Li Hai 159–60, **160**
Li Jingbo 169
Li Yisu 194
Liang Qichao 166
Lim, Genny 6
Lip 130–1
Liu, Newton 5
Liu, Wan 5
Liu Gongquan 10, **11**
Liu XX, 174, **175**
Livingston, California 21
location codes 16–17
Lodi, San Joaquin County 42
London 221
Long live the Great Japanese Empire! 272, **272**
Longing for the Homeland by a Student Refugee (Lip) 130–1
Los Angeles 29, 150
Los Angeles Times (newspaper) 20, 53, 257
Lou, Chung Hing, Angel Island Memoir 192
Love Songs (Tanaka) 80
Lowe, Felicia 194, 195
LPC 222, 239

McKinley. James W. and Lillian 33
Magnuson Act 153
Man of Yaksan Mountain 142
March 1 Movement 128
marriage 185–6
Maurer, Katherine 62
May Fourth Movement 179
medical examinations 37, 48, 63–4, 170, 188, 254

Meiji and Xuantong dates 24–5
Meizan 63
melancholy 7
Mennonite emigration 228–9
merchant seamen 201, 239–44
Mexican border 4
Mexico 180, 229, 244, 245, 246
military naturalization 118–19, 121, 146–7, 242
Miller, Arthur 215
Mine Village, Usui District, Gunma Prefecture, Japan 67
Minejima, Giichi 105–6
mirrors 84
Miyamoto, Chiyokichi 25, 26, 27
Miyamoto, Masaru and Kinuyo 25–31, **27, 28, 30**
Miyamoto, Masato 31
Miyamoto, Minoru 303n25
Miyamoto, Mitsuyo 25, 26
Miyata, Masami 36–7
Miyata, Toshie 37
Model, Samuel 218–19
Moldova 229–30
Molokan Church 211, 213
Month of March, The (Shimizu) 67–8
Mount Vernon, SS 218–19
My Hometown (Koso) 85

Naganuma, Joanne Chizumi 35
Naganuma, Michiko 34
Namba, Daisuke 71
Nanhai 161–2
Nanking SS, 177
nationalist sentiments 145–7
naturalization 153, 231, 244
  Declaration of Intention 119
  military 118–19, 121, 146–7, 242
Naturalization Act 1790, 152
Neufeld, Helena 229
Neufeld, Jacob 228–9
Neufeld, Jakob Heinrich 229
Neufeld, Jakob P. 229
New Year 85–8, 94, 99, 102, 104, 109
New York 126, 220
New York Times (newspaper) 29, 320n8

New Zealand 240–1, 243
Nicaragua 244
Nichibei Shimbun [The Japanese-American News] 22–3, 40, 46–112
   Angel Island Immigration Station 46–57
   discrimination 107–12
   picture brides 53–66
   poetry 59–105
   Shimizu poems 67–8
   Suicide Note of a Picture Bride 58–9
   transcription 305n81
   Yamato Colony 90–106
   Yoneda poems 69–75
Nizenkoff family 225–8, **225**, **226**
Nodan 96, 108
Nonkibo 78
Nukui, Kawauchi Village, Asa District, Hiroshima Prefecture, Japan 26, 31, 303n34
Nuremberg Tribunals 29

Obata, Chiura 68
Okina-rokkei 95
Oku, Motoichi 37–8
Oku, Shizuno 37–8
Oku, Ume 37
Okusuke 98
Okuye, Take 106
One Who Laments the Times 143–4
Onoyama, Yoshiki 34
oral histories 6
Ota, Peter 255–6
Ota, Tamekichi 57
Otsuka, Hajime 275
Overthrow American imperialism! 44

Pacific Mail Steamship Company 5
Page Act 1875, 150–1
Page Law 1875, 197
painting campaigns 5
Pak, Wun-Chung 123
Panama Canal 1
Pantsu 62
Papeete 239–40
parasitic diseases 188

Park, Yang N. 136
Pearl Harbor, attack on 248, 258, 267
People of Yamato 42–3
personal sacrifices, Japanese immigrants 32–5
picture brides 20, 53–9, 107–8
   deportation 57
   numbers 57
   suicide note 58–9
pictures, 14
   ancestral altar **189**, 190–2, **190**, 299
   bird sketch **45**
   cartoon **46**, 298
   good luck money 182, **183**, **184**
   Japanese POW cartoon **279**, 300
   rooster carving **45**, 298
   sailing ship **160**, 299
   scaly fish **14**, 298
   two birds 159, 298
   wall locations 298–300
Pioneer (Okusuke) 98
Piton, Enrique E. 244–6, **245**
Po, Han-Pyung 123, 135–6
poem numbers, *Island* 287–9
poetry
   Chinese 5–8, 155–88
   European Sitting Room 164–7, **166**
   Japanese 59–105, 307n117
   Japanese Hawaiian 266–9
   Korean 122–47
   Punjabi 237–8
   recent-style verse 8
   Russian 231–4
   shi forms 6
   Shimizu 67–8
   Soga 266–9
   Tet Yee manuscript 293–5
   Yoneda 69–75, 307n117
political activism 213–16
post-war deportees 281–4, b285
prisoners-of-war 3, 219, 249–51
   boy soldiers 255–6
   daily schedule 252
   diet 254
   discipline 252

German 249–50, 252–3, 270, **271**
Italian 250
Japanese 250–1, 253–7, 255–7, 267–8, 270–81, **272**, 272–4, **278, 279, 280**
  medical examinations 254
  repatriation 256–7, 320n8
  wall inscriptions 270–81, **271, 272,** 272–4, **278, 279, 280**
Prohibition 109
Prokofiev, Sergei 200
prostitution 151, 197
Punjabi poetry 237–8
Pyongyang, Floating Jade Tower 133, 134

Qingming (Tomb Sweeping) Festival 191
Quan, Daniel 5
Quiet Night Thoughts 168
Quota Act 1921, 219–20

racial bias 38, 119
racism 149
Ram, Avithal 221
Ram, Lazar 220–1
Random Thoughts Deep at Night 7
Random Thoughts (Li Jingbo) 169–70
Reagan, Ronald, 29
record-keeping 3
Rhee, Syngman 128
Rogovsky, E.F. 200
Rohwer War Relocation Center 38
Roi 102
Roosevelt, Franklin D. 28–9, 248
Roosevelt, Theodore 19, 115
rooster carving **45**, 298
Rowland 37
Rule 10, 201
Russia 113–14, 114
Russian American Society 216
Russian immigration and immigrants 200
Russian poetry 231–4
Russian Revolution 200, 204, 219, 228, 232
Russian wall inscriptions 201–31

Russkii Golos [Russian/nlVoice] (newspaper) 231–4
Russo-Japanese Wa, 1904-1905, 179
Ryu, Gen-Ye, 118

Sacrament, 43
sailing ship **160**, 299
Saipan and Tinian inscription 273, **274**
Sakamaki, Ensign Kazuo 249, 267
Sakata, Teruo 88
Sakihara, Mitsugu 256
Sakoi, Joichi 42
Sakoi, Maichi 42
San Francisco 27, 51, 54, 115, 116, 133–4, 141, 193, 195
  school plan 19
  South Park 86–7
San Francisco Earthquake 1906, 153
San Francisco General Strike 1934, 214
San Quentin 244, 245
Sanfuro 76
Sansh 101
Sansho 91
sardine industry 81–2
Sayad, Nurdin 236
scaly fish **14**, 298
Scott Act 1888, 152
Seattle 53, 105
Second Brother from Nanyi 187
Second War Powers Act 1942, 121
Second World War 4, 21, 23, 34, 41, 121, 204, 207, 214, 217, 224, 227, 242–3
  Battle for Attu 270–1
  Battle of Okinawa 255
  Battle of Peleliu 282
  Battle of Saipan 274, 275
  Battle of Tinian 274–5
  boy soldiers 255–6
  Hiroshima bombed 31
  internments 21–2, 23, 28–9, 36, 38, 70, 248, 248-9
  interrogation center 250
  Japanese Hawaiian inscriptions 257–69, **260, 261**
  post-war deportees 281–4, **285**

prisoners-of-war 249–51, 252–7, 270–81, **271**, **272**, **272–4**, **278**, **279**, **280**
wall inscriptions 247–85
Sekiki 104
Selective Service Act 112
Send Off (D. W.) 139
separateness 42–3
Shaonian Zhongguo chenbao [Young China Morning News] (newspaper) 173
Shi Ning 173
Shige, Tomishima 59
Shihyo 89
Shimizu, Kashin 67–8, **68**
Shimonishi, Taichi 27, 31
Shimonishi, Toshio 31
Shindo, Takuji 257–60, **261**
Shinji 94
Shinroku 111
Shisei 90
Shoei 86, 94
Shoichi 109
Shoin, Yoshida 279
Shunkan 54, 56
Siberian Ice March 200
Sikhs 200–1
Sinhan Minbo [New Korea] (newspaper) 116
  poetry 122–47
Sino-Japanese War 1894-1895, 114, 179, 276
Slavin, Moisei 218
Smiley Jann manuscript 169, 177, 178, 295–8
Soga, Yasutaro 266–9
Son, Jin-Sil 127–8
Son, Jong-do 128
Songs of the Immigrant Land (Okina-rokkei) 95
South Asian wall inscriptions 235–6, **235**
South Asians 200–1
South Park, San Francisco 86–7
Spain, Bilbao 239
special board hearings 258–9, 262–3
Stark, Admiral Oskar 200, 228

Statue of Liberty in the New York Port, The (Han) 126
Steinbeck, John, *Cannery Row* 81
sterilizations 198
Straus, Ulrich 250–1
Sueoka, Robert Iju 261–3, **261**
Suicide Note of a Picture Bride 58–9
suicides 58–9
Sukovitzen, John 213
Sun Yat-sen 168, 173
Surugaya Company 51
Suzuki, Kyosen 80
sympathy 57

Tahara 59
Tahiti 240
Taizan 91
Takata District, Japan 42
Takebo 91
Tanaka 80
Tangxi, China 176
Tanoji 86–7
Tara Singh inscription 235–6, **235**
tenant farmers 40–1
Terminal Island 36
Tet Yee manuscript 169, 177, 293–5
There are worms growing 188, **188**
There's a Long Way Ahead (Jangbaek Mountain Recluse) 132–3
Tientsin, Convention of 1885, 114
The time has come for me to fulfill my duty 284, **285**
To Leave or Not? (Itoshima) 82
Tobi 99
Tokiro 77
tolerance 41
Tolstoy, Alexandra 200
Tomenro 81–2
Tominaga, Gusuke 55, 56
Tominaga, Kotoko 53–6
Tominaga, Sumi 56
Tonkyo 96
Topaz War Relocation Center 37
toso wine 60
trachoma 63–4
Transcontinental Railroad 149–50, 311–12n3, 311n2
transcription 17, 305n81

translation 17
Trans-Siberian Railway 114, 200, 205, 227, 232
travel records 33
truth, speaking 5–6
Tsujitaka, Kinzo 35
Tsunemichi, Nakata 275–6
Tule Lake War Relocation Center 38
two birds 159, 298
Tydings-McDuffie Act 199

Umesho 88
uncinariasis 25, 32, 68, 123
United Korean Association 115
United States Army Air Forces 121
Unnunbo 100
US Constitution
   Eighteenth Amendment 109
   Fourteenth Amendment 152
Ushijima, Chairman 49, 52–3
US-Japan Treaty of Commerce and Navigation 19

Valentino, Rudolph 33
venereal disease 58–9
Vincent, Vivian 239–40
V-J Day 256
Vladivostok 200, 218, 218–19, 219
Vodniak, Ionia and Abraham 222–5
Vodniak, Ishiker 222

wall locations
   Island poems 289–93
   pictures 298–300
   Smiley Jann manuscript poems 295–8
   Tet Yee manuscript poems 293–5
Walsh, George 216–17
Walsh, Nadia 216–17
Wandering (Il), 125–6
Wang, Xing Chu 5
Wang Wei 166–7
War Relocation Authority 248
Washington, University of 227
Washington Post (newspaper) 1
Watching a Friend Send Her Children Back to Japan (Ijiri), 79
Weaving Maid, the 66

Weiss, Alexander 14–15
When you go downstairs for meals 171, **172**
White Russians 200, 228
White-Slave Traffic Ac, 1910, 197
Whitlock, Major John , 253–4, 254
Wilfong, Maj Albert E, 252
Wilson, Woodro, 199
women
   Chines, 151
   class selectio, 197
   Korean 127–8
   picture brides 20, 53–9, 107–8
   Yamato Colony 96, 97, 99
Women's Home Missionary Society of the Methodist Episcopal Church 55–6, 62
Wong, Eddie 310
Woodnick, Abe 223–4
Woodnick, Joseph 222–5
Woodnick, Seymour 224
Workingmen's Party of California 150
writers 9

Yaji 103
Yakkodako 103
Yaksan Mountain 142
Yamashita, Junwo 41
Yamashita, Kimiye 39, 40–1
Yamashita, Nao 39–41, 40
Yamashita, Shigeru 41
Yamashita, Tsurukichi 39–42, **39**, **40**, 49, 53
Yamato 42–3
Yamato Colony 21, 23, 90–106
Yan Hui 163
Yan Zhenqing 10, **10**
Yasui, Masanosuke 40, 46–52
Yasumi, Chika, 33–4
Yasumi, David, 35
Yasumi, Fumi, 34
Yasumi, Hide Okamura, 33
Yasumi, Hideo, 34, 35
Yasumi, Ichitaro 32–5, **32**
Yasumi, Midori 34
Yasumi, Saburo 33
Yasumi, Sachiko 34
Yasumi, Yorito 33–4, 34

Yee, Tet 169, 177, 293-5
Yi, Kwang-su 132-3
Yim Lee, E. 195
Yoneda, Karl Goso 69-75, 307n117
Yoshio 89
Youli 169
Yuan Shikai 168
Yun, Chi-Chang 128
Yung, Judy 3, 4, 6
Yuqing from Tangxi 175-6

Zeitlin, Abram 205
Zeitlin, Jacob 201, **202, 203,** 204-7
Zeitlin, Leib 205
Zeitlin, Peshe 204, 205, 205-6, 206
Zeng Shen 163
Zeng Yuan 163
Zenzinov, Vladimir 200
Zhao Zilong 179-80
Zhu 187
Zou Xiwen 172-3

www.ingramcontent.com/pod-product-compliance
Lightning Source LLC
Chambersburg PA
CBHW072120290426
44111CB00012B/1723